Entropic Philosophy

Philosophical Projections

Series Editor: Andrew Benjamin, Distinguished Professor of Philosophy and the Humanities, Kingston University, UK, and Professor of Philosophy and Jewish Thought, Monash University, Australia.

Philosophical Projections represents the future of Modern European Philosophy. The series seeks to innovate by grounding the future in the work of the present, opening up the philosophical and allowing it to renew itself, while interrogating the continuity of the philosophical after the critique of metaphysics.

Titles in the Series
Foundations of the Everyday: Shock, Deferral, Repetition
Eran Dorfman
The Thought of Matter: Materialism, Conceptuality and the Transcendence of Immanence
Richard A. Lee
Nancy, Blanchot: A Serious Controversy
Leslie Hill
The Work of Forgetting: Or, How Can We Make the Future Possible?
Stephane Symons
Political Loneliness: Modern Liberal Subjects in Hiding
Jennifer Gaffney
On the Brink: Language, Time, History, and Politics
Werner Hamacher; edited by Jan Plug with an Introduction by Andrew Benjamin
Fraught Decisions in Plato and Shakespeare
Dianne Rothleder
Refugees: Towards a Politics of Responsibility
Nathan Bell
Remains of a Self: Solitude in the Aftermath of Psychoanalysis and Deconstruction
Cathrine Bjørnholt Michaelsen
Entropic Philosophy: Chaos, Breakdown, and Creation
Shannon M. Mussett

Entropic Philosophy
Chaos, Breakdown, and Creation

Shannon M. Mussett

ROWMAN & LITTLEFIELD
Lanham • Boulder • New York • London

Published by Rowman & Littlefield
An imprint of The Rowman & Littlefield Publishing Group, Inc.
4501 Forbes Boulevard, Suite 200, Lanham, Maryland 20706
www.rowman.com

86-90 Paul Street, London EC2A 4NE, United Kingdom

Copyright © 2022 Shannon M. Mussett

All rights reserved. No part of this book may be reproduced in any form or by any electronic or mechanical means, including information storage and retrieval systems, without written permission from the publisher, except by a reviewer who may quote passages in a review.

British Library Cataloguing in Publication Information Available

Library of Congress Cataloging-in-Publication Data

Names: Mussett, Shannon M., author.
Title: Entropic philosophy : chaos, breakdown, and creation / Shannon M. Mussett.
Description: Lanham : Rowman & Littlefield, [2022] | Includes bibliographical references and index. | Summary: "Taking an interdisciplinary approach, this book traces the development of entropic themes, capturing phenomena ranging from chaos, disorder, homogenization, slackening, dissipation, and ultimately, creation"—Provided by publisher.
Identifiers: LCCN 2021038833 (print) | LCCN 2021038834 (ebook) |
    ISBN 9781786612465 (hardback) | ISBN 9781538165188 (paperback) |
    ISBN 9781786612472 (epub)
Subjects: LCSH: Order (Philosophy) | Entropy.
Classification: LCC B105.O7 M87 2022 (print) | LCC B105.O7 (ebook) |
    DDC 117—dc23
LC record available at https://lccn.loc.gov/2021038833
LC ebook record available at https://lccn.loc.gov/2021038834

To Cleo and Milo, in reverence and care

Contents

Acknowledgments	ix
Preface	xi
Introduction	1
1 Entropy in Science and Metaphor	17
2 Entropy in Ancient Greek Thought	35
3 Entropy in German Philosophies of Nature	61
4 Leveling Modernity: Entropy in Freud and Lévi-Strauss	83
5 Old Age and Entropic Decline	107
6 Entropic Excess: Reconfiguring Matter and Waste	131
7 Destruction and the Joy of Creation	155
Conclusion	177
Bibliography	185
Index	195

Acknowledgments

To write a book about entropy is a task that seems at odds with itself. To complete a book on entropy during a global pandemic is something else altogether. I could not have accomplished this task without the support of friends, family, and colleagues over the many years.

Thank you to Andrew Benjamin for encouraging the book from the beginning, and to Frankie Mace at Rowman & Littlefield and Monica Sukumar at Deanta for their assistance with publishing. Thank you to Ethan Johnson for help with the early research, and Dina Schapiro and Danielle Epstein at *The Marble House Project* for providing me with the time and place to think through this endeavor in its infancy.

This book casts a wide intellectual net that needed many readers to keep it on track. My deep gratitude to Michael Shaw for reading multiple drafts and helping me see the power of the *entrepic*. I am also indebted to Nathan Gorelick, Jackie Radigan-Hoffman, Kristi Sweet, Sara Brill, and C. Thi Nguyen for reading chapters and providing invaluable feedback and support. Finally, Madeline Brenchley's help with research, editing, and indexing is the only reason I finished this book on time.

Thank you to my daughter for showing me the Asimov story and to both of my children, Cleo and Milo, for making me want to envision a different future.

Preface

> For there are no new ideas. There are only new ways of making them felt.
>
> Audre Lorde, "Poetry Is Not a Luxury"[1]

> The value and interest of the sciences always increases in proportion with the extent to which they are seen as capable of a deep and real relation to the highest of sciences, philosophy, and people who try because of a regrettable misunderstanding to tear their particular science as far as possible away from philosophy do not know what they are doing.
>
> F. W. J. Schelling, On the History of Modern Philosophy[2]

This book is entirely motivated by the desire to say something at a time filled with palpable anxiety about the state of the world. Deep social and cultural divisions are everywhere apparent, even among those fields that most desperately need each other for support and mutual discovery. If we listen to the harbingers of the death of humanities, philosophy has nothing to offer for the future of humankind. Artificial Intelligence can already write opinion pieces on its own worth,[3] works of literature,[4] and ultimately cobble together a convincing enough theory. Philosophy has often been both condemned and praised for its uselessness, that is, as a mode of thinking and questioning not immediately undertaken for practical results. What then can philosophy do at this moment of great global crisis? This question drives the following studies of entropic philosophy.

Recently, philosophy has been a favorite target of a number of prominent American physicists. Perhaps the most audacious shot against it was fired in 2011 by Stephen Hawking, who told Google's Zeitgeist conference that "philosophy is dead."[5] In a pale imitation of Nietzsche's critique of Christianity, Hawking declared the death of philosophy and the ascension of science. Speaking to Google, his exact words were, "Most of us don't worry about these questions most of the time. But almost all of us must sometimes wonder: Why are we here? Where do we come from? Traditionally, these are questions for philosophy, but philosophy is dead." He added, "Philosophers have not kept up with modern developments in science. Particularly physics."[6] In other words, philosophy is guilty of the crime of not being science. While philosophers of science may disagree, Hawking went on to claim that "scientists have become the bearers of the torch of discovery in our quest for knowledge," because philosophy has lost its way in the modern era.[7] Indeed, he seems to imply, with the development of the Hadron collider, deep-space telescopes, and super-computers, what use are the questions: Why am I here? Where do I come from? What is the purpose of existence? What ought I to do? Leaving aside the foolishness of believing that science could definitively answer the questions about life's meaning, such discourse reveals the underlying assumption that the methodology of philosophy is no longer useful because science has effectively answered (or will answer) all of the big questions. Whatever queries remain will either be unanswerable or ultimately unimportant. Presumably, this is because natural science gets things right and philosophy gets lost in the exercise of anachronistic pointlessness.

Another critic of philosophy, Neil de Grasse Tyson, announced to his interviewers in 2014: "My concern here is that the philosophers believe they are actually asking deep questions about nature. And to the scientist it's, what are you doing? Why are you concerning yourself with the meaning of meaning?"[8] Philosophers, he believes, are misguided about their investigations into nature insofar as they think they are asking profound questions, when in reality they are simply doing late-stage navel-gazing. He goes on to illustrate the stupidity of philosophy using a tired example:

> How do you define "clapping?" All of a sudden it devolves into a discussion of the definition of words. And I'd rather keep the conversation about ideas. And when you do that, don't derail yourself on questions that you think are important because philosophy class tells you this. The scientist says, "Look, I got all this world of unknown out there. I'm moving on. I'm leaving you behind. You can't even cross the street because you are distracted by what you are sure are deep questions you've asked yourself. I don't have the time for that."[9]

Not only infantilizing and dismissive of philosophy as a whole, de Grasse Tyson actually warns against the pursuit of philosophy. One will be too busy clapping a hand rather than contributing to human progress. If one has big questions, the answers are to be found in science.

More recently, Bill Nye replied to a philosophy major in an online platform that philosophy won't land a job. In a rambling and uninformed monologue, Nye continues the narrative of the uselessness and impracticality of philosophical knowledge. He asks rhetorically, "Is reality real or is reality not real and we are all living on a ping pong ball as part of a giant interplanetary ping pong game and we cannot sense it?"[10] While acknowledging it's a good question, he continues by dismissing philosophy as outdated. Just as de Grasse Tyson imagines philosophers sitting around clapping one hand, Nye imagines philosophers spending time contemplating ridiculous and unprovable hypotheses on the nature of reality, rather than contributing to the unfolding of truth.[11]

But natural science cannot provide answers and solutions on its own. Today, the United States and a growing number of countries throughout the world face the domination of internet culture's darkest, most dangerous side. Not merely lacking but outright despising a critical attitude toward objective truth and what constitutes sound argument, we face a terrifying proliferation of "alternative facts" and indemonstrable conspiracy theories growing like mold in the walls of community, thwarting common ground, and hastening continued world destruction. The most recent scourge facing philosophical endeavors in the United States (but spreading across the globe), QAnon travels far and wide largely because of untamed (and so far untamable) social media platforms that promote an anything-goes, the-more-extreme-the-better attitude toward truth. QAnon is a perfect conspiracy theory because it is all-encompassing: blanketing everything, going everywhere, and, thus, going nowhere constructive. It could be an entirely new force of unreason, or, as Hari Kunzru writes, it: "Could also just be a late stage of the usual thinking, a kind of entropic decay that's inherent to conspiracy."[12] In other words, this mountain of entanglements and fantastic mythologies is really just a sign of the devolution of information into noise. I believe that science on its own is not equipped to challenge this kind of thinking without the aid of philosophy. In fact, philosophy should take the lead.

This book strives to bring philosophy back into relevant conversation with various disciplines, including science. Although most of the themes developed in the following pages are grounded in philosophy, art, and social science, "entropy" is a scientific law. The second law of thermodynamics names a law of nature that, although not explicitly discovered as a law until the nineteenth century, was an observable (if unnamed) constellation of phenomena addressed by all of the thinkers I explore. It is my position that entropic philosophy grants access into a way of questioning and analyzing both historical and contemporary phenomena in such a way that unveils a key component of our growing anxiety and despair.

We live in a time when human beings must face the realization not only of their individual and species mortality but also of the role we have played in escalating the state of global precariousness. Entropic philosophy provides a framework for speaking about occurrences of chaos and breakdown. While this book is in no way exhaustive, it tackles certain approaches in thinking that disavow or intensify entropic forces to the detriment of the species and the world. Illusions of control lead to much of the obscene damages produced by modern forms of advanced capitalism. While this study humbly takes up a selection of sites where this confounding relationship to entropic forces is evident—the creation of philosophies seeking to rule disorder, the domination over and leveling of natural diversity, the production of unutilizable waste, and the mistreatment of vulnerable populations—there are many other directions opened up by this approach.

Ultimately, we are presented with an ethical demand to rethink the human relationship to the various systems and energies that compose our shared yet fractured world. The counter-narrative to the bombastic practices of disregard and waste has a difficult time being heard, but it is never far away, and always waiting to be received. The call for care and respect in the face of finitude must be amplified because we are not locked into a determined death spiral, even as many have become resigned to attitudes of hopelessness or cynicism. Entropic philosophy offers vital insights into the contemporary condition in which humanity finds itself. Perhaps this wild and variable metaphor can help to confront the present without invoking some of the more pernicious metaphysical illusions conjured when faced with our own possible annihilation. It is in this spirit that I offer the following pages.

NOTES

1. Audre Lorde, *The Selected Works of Audre Lorde* (New York: W. W. Norton & Company, 2020), 7.

2. F. W. J. von Schelling, *On the History of Modern Philosophy*, ed. Andrew Bowie (Cambridge: Cambridge University Press, 1994), 131.

3. GPT-3, "A Robot Wrote This Entire Article. Are You Scared Yet, Human?" *The Guardian,* September 8, 2020, https://www.theguardian.com/commentisfree/2020/sep/08/robot-wrote-this-article-gpt-3.

4. Marta Torres Briegas, "Artificial Intelligence Has Made Its Way to Literature," *BBVA,* November 6, 2018, https://www.bbva.com/en/artificial-intelligence-made-way-literature/.

5. Matt Warman and Mattwarman, "Stephen Hawking tells Google 'Philosophy Is Dead,'" *The Telegraph,* May 17, 2011, http://www.telegraph.co.uk/technology/google/8520033/Stephen-Hawking-tells-Google-philosophy-is-dead.html.

6. Ibid.
7. Ibid.
8. George Dvorsky, "Neil deGrasse Tyson Slammed for Dismissing Philosophy as 'Useless,'" I09, *Gizmodo,* May 12, 2014, https://gizmodo.com/neil-degrasse-tyson-slammed-for-dismissing-philosophy-a-1575178224.
9. Massimo Pigliucci, "Neil deGrasse Tyson and the Value of Philosophy," *Huffpost,* May 16, 2014, https://www.huffingtonpost.com/massimo-pigliucci/neil-degrasse-tyson-and-the-value-of-philosophy_b_5330216.html.
10. BigThink, "Hey Bill Nye, 'Does Science Have All the Answers or Should We Do Philosophy Too?," *YouTube,* February 23, 2016, https://www.youtube.com/watch?v=ROe28Ma_tYM.
11. Olivia Goldhill, "Bill Nye, the Science Guy, Says I Convinced Him that Philosophy is Not Just a Load of Self-Indulgent Crap," *Quartz,* April 15, 2017, https://qz.com/960303/bill-nye-on-philosophy-the-science-guy-says-he-has-changed-his-mind/. Unlike his colleagues, however, Nye was at least persuaded to revisit his uninformed assessment and changed his mind a year later.
12. Hari Kunzru, "Easy Chair: Complexity," *Harper's Magazine* January 2021, 7.

Introduction

> Von Neumann, Shannon reports, suggested that there were two good reasons for calling the function "entropy." "It is already in use under that name," he is reported to have said, "and besides, it will give you a great edge in debates because nobody really knows what entropy is anyway."
>
> Myron Tribus, "Information Theory and Thermodynamics"[1]

Set in the near future, Ursula K. Le Guin's novel, *The Lathe of Heaven*, tells a story about a struggle for power between two men. George Orr suffers from dreams that rewrite reality, leaving him alone in the knowledge of what once was but is no longer. In an attempt to suppress his dreams, he overdoses and is consequently sent to Dr. William Haber, a dream specialist. Haber quickly learns that Orr is not delusional but does in fact have the ability to transform the world. However, this ability is filtered through dream logic and so the consequences are unpredictable in their effects and scope. Nevertheless, Haber builds a machine capable of inducing Orr's effective dreams and tries to better the human condition through suggestion and manipulation of Orr's unconscious.

Haber uses Orr's dreams in a misguided desire to cure the calamities of the world: overpopulation, pollution, war, and racism. Yet, each time he does so he manages to do unanticipated harm while simultaneously shoring up power and prestige for himself. He tells Orr to dream of feeling uncrowded, causing six billion inhabitants of the planet to die from plague. The erasure of the majority of humans does not solve war, so Haber suggests that Orr dream of world peace, only to create an alien invasion. Despite ending war between earthlings, the alien invasion does not cure racism, so Haber suggests an end to the question of race, producing a world in which everyone is grey. While Haber believes his intentions are good, fostering the spirit of scientific and humanitarian progress, he is in fact a destructive and nihilistic force. His goals work against diversity and encourage homogenization. Humanity, architecture, work, and nature increasingly coalesce into flavorless, colorless indistinction.

Le Guin's characters come to voice two opposing takes on the human relationship to entropy. With his monocular view set on the expurgation of human weakness and the centralization of power into his own hands, Haber accelerates entropy while simultaneously disavowing his role in doing so, instead positioning himself as a champion of life. As the world slides into eugenics, Orr pleads with the obsessed doctor to stop his relentless pursuit of progress. Haber counters that he is only working within the constant flux and danger of life where change is the rule, arguing that "when things don't change any longer, that's the end result of entropy, the heat-death of the universe."[2] The doctor regards entropy as a force to be eradicated, rather than a law to work within. He thinks that he is approaching the "brink of discovering and controlling, for the good of all mankind, a whole new force, an entire new field of antientropic energy, of the life-force, of the will to act, to do, to change!"[3] In this declaration, Haber espouses a particularly dangerous yet pervasive ideology that equates progress with domination and control of the laws of nature. He articulates the audacious claim that a single human can *and should* bend the world to their vision of progress, one that is built upon the forced movement toward natural and cultural uniforming. Orr beseeches Haber to relinquish his delusions of power and control by imploring him to realize that human beings are

> in the world, not against it. It doesn't work to try to stand outside of things and run them, that way. It just doesn't work, it goes against life. There is a way but you have to follow it. The world *is*, no matter how we think it ought to be.[4]

Orr understands that there is no antientropic power and that the only way to promote life is to work within, rather than against, entropy. He is a voice advocating for operating inside the parameters of the world's limitations and possibilities, rather than trying to efface or dominate them. As such, George Orr exemplifies the spirit of this book.

Entropic philosophy takes breakdown, decay, slackening, and creation as central to understanding the human condition. These phenomena are pervasive and have preoccupied philosophers, scientists, and artists for millennia. While awareness of them precedes the discovery of entropy as a scientific law, entropic philosophy provides a unique framework through which to understand their hold on thinking. Entropy is a multivalent concept that has had, according to Peter Lloyd Jones, an "extraordinary, even extravagant impact" on the layperson and for a good reason.[5] In many ways, it is conceptually overdetermined insofar as it appears in multiple scientific, philosophical, and artistic registers, taking on a variety of meanings. The most common understanding of entropy is the perceived (or imagined) movement from order to disorder. This expression of entropy can be felt in our very bones; every project, from the smallest act of tidying a house to the largest act of developing complex language for artificial intelligence, falls prey to the gnawing forces of disorder without constant influx of energy. Homes become messy and language can never be entirely purged of noise. But more is at work in entropic thinking than following the movement from stability to disarray.

There is a general sense of everything falling to pieces, particularly at this historical juncture—a pervasive, uneasy feeling that stability is impossible and everything, absolutely everything, is unraveling across political, social, economic, and individual lines. Entropic philosophy directly interrogates this existential anxiety about demise. If everything tends toward dissolution, what does this say about the meaningfulness of existence? Are we condemned to nihilism and despair in the face of death? Or, is there a way to acknowledge dissolution, working within its parameters, and in so doing fostering creativity and care?

This book approaches the fraught and distinctly modern sense of undoing through both historical and contemporary analyses of entropic phenomena. I submit the following studies to broaden the vocabulary diagnosing an aspect of modern nihilism and to envision ways out of it. The philosophy of entropy, often referred to as "entropics," provides a context for understanding expressions of chaos, breakdown, slackening, and creation. What follows will illuminate how these phenomena have been an ongoing concern for humanity and so must be taken into consideration and incorporated into whatever future is to come. This is a timely issue as we live in an age of global interconnection and shared precariousness. Working through entropics opens up a possible future that focuses on care and reverence for finite life, rather than the denial or acceleration of death.

For all of its ubiquity and familiarity, entropy remains a surprisingly vague and ambiguous notion. This nebulousness can create arguments between disciplines about imprecision and misuse of the term, but in this plasticity lies its strength. The concept is highly adaptable and lends itself to multidisciplinary applications. Outside of the scientific and technological disciplines, this is a secret known by select artists and writers: entropy is real, it is complex, its meaning malleable, and it reveals the nature of the universe and our place within it in important ways. Although most of the themes I develop are based in philosophy, art, and the social sciences, entropy is first and foremost a scientific concept. The Second Law of Thermodynamics names a law of nature that, although not explicitly discovered as such until the nineteenth century, was evident to many great thinkers who contemplated life and the forces that work within and against it.[6] These minds knew that humanity is engaged in a constant struggle with forces that sap vitality. While disorder is often met with denial or attempts to control or eradicate it, entropy does not have to figure as the enemy. Thinking through and working within it provides a far more powerful countermeasure to nihilism than merely denying or fearing it.

A basic existential fact is that preservation and maintenance are *exhausting*. It is an understatement to say that a great deal of energy expenditure is required to create and maintain both life and culture. Entropy is constantly exerting its unsettling effects in all aspects of life. It is so common as to be unobtrusive in most cases: fruit rots, tea cools, bodies slow. Sometimes, the entropic interrupts awareness in stark and obvious ways: arriving home from a trip only to find a neatly packed suitcase throwing up its contents, finding childhood neighborhoods taking a stark turn toward dilapidation, and the aging body injuring and taking more time to heal than it once did. Rarely are these occurrences overtly attributed to "entropy," but once they are, it seems to make them meaningful in an inimitable way. Whether or not one knows precisely what it means to assign these phenomena to the workings of the second law of thermodynamics, the metaphor retains a rather striking hold on the collective imagination.

While slackening and disorder are core components of the subsequent analyses, I also explore other aspects of the entropic as it permeates the past and present. Chaos, for example, can be understood to be complete heterogeneous dispersal where nothing is held in common and everything is separate and scattered at random. Additionally, chaos can indicate the drive toward homogenization: the evening out of differences, the cessation of movement and change, the principle of stability where all is at rest. This latter meaning, taken to its limit, necessarily ends in nothing less than the heat death of the universe, what physicists now refer to as the "Big Freeze."[7] Such a thought causes a different, though not unrelated kind of anxiety—the anxiety of death, the organism, and the universe itself dissolved into cold, uniform matter, the lack of distinction between parts and wholes. Total annihilation.

These multiple senses of entropy infuse aspects of the history of Western ideas, ultimately leading to another sense in which entropy is necessary for creation. Focusing solely on disorder, leveling, dissolution, and death almost invariably leads to pessimism, creating the feeling that no matter how mightily we struggle, all our efforts are ultimately in vain. Despite the labors to persevere, to live, and to thrive, everything will succumb, like Ozymandias, to what Sir Arthur Eddington coined "time's arrow."[8] Attempts to construct order for ourselves, our families, communities, and the planet are at best temporary and at worst illusory. This beguiling line of thinking can foment inaction and despair. However, there is more to be garnered from our forays into the entropic than abyssal dread or paralyzing resignation. Turning the focus to the other side of entropics may reveal a different way to imagine the direction of the world and the human place in it. This sense of entropy is one taken from artists and philosophers who are best at de-romanticizing and de-anthropomorphizing the machinations of entropy, thereby avoiding the snares of cynicism or naive enthusiasm. These writers and artists show how breaking down systems and demolishing order can give rise to the new. I hope that such insights will unearth possibilities for transformation rather than disquiet. Because if we cannot find different opportunities in the chaos, we have essentially given up; but it is too soon, and should always be too soon, for that.

This book is necessarily interdisciplinary in its approach because the entropic metaphor is variegated and its application far-reaching. This metaphor appears in science, philosophy, anthropology, psychoanalysis, and art, and it morphs and influences accordingly. Thus, rather than maintaining strict divisions between the various disciplines taken up in the following chapters, I aim to blur them so as to develop the fecundity of entropic philosophy. Despite the sometimes bizarre and often misguided attempts to keep science and humanities apart—even at war with each other—such border-drawing, gate-keeping tactics promise no viable vision of the future. In fact, the sciences and the humanities must work together in building a program for how to cope with impending energy diminution.[9] This study provides an orientation to entropic philosophy that is in line with the historical-scientific interpretations of the law, while eschewing overly rigid constraints often found in scientism. What entropy "means" is highly dependent upon the epistemic category under consideration, whether it be information theory, life sciences, psychology, thermodynamics, chemistry, literature, art, or economic theory. Given its appearance in such vastly different disciplines, as well as its omnipresence in lived experience, much can be gained by grappling with the underlying cluster of concepts that inform the term, particularly at this moment, where so much seems to be coming apart.

Focused readings into key moments in the history of Western ideas reveal ways in which thinkers engage or resist entropics. In their confrontations or disavowals, varied presentations of entropism arise that either open or foreclose pathways of thought, revealing a monumental battle between the disordering forces of chaos and the ordering demands of reason and *logos*. As a scientific law, entropy provides a way to understand how time not only moves forward but also why systems degrade without external contributions of energy. As a metaphor, entropy makes a multivalent net that far exceeds the strictly scientific applications of the law. As a result, entropic philosophy provides special parlance to talk about core aspects of human finitude involving scarcity, lack, disorder, and chaos. To enter the labyrinth of entropic philosophy is to embark on a journey of attempts to work against and within the chaos, with the hope of overcoming nihilistic fatalism when ruminating about the future.

DIFFERENT THREADS

In 1855, the physicist Rudolf Clausius, refining earlier work done by Nicolas Léonard Sadi Carnot in 1824, coined the term "entropy" from the Greek word ἐντροπία (*entropia*). While the main storyline of this book leads up to contemporary interpretations of entropy as a lawful movement toward homogenization, disorder, and destruction, there is another formulation of entropy hidden in ancient understanding. The earliest Greek usages of the term evoke a sense of care and reverence in the face of finitude and death. Hesiod's understanding of chaos, as discussed in chapter 2, will speak of two entropic paths (chaos and disorder) that grow and transform continuously until the development of thermodynamic theory. However, another expression of the entropic, what I call the "*entrepic*" (or "*entrepics*"), emerges from a philological analysis of the original Greek term. Ἐντροπία (*entropia*) or the Attic ἐντροπή means (1) a turning toward, (2) respect or reverence, and (3) shame or reproach.[10] This noun is derived from the verb ἐντρέπω (*entropia*). The middle voice form, ἐντρέπομαι, means "to turn about," "hesitate," or "feel misgiving," as well as "to turn toward," "give heed or regard to," "respect," or "reverence," as seen in Homer, Sophocles, and Plato.[11] Of utmost importance is the uniqueness of the middle voice in this context. The one who engages in hesitation or turning is not simply actively *doing* it or having it *passively* done to them but is rather co-responsible in the movement with the thing or the person being turned toward. The subject turns and that to which the subject turns is calling for this connection. This implies a mutual responsibility within the subject and the world that calls to it.

The uses of *entrepomai* (ἐντρέπομαι) in Homer and Sophocles show powerful countercurrents to the largely pessimistic bent found in Hesiod and the majority of thinkers who follow. Pointedly, the appearances of *entrepic* thinking as a "turning toward" in Homer and Sophocles occur in relation to death, thus signaling a special alignment to demise (a key component of the entropic). However, these *entrepic* inclinations indicate respect and reverence for life and for the human need to care for what is finite and vulnerable, not later but right now.

The most ancient instances of the verb ἐντρέπομαι occur in *The Iliad* and *The Odyssey* and convey a sense of veneration or esteem in the face of death.

In the heat of battle in *The Iliad*, the Trojan, Dolops, faces the Greek hero, Meges, in one of the many grisly confrontations during the Trojan onslaught of the Achaean forces. Menelaus steps in to protect Meges and spears Dolops through the back, killing him instantly. As the two Achaeans rip the armor from the Trojan's corpse, Hector calls to Melanippus, chiding him into action, crying, "Are we going to slacken like this? Has your dear heart no *regard* (ἐντρέπεται) for your kinsman who is slain?"[12] With these words, Hector asks Melanippus to turn toward and show regard for the fallen fighter, to honor and respect him through this turning, thereby soliciting respect for the dead.

Reinforcing this *entrepic* conception, *The Odyssey* opens with the eponymous hero languishing on Calypso's island and Athena pleading to her father on his behalf. The first words that Zeus speaks in the epic poem are a chastisement of the shamelessness of mortals who blame the gods for all of their calamities: "But they themselves, with their own reckless ways, compound their pains beyond their proper share."[13] Zeus then recounts the self-imposed tragedy of Aegisthus, infamous for plotting the demise of Agamemnon with Clytemnestra. Despite having sent Hermes to warn Aegisthus that Orestes would avenge his father's murder, the schemer pursues his doomed path, meeting his death through his own actions. In response, Athena draws Zeus' attention to the true and valiant warrior, marooned on the island: "Odysseus [who] longs to die."[14] Saddened by his hopelessness and despair, yearning to die far from his homeland and family, Athena entreats her father: "Olympian Zeus, have you no care (ἐντρέπεται) for *him* in your lofty heart?"[15] This petition conjures the same meaning from *The Iliad* of a plea to turn toward and care for suffering in the face of death. Without Zeus' aid, Odysseus will die miserable, separated from family and home.

In both *The Iliad* and *The Odyssey*, Homer depicts a revered character reprimanding another for failing to turn toward an aching individual. Hector implores Melanippus to honor the dead; Athena chastises Zeus for failing to care for suffering Odysseus. Here, in its earliest uses, long before the trajectory of European philosophy and science had settled on the entropic as a necessary tendency toward disorder and decline, Homer provides a complementary understanding. The inevitability of suffering and death for mortals requires reverent attention to their needs in order to forestall the destructive forces of decay. The *entrepic* demands a constant turning toward distress in order to ward off misery and decline.

The oldest extant use of ἐντροπή (*entrope*) as a noun comes from Sophocles' *Oedipus at Colonus*, where Sophocles tells the story of the king nearing the end of his life. Having been exiled from Thebes, Oedipus wanders around looking for his final resting spot. Along the journey, the blind old man implores the chorus not to despise him but to hear his story. Asking for the king of the country to come visit him, Oedipus asks, "Do you not believe that he will care (ἐντροπὴν) so much to give a thought to a blind man—that he will come himself to see me?"¹⁶ The fallen king questions whether the ruler of the land will turn toward him, respect and heed his plight. Later, he meets Theseus, to whom he reveals where his final resting place will be. He begs Theseus to keep the location a secret. Clearly alluding to the ultimate secret of death itself, Oedipus echoes Zeus' judgment in *The Odyssey*: human beings are wont to disregard the sage council of the divine which ultimately leads to madness. Following this proclamation, Oedipus says to his companion: "Let us now go to the place—a pressing summons from the god forces me—and delay (ἐντρεπώμεθα) no more."¹⁷ The meaning of ἐντρέπομαι conveys a hesitation or pause, but also a *turning about* as Oedipus asks that they not turn away from the secret site of his impending death. They must not hesitate to embrace the death that will protect Athens for eons. A divine summons calls Oedipus to this site, and together with Theseus, king of Athens, they must turn toward mortality with reverence and respect. This *entrepic* prohibition or hesitation in the face of Oedipus' final rest voices an opposing current to entropy understood only as the ceaseless and gloomy passage to death.

In yet another usage of ἐντρέπω, Sophocles' *Ajax* tells the story of the once-great warrior who, in a rage, slaughters all the animals in the Greek camp at Troy. Agamemnon granted Achilles' armor to Odysseus instead of Ajax and the latter becomes consumed with anger at the perceived dishonor. Athena caused a madness to deceive his eyes such that Ajax believes that he has willingly killed the Achaean kings who denied him the honors. As Ajax, fresh from massacre enters the stage, Athena calls to him, "Is this how much you care (ἐντρέπει) for an old ally?"¹⁸ Once again, in the face of death, Athena evokes an *entrepic* sense of care, essentially asking Ajax whether or not he has concern for his comrade and the sacred bond to the divine. Believing that he has in fact just killed his fellows, it is clear that Ajax lacks this necessary reverence for the sacredness of life.

Finally, Sophocles' *Oedipus the King* portrays Oedipus in the moment of recognition, speaking of his terrible crimes to his wife and mother, Jocasta. As he begins to tell her that Creon has informed him that he is his own father's murderer, Jocasta pleads with him not to confront the horrible truths revealed by death. As she attempts to convince him that the oracles failed in their prophecy portending Laius' death by his own son, she entreats, "so clear in this case were the oracles, so clear and false. Give them no heed (ἐντρέπου)."¹⁹ While the other uses of *entrepo* beseech those who do not give proper care to vulnerable, finite life, Jocasta offers a warning to Oedipus to *turn away* from the truth as it will ultimately lead to his own demise. This usage provides one more example of the *entrepic* as a kind of turning in the face of death.

The Homeric-Sophoclean formulations convey a sense of turning toward something worthy of respect, honor, care, and reverence, to someone who is not properly focused on it.[20] Homer and Sophocles use the verb *entrepomai* in the context of death (the ultimate dissolution) albeit in different ways. Homer's use in *The Iliad* and *The Odyssey* is one of giving regard, respecting, or revering. Sophocles' usage focuses more on turning about or hesitating when encountering death. Whether Hector's demand of respect for his comrades and polis, Athena's insistence that Zeus not allow Odysseus to succumb to suicide, or Athena and Oedipus' call for honoring the lives of citizens and animals, the *entrepic* appeals to heed the many expressions of finitude. As this project ultimately returns to challenge the modern scientific and metaphorical senses that have *lost* this understanding, it is critical to lay out these alternate threads at the beginning. While it will only return in the later chapters, the *entrepic* always shadows the noisier claims of its entropic sibling, never lagging far behind. In the spirit of bringing to light a kind of reverence and care that the *entrepic* induces, the final chapters take up matter, art, and philosophy that recover this meaning.

Creation emerges in the immense spaces between the maximal entropic states of the universe's beginning and end. As structures fall apart and die, others borrow from the waste and new ones are born. The end of time may be the total dispersal of all systems and parts, yet creation is this vast journey. Exploring entropic philosophy allows for a reorientation toward the terrifying for a new understanding of ruin as essential to creation. My approach in exploring the richness of the entropic metaphor is philosophical-historical and interdisciplinary. The chapters trace a line of thought beginning in select texts and culminating in entropy's appearance in contemporary formulations of age, waste, matter, and art. The thinkers and works I take up were chosen specifically because of how they illustrate the arc of entropic thinking that moves from attempts to dominate and control disorder, to a fatalism regarding its inevitability, to a consideration of entropy beyond the human, and finally to an affirmation of creation and care.[21]

While decline and slackening are inescapable and intrinsic to all systems, there is no reason either to deny or unnecessarily accelerate entropy through cultural, economic, or bodily ways of being. The task is to see these fissures not only as collapses but also as fertile settings for new ways of acting, thinking, and being. Ultimately, universal heat death does not concern humanity given the scope of time in which it will happen. However, time's irreversible arrow does, and although it cannot be reversed, it can certainly be lived otherwise. Facing entropy directly can lead to a different kind of discovery: finding ways to endure and creatively reimagine social and individual practices that reconfigure instead of hasten the decline. Humanity can choose to accept destruction as essential to life and thus embrace it by refusing ignorance, exploitation, and environmental ruin. In brief, we can turn with reverence and care to the preciousness, fleetingness, and beauty of finitude.

In the Western tradition, the entropy law has theoretical roots reaching back at least to the Presocratic philosophers. What follows does not claim to tell *the* story of the development of ways of thinking about the world that necessarily led to the formulation of the entropy law. Instead, it tells *a* story of certain tendencies in thinking that lead to a dangerous form of pessimism, and potentially to an orientation of care and reverence for life. Each chapter explores the manifold ways in which thinkers work against and within the many senses of entropics by utilizing key senses of entropy as a metaphor: entropy as (1) chaos (both as disorder and homogenization), (2) slackening and breakdown, and (3) a force of creation and a site of nurture.

Once entropy became a known law, it not only influenced the future of science (as well as economic theory, literature, philosophy, information theory, art, etc.) but also retroactively modified the understanding of past thinkers and ideas. In this spirit, chapter 1, "Entropy in Science and Metaphor," explores the relationship between the science of entropy and its metaphorical applications. Originally discovered as a way to measure energy unavailable for work in steam engines, entropy came to describe various phenomena of loss, time, chaos, and noise. Entropy's scientific power also gave rise to a proliferation of metaphorical formulations. I utilize Eric Zencey's claim that entropy functions as a ubiquitous modern root metaphor that anchors world interpretation and shared experience to mine these metaphorical riches.

Chapter 2, "Entropy in Ancient Greek Thought," addresses the appearance of chaos and disorder in ancient Greek philosophy and literature, specifically in the works of Hesiod, Homer, Anaximander, Anaxagoras, Plato, and Aristotle. Beginning with Hesiod, chaos appears in the establishment of the cosmos itself and in the human advice to order one's life well. As Hesiod tells his brother in *Works and Days*, "For mortals order is best, disorder is worst."[22] While Hesiod poetically chides his wayward brother to sort out his life, Anaximander speaks of the penalty of existence as a return to chaotic origins. Anaxagoras posits a primary sense of cosmic chaos existing before the ordering movement of Mind. Chaos, in the Anaxagorean sense, is total entropy in the form of disorder of homogenous inert matter, the universal mixture before Mind introduces motion and time. Plato's *Timaeus* also speaks of an originary chaos existing before a demiurge arranges the universe out of elemental disorder. Unlike Anaxagoras, Timaeus' universe includes divine mechanisms to ensure that this originary state of chaos never returns. Plato's *Statesmen* provides an additional challenge to the inevitability of time's forward arrow through its portrayal of divine intervention in the material cosmos. Plato's emphasis on form and order as victorious is reiterated through a different framework by Aristotle's subordination of lack to an organizing principle. For Aristotle, privation can only be predatory, and never primary or causal in any given entity, thereby bringing its threat fully under control of the formal principle.

Chapter 3, "Entropy in German Philosophies of Nature," builds upon the insights gleaned from the conception of nature emergent in dialogue with ancient Greek formulations. German thinking of the eighteenth and nineteenth centuries presents the entropic as a threat to rational breakdown and as a kind of melancholy pervading finite life. Immanuel Kant sets up a problem between rational cognition and the natural world that both F. W. J. von Schelling and G. W. F. Hegel attempt to address. While Kant dallies in considerations of geological and rational chaos in *The Critique of Judgment*, he fundamentally embraces a belief in human belongingness to the world. While Schelling's philosophy of nature gives a real place to forces that work against the divine order, ultimately, the divine principle of light ascends over the irrational chaos. Following a brief treatment of Kant and Schelling, I turn to a more careful study of Hegel's *Philosophy of Nature* and the treatment of mortal life, exposing how irrationality pulls entities relentlessly toward dispersal. Hegel's ultimate demand for nature's self-sacrifice in the service of spirit's ascension shows how far-reaching the forces of chaos infiltrate nature's materiality and the extreme measures philosophy often takes in order to rise above and subdue them.

Chapter 4, "Leveling Modernity: Entropy in Freud and Lévi-Strauss," traces the explicit effects of the law into the twentieth century. By the time Freud and Lévi-Strauss name the retrograde character of psychic and social life, the second law of thermodynamics has been firmly established as a natural law with far-reaching repercussions. Freud and Lévi-Strauss are two central figures inheriting the repercussions of the entropy law's discovery, showing how its power as a metaphor extends beyond natural science. Using psychoanalysis and anthropology, both authors provide profound expressions of entropics by describing universal tendencies toward leveling life and civilization. Whereas Freud weaves a tale of life emerging from and desiring a return to the inorganic, Lévi-Strauss depicts all human society devolving into a uniform state, away from complexity and difference and toward simplicity and homogeneity. Both thinkers bring out the fatalism lying at the heart of entropics, insofar as human beings on psychological and social levels are no different than any other system that uses limited energies for self-maintenance.

The heavy weight of entropic pessimism and the misguided relationship to it produce damaging contemporary social practices. Chapter 5, "Old Age and Entropic Decline," builds upon the psychological and anthropological insights gleaned from Freud and Lévi-Strauss. This chapter studies the excesses produced by contemporary advanced capitalist structures, which are fundamentally built upon the *denial and acceleration* of entropic breakdown. Focusing on the working elderly through the work of Simone de Beauvoir and Karyn Ball, I describe how the body, which has been conceived as a machine since the industrial revolution, is conditioned for maximal output. This machine, as all machines, cannot exist in perpetual motion but necessarily capitulates to breakdown as it ages and wears out. Rather than conceding this, all but a handful of materially over-privileged individuals must work well into an age of diminishing returns. Capitalism extracts as much labor and consumption out of aging bodies as possible before they perish, using every last drop of energy before discarding them to the chaos of death.

At the moment of glimpsing the most harrowing aspects of entropic thinking, I bring back *entrepic* thought, with its focus on reverence and care. A primary goal of this book is to show how entropy functions as a scientific, philosophical, and sociological metaphor charting breakdown and disorder. However, it additionally advocates for reconceiving humanity's place in the various spiraling systems of which it is a part. In this spirit, the final two chapters challenge the pessimism that all too easily arises from ruminations on decline. Chapter 6, "Entropic Excess: Reconfiguring Matter and Waste," employs Jane Bennett's vital materialism and Robert Smithson's entropic artworks to contest the notion that entropy is necessarily a one-way ticket to cynicism and despair. This chapter investigates the possibilities of thinking about entropy in specifically *nonhuman* ways, thus destabilizing anthropocentric privilege so as to see the world anew. Organic and inorganic systems overlap and interweave, sharing amorphous and porous boundaries that far exceed the human. Meditating on different formulations of bodies helps to shake free from toxic, sedimented forms of thinking by conceiving materiality as a dynamic web of overlapping systems constantly borrowing from and impacting each other.

This book is inspired by many thinkers, but perhaps the most profound source is the artist, Robert Smithson. Creator of one of the most important works of art in the twentieth century, the *Spiral Jetty*, Smithson, approaches entropy as the place of emergence and creation. Through understanding many of the ways that chaos, decay, and dissolution have been and continue to be of paramount material, psychological, social, and philosophical concern provides critical insight into how to use them as transformative and creative. The book thus concludes by re-envisioning the relationship between form and destruction. Chapter 7, "Destruction and the Joy of Creation," questions the very power of entropy as unbreakable law, while also celebrating its inevitability. When Heraclitus remarks, "The fairest order (*kosmos*) is a random heap of sweepings,"[23] he alerts us to a force that not only destroys order but may, in fact, *give rise to* order and beauty. Just as Chaos is the first god in Hesiod's cosmogony, the return to this paradoxically generative principle provides a counterpoint to the disquiet about disorder. II turn finally to Nietzsche, who concludes his praise of the Dionysian in the *Twilight of the Idols* with the observation that the link between tragic insight and life-affirmation hinges on a kind of joy, the "eternal joy of becoming—that joy that also includes in itself the *joy of* destruction."[24] Here, the fecundity of entropy becomes a creative force. I turn once more to Smithson as an embodiment of the artist capable of transforming entropy into aesthetic creation and, in so doing, revaluing pessimism into affirmation.

A sense of certainty regarding the inevitable heat death of the universe leads to a kind of fatalism that allows us to sit passively by as our shared world crumbles and burns. Yet, entropic inevitability does not prohibit contemplating different modes of living and acting that promote creativity and affirmation. While the disordering principle of entropy is rife with danger to living beings that organize and are organized, reworking the philosophical priority of order and stability opens a wealth of new perspectives. The goal is to forge different pathways of thinking, doing, and being that honor not only the human but the world in all of its untold materializations.

NOTES

1. M. Tribus, "Information Theory and Thermodynamics," in *Heat Transfer, Thermodynamics and Education: Boelter Anniversary Volume*, ed. H. A. Johnson (New York: McGraw Hill, 1964), 354.
2. Ursula K. Le Guin, *The Lathe of Heaven* (New York: Avon Books, 1971), 135.
3. Ibid, 135–136.
4. Ibid, 136.
5. Peter Lloyd Jones, "Some Thoughts on Rudolf Arnheim's Book 'Entropy and Art,'" *Leonardo* 6 (1973): 29. Jones attributes the grandiose allure of the second law as a metaphor for degeneration to the fact that it is an extremal principle and these "easily acquire anthropomorphic overtones." Ibid, 30.
6. The three laws of thermodynamics are: (1) The Law of Conservation of Energy, which states that in an isolated system, energy can be neither created nor destroyed, it can only change form. (2) Within an isolated system, entropy always increases, moving toward a state of systemic equilibrium. (3) The entropy of a system approaches a constant value as the temperature approaches absolute zero (the lowest theoretical temperature possible). In addition, there is also a "zeroth" law that precedes these three that states if two thermodynamic systems are in equilibrium with a third, then they are in thermal equilibrium with each other. Taken together, these laws are important because of their necessity as well as their scope—excepting the very smallest quantum phenomena, they apply to all systems. While the laws of thermodynamics are often capitalized, I will be referring to them in lower case in all further discussions.

7. Eric Betz, "The Big Crunch Vs. the Big Freeze," *Astronomy* (January 2021), 50–52.

8. David Layzer, "The Arrow of Time," *Scientific American* (1975): 56–69.

9. Many of the greatest minds of the twentieth century, such as Maurice Merleau-Ponty, Edmund Husserl, Simone de Beauvoir, Claude Lévi-Strauss, and Sigmund Freud, understood their theoretical work to be an exchange and cross-pollination between natural sciences, social sciences, economic theory, mathematics, and humanities.

10. Henry George Liddell and Robert Scott, *A Greek-English Lexicon*, 9th ed. (Oxford: Clarendon Press, 1940), 575–576.

11. Ibid, 575.

12. Homer. *The Iliad*, trans. Robert Fagles (New York: Penguin Books, 1991), 4.554. Italics my own.

13. Homer, *The Odyssey*, ed. and trans. Robert Fagles (New York: Penguin Books, 1999), 1.40.

14. Ibid, 1.70.

15. Ibid, 79, 1.71–72.

16. Sophocles, "Oedipus at Colonus," in *Sophocles I*, ed. David Grene and Richard Lattimore, trans. Richard Lattimore, 2nd ed. (Chicago: University of Chicago Press, 1991), 299. As I go on to discuss, the more ancient verb occurs in Homer, Sophocles, and Plato which all reinforce the notion of turning toward, care, and reverence. I return to *Oedipus at Colonus* in chapter 5.

17. Ibid, 1759.

18. Sophocles, "Ajax," in *The Complete Greek Tragedies*, ed. David Grene and Richmond Lattimore, trans. John Moore, vol. 2, Sophocles II (Chicago: The University of Chicago Press, 1969), 90. While I have explored almost all of the references to ἐντρέπω in Greek literature, there remains one other worth mentioning. In Plato's *Crito*, the laws chide Socrates for saying that he preferred death to exile during his trial, "Now, however, those words do not make you ashamed, and you pay no heed (ἐντρέπει) to us, the laws, as you plan to destroy us." Plato, "Crito," in *Plato: Complete Works*, ed. and trans. Donald J. Zeyl and John M. Cooper (Indianapolis: Hackett Publishing Company, 1997), 52d. Even in this later usage, the meaning of respect and care is central to the notion of the *entrepic*.

19. Sophocles, *Oedipus the King*, in *Sophocles I*, ed. David Grene and Richard Lattimore, trans. Richard Lattimore, 2nd ed. (Chicago: University of Chicago Press, 1991) 723.

20. *Entrepic* care is not unlike the notion of love running throughout bell hooks' later works, which is a love that "combines acknowledgment, care, responsibility, commitment, and knowledge." This feminist love, coupled with justice, "has the power to transform us, giving us the strength to oppose domination." bell hooks, *Feminism is for Everybody: Passionate Politics* (Cambridge: South End Press, 2000), 104.

21. To be clear, although there is a noticeable and unavoidable air of pessimism around the scientific assessment of life on Earth, the majority of authors tackling our gloomy future offer urgent pleas to change, adapt, reimagine, and wake up. See, for

example, Bill McKibben, *The End of Nature* (New York: Bloomsbury Publishing PLC, 2003), Peter F. Sale, *Our Dying Planet: An Ecologist's View of the Crisis We Face* (Oakland: University of California Press, 2011), and Jedediah Purdy, *After Nature: A Politics for the Anthropocene* (Cambridge: Harvard University Press, 2015). Unfortunately, many works also elicit a profound sense of fatalism. I want to challenge this despair and ask instead how we can take the very worst aspects of entropic devastation: waste, pollution, abuses of humanity and life itself, and rather than imagining them as inevitable, envision them as sites calling out for attention. Bronislaw Szerszynski has a similar goal to forge passages between physical and social sciences to "to grasp the heterogeneous, shifting and contested nature of the Earth's spiritual body, and thereby to start to develop a postsecular analysis of a dynamic planet." Bronislaw Szerszynski, "Gods of the Anthropocene: Geo-Spiritual Formations in the Earth's New Epoch," *Special Issue: Geosocial Formations and the Anthropocene* in *Theory Culture & Society* 34 (2–3), 2017, 255. Martin Flament Fultot believes that any macroethics needs "to embrace all aspects of reality, including, ironically, entropy itself," a conclusion with which I wholeheartedly agree. Martin Flament Fultot, "Ethics of Entropy,": *The American Philosophical Association's Newsletter on Philosophy and Computers* 15 (2) Spring 2016, 8.

22. Hesiod, *Works and Days* in *Theogony, Works and Day, Shield*, trans. Apostolos N. Athanassakis, 1st ed. (Baltimore: Johns Hopkins University Press, 1983), 472.

23. Heraclitus, Fr. B46, in *The Texts of Early Greek Philosophy Greek Philosophy*, trans. Daniel W. Graham (Cambridge: Cambridge University Press, 2010). Greek *kosmos* can mean either order in general or a world in particular, therefore serving as a model for the kind of systems under discussion throughout this book.

24. Friedrich Nietzsche, *Twilight of the Idols* ed. and trans. Richard Polt (Indianapolis: Hackett Publishing Company, 1997), 91. Also pulling on Nietzschean themes, Apple Zefalius Igrek discusses entropic philosophy in his book, *Entropic Affirmation: On the Origins of Conflict in Change, Death, and Otherness*. Whereas I am concerned more with the human response to finitude, Igrek deals with developing an approach to radical, infinite otherness. Apple Zefalius Igrek, *Entropic Affirmation: On the Origins of Conflict in Change, Death, and Otherness* (Lanham: Lexington Books, 2018).

Chapter 1

Entropy in Science and Metaphor

If your theory is found to be against the second law of thermodynamics I can give you no hope; there is nothing for it but to collapse in deepest humiliation.

Sir Arthur Eddington, The Nature of the Physical World[1]

I am part of the part that once was everything,
Part of the darkness which gave birth to light,
That haughty light which envies mother night
Her ancient rank and place and would be king—
Yet it does not succeed: however it contend,
It sticks to bodies in the end.
It streams from bodies, it lends bodies beauty,
A body won't let it progress;
So it will not take long, I guess,
And with the bodies it will perish too.

Goethe, Faust[2]

In the novel, *A Wild Sheep Chase*, Haruki Murakami tells the story of a man at the threshold between youthful carelessness and the weight of adult responsibility. The novel begins with the death of one of the protagonist's past lovers. Following this death, the story moves into a staccato recapture of the unnamed protagonist's divorce from his wife and discovery of a new woman with irresistible ears. The character's thoughts, as well as his relationships, are fractured and broken. Despite the opening chapter offering only the scattered pieces of a life whose story begins in an undetailed death, the reader desires to take these splinters and make them whole. Put another way, the reader is encouraged to take the chaotic disarray of a broken existence and make it coherent. But this act of unification requires energy on the reader's part.

At the conclusion of the novel, the protagonist ultimately finds himself confronting death once again. But instead of the disjointed and one-dimensional death of a girl, this death is of a friend who returns to provide meaning for what initially seemed like a nonsensical journey to find a sheep who may or may not have an immoral, authoritarian-driven plan for world domination. Murakami's tale begins and ends with death, in between which unfolds moments of entropic chaos. The protagonist commences with the realization that he is an impossible point of rest in the eternal flux of the universe,[3] and ends experiencing his friend's self-sacrifice to prevent the sheep's plan to achieve the goal "of total conceptual anarchy. A scheme in which all opposites would be resolved into unity."[4] Despite the seemingly chaotic and disjointed story, it provides a profoundly *anti*-entropic exposition. In fact, something about the way in which much of the story is pieced together feels somewhat *backward*, as if the flow of time wants to move in reverse and the reader must work against this. The seemingly random events and thoughts of the main character only become coherent at the conclusion providing the reader a feeling of relief at randomness coalescing into calm. Hideaki Yanagisawa describes this phenomenon in the novel as the experience of joy resulting from a temporary artistic decrease in entropy.[5] This entropic decrease is joyful precisely because it runs counter to the way in which time and systemic breakdown are experienced phenomenologically. The pleasure of overcoming entropy is central to this narrative and certainly many other aesthetic experiences. But what exactly is entropy?

THE SCIENCE OF ENTROPY

Entropy has been called time's arrow, the only real proof for the movement forward between the past and future.[6] Although based in probability, it is perhaps the only law that is certain. Entropy's lawfulness may be best illustrated by counterexamples. The uncanniness of film played in reverse results from the realization that outside of artificial manipulation, time only moves forward. We are familiar with knocking a glass off the table, watching it shatter into a hundred pieces. But none of us, without the imposition of cinematic or digital alteration, has ever seen a shattered glass reform and leap back onto the table; and outside of virtual reality or film, no one ever will. Because it unfailingly moves toward a maximum, entropy relentlessly drives time (and thus a certain way of experiencing the world) forward. Forward to what is another question altogether.

Classical mechanics, exemplified by Newtonian physics, deals with force, energy, position, and velocity of objects of a nonzero size (rather than those existing on the quantum level). Important within classical mechanics is the emphasis on locomotion, which is both without quality and, significantly, *reversible*. An object can move or can stop; the laws of physics are not violated by objects relocating in opposite directions from other objects of similar makeup. Going in one direction does not prevent an object from going in the opposite. Predictability is central to classical mechanics in that the same set of conditions will yield the same outcome. Thus, one should be able to work from either the original conditions to the outcome or from the outcome back to the original conditions. The second law of thermodynamics, or the entropy law, is *not* reversible, however. Rather, entropy necessarily increases. As such, entropy tells a different story about the universe than does classical mechanics. As the economist Nicholas Georgescu-Roegen notes, physicists discovered "that heat always moves by itself in one direction only, from the hotter to the colder body. This led to the recognition that there are phenomena which cannot be reduced to locomotion and hence explained by mechanics."[7] Even if *locally* entropy decreases (heating with natural gas increases the temperature of the closed system of a home, for example) it increases *globally* (as gas must be harvested, using more energy in the extraction and delivery of it than captured for the sake of heat, thus contributing to the overall increase of unusable waste). Locally, entropy can be staved off through systemic borrowing, but universally, it increases without exception. Ultimately, therefore, the entropy law is unidirectional. Or, as Ilya Prigogine observes, "only irreversible processes contribute to entropy production. Obviously, the second law expresses the fact that irreversible processes lead to the one-sidedness of time."[8] In any closed system, energy decreases without additional energy from another system, for which the same rule applies, ad infinitum, until the absolute end of the universe itself. Pandora's box has been opened and the contents have spilled out in such a way that stuffing them all back in would require more energy than is available in the cosmos as a whole to accomplish.

Thermodynamics emerged out of the study of the proficiency of machines, ultimately proving the impossibility of perpetual motion devices.[9] In 1824, Sadi Carnot penned a memoir wherein he analyzed the efficiency of steam engines based on temperature differentials. Classical mechanics was unable to account for unidirectional movement because it recognized only those laws that are reversible. However, Sadi Carnot observed that heat always moves unidirectionally from hotter to colder bodies and spaces, thus giving rise to a new branch of physics devoted to explaining this singular natural law. Rudolf Clausius, who coined the term "entropy," was the first to clearly formulate the second law of thermodynamics in the mid-nineteenth century as one that measures how much thermal energy is unavailable for work in any given closed system (as with Sadi Carnot, the initial case being in a steam engine). Clausius discovered two laws regulating energy circulation in thermodynamics: (1) the energy of the universe remains constant, that is, matter and energy are neither created nor destroyed but only transformed and (2) entropy in the universe always moves toward a maximum. This may appear to present a conundrum, insofar as there is no net loss of energy, and yet entropy charts an increasing loss of it. However, if entropy is understood to measure the transformation from hotter to cooler, or available to unavailable energy, it becomes easier to couple the first and second laws. The quantity of energy remains constant, while the quality of energy changes from useful to useless.

Energy is understood as either *free* (energy available for mechanical work) or *bound* (unavailable mechanical energy). Once free energy has been exploited, it transforms into bound (or latent) energy. While there is no overall loss of energy in the universe, "the final outcome is a state where all energy is latent, the Heat Death as it was called in the earliest thermodynamic theory."[10] In addition to signaling the lawful degradation of the universe into maximum entropy (complete loss of available energy for work, or "the Big Freeze") the second law also shows that time itself is unidirectional. To move from lesser to greater states of entropy requires earlier and later states in time, so time always walks *forward* and never in reverse.[11] Such a conception accordingly challenges any other formulation where time might be conceived as cyclical, reversible, or simply the product of human experience alone.[12]

It is helpful to remember that the second law charts the dissipation of heat energy available for work in a *system*. Although systems can take different forms on microcosmic and macrocosmic levels, to be a system means to be in some way bounded. Thus, a body can be a system, as well as a geographical place, a cell phone, or a collection of planetary bodies connected by gravity. Clausius noted that without external energy, a machine system could not convert heat from one body to another at a higher temperature. Without the input of additional energy from outside the "closed" system (in this case of heat-producing machines) breakdown occurs. This is because, as Brian Greene observes, entropy "declares that the production of waste is unavoidable," therefore revealing "that everything in the universe has an overwhelming tendency to run down, to degrade, to wither."[13]

Despite the fact that Clausius was mistaken about the nature of heat (he believed it to be a fluid), he crystalized the nature of entropy as a measurement of that which is *lost* in energy exchanges. Heat always moves from a warmer body or system to a cooler one and never (without additional energy input) in reverse—from cooler to warmer. This unidirectional movement thus means that machines always lose energy with entropy gauging the decrease in the total amount of energy available for work. Free energy, therefore, is energy available for work (a state of low entropy) whereas bound energy is energy that is unavailable for work (a state of high entropy).[14] For example, coal is in a state of low entropy and can therefore be used as a fuel source, but utilizing it thus produces the high entropy waste of coal ash and scrubber sludge, that is, waste substances unable to fuel any kind of work.

Ludwig Boltzmann proposed that entropy is that which measures the movement toward the *homogenous* distribution of heat in a sealed system, much like the plan formulated by Murakami's diabolical sheep. Entropy increases because probability increases. In what may seem to be counterintuitive, this homogeneity is actually a movement toward randomness, an orderless state with no differences between the elements within the system. Think, for example, of how ink dropped into a glass of water fans out until only an even dispersal of the color remains. The movement toward homogeneity brings the second law into an interesting relationship to the first law (the conservation of matter and energy). Assuming a closed system, entropy never decreases such that entropic loss is *inevitable*. However, this does not mean that energy is *destroyed*, only that the distribution of it evens out, thereby preventing movement from low to high entropic states altogether. Change, in other words, slows down and inescapably ceases, even as matter and energy neither come into nor pass out of existence. This is largely due to the fact that the parts do not inherently cohere with each other and tend toward randomization (followed by homogenization) without energy added to forestall this disordering movement. Boltzmann formulated entropy as a probability function, a movement toward randomness, thereby moving beyond the understanding of entropy as a measurement of energy unavailable for work in heat engines and toward entropy as molecular homogenization.[15] Closed systems lead to greater statistical probability, or the leveling of difference into homogeneity.

Clausius' more notable observation was that the entropy of the universe tends toward a maximum. Regardless of what the first law states regarding energy conservation, the tendency toward entropy points not to a stable self-renewing universe but rather to a universe that is hemorrhaging heat. As machines, information, and bodies necessarily undergo change, there is an ever-increasing repository of unavailable energy (what often appears to human beings as "waste"). Luciana Terranova and Tiziana Parisi explain that

> although the amount of energy in the system and its environment stays the same (i.e., the first law of thermodynamics, of conservation of energy, holds), the amount of energy available to do work decreases and entropy, as heat, noise and uncertainty, increases.[16]

Even as we can stave off entropy on the local level (transferring energy from one system to another, such as when I eat an apple from the tree in my yard to maintain bodily integrity) given enough years, there will be no more systems from which to borrow. Inevitably, the second law dictates thermal equilibrium and the eventual "heat death" of the universe, trillions of years into the future, when change ceases and all elements are equally dispersed throughout. Although this is an oft-repeated and highly useful way to talk about entropy, it is also, in some senses, an oversimplification. Jeff Hester clarifies that

> entropy is actually a quantitative measure of how many different ways you can rearrange the components of something without changing its bulk properties.... Rather than "disorder increases," what the Second Law of Thermodynamics actually says is that random changes tend to move things toward statistically more likely configurations.[17]

In other words, a sister notion to entropy as *disorder* is one wherein entropy registers the movement toward statistically more likely states or *decreasing complexity*. In this way, Hester explains the entropy law as being "as much about building structure and complexity as it is about tearing them down."[18]

This important dual quality of entropy allows for not only observing dissipation and decline but for also understanding a central element in creation. For example, Hester describes an interstellar gas cloud collapsing to form a young star with planets as illustrative of marvelous creation emergent from entropic forces. Even though cosmically entropy increases due to the nature of the second law as a *law*, locally entropy is temporarily lessened through the blending and borrowing of systems. Here is where we find not only destruction but creation in all of its manifestations—galaxies, planetary systems, amoeba, forests, and the Caves of Lascaux.

One of the more creative and memorable challenges to the irreversibility and pervasive destructiveness of entropy came from an unusual thought experiment. In 1871, J. Clerk Maxwell proposed a hypothesis wherein a tiny demon ("Maxwell's Demon") is positioned at a door between two chambers. In this thought experiment, the demon (mysteriously contributing no energy itself) separates molecules between the two chambers such that it can create differences in temperature between them without doing any work. The demon would effectively allow swifter molecules to pass through a small hole in one direction and the slower molecules to pass through from the other. In doing so, this molecule-sized demon would raise the temperature of the first chamber, while lowering the temperature of the second (thus refuting, hypothetically, the idea that heat always dissipates according to entropy). In other words, the demon "can unbind bound energy and, hence, defeat the Entropy Law of statistical thermodynamics."[19] Maxwell's anti-entropic demon does, theoretically at least, call into question entropic lawfulness, since it is possible to conceive, if not a demon, then a semipermeable membrane that *could* do this kind of separation. Yet, the demon, or membrane, cannot sufficiently serve as a perpetual motion sorting machine, even in thought. The demon needs information and energy, thereby effectively showing the possibility of cheating or reversing entropy. While only a hypothetical thought experiment, Maxwell's Demon provoked scientists to challenge the inevitability and necessity of entropy's effects as well as to explore other areas where entropy might be functioning.

The debate about Maxwell's Demon led to the expansion of entropy into the burgeoning field of information theory. Leon Brillouin associated information with entropy (that which can be transmitted and preserved from randomness and confusion). Further developing the definition beyond machines, Claude Shannon developed information theory in 1948 on the basis of Boltzmann's equation for entropy.[20] In his 1939 paper, "A Mathematical Theory of Communication," Shannon describes entropy as a measure of information in the transmission of a message, ushering in a different way to think about entropy's application. Rather than measuring an increase toward disorder or homogenization, Shannon's entropy assesses information in terms of novelty or what was not already known. Entropy, in communication theory, charts surprise. Information is measured by learning something new, whereas redundancy provides no fresh knowledge. This is why Shannon evaluated information in terms of low and high entropy depending upon how predictable or unpredictable it is. For Shannon, entropy is the measure of uncertainty in the transmission of information. A low-probability event yields more information because it contains a greater element of surprise (the appearance of a green ladybug, for example). A high-probability event offers less information and is thus unsurprising (a red ladybug, for example). Entropy in information theory appraises the loss or lack of information, delineating the number of possible answers to a given question. The more information there is, the fewer possible answers to a question, whereas less information produces a greater number of possible answers.[21] Redundant information yields nothing new, whereas randomness and unpredictability generate informational novelty. For example, if I flip a coin, there are only two possible outcomes: heads or tails. Therefore, less information is garnered from the various outcomes of my coin tosses. However, if I role six Yahtzee dice, I have increased information because the arrangement of the dice offers more variables than either heads or tails; there are more possible answers to the question: what will I roll next? Thus, the dice provide *more* information *because* their arrangement is less predictable, thereby exhibiting entropy through unpredictability and novelty, rather than redundancy (understood in terms of regularity).

Information transmission is never perfect; consequently, whatever form it takes inevitably undergoes loss in terms of noise. As with other forms of entropy, what one system accomplishes through order and predictability comes at the cost of increased disorder elsewhere. However, Shannon's equivalence of high entropy with unpredictability gives rise to a sense of entropy as productive rather than merely negative. Patricia Clough explicates that

> information is a local organization against entropy, a temporal deferral of entropy—that is life. Even as entropy increases in the universe as a whole, information can prevent entropic collapse temporarily as extrinsic resources of informational order or energy arise.[22]

Entropy is at a maximum when all outcomes of the units involved in information transmission are equally likely (true randomness), and entropy decreases as the predictability of the informational units increase. Whereas high entropy makes *understanding* the information transmitted more difficult, the information (*because* it is less predictable) actually contains more novelty. By "identifying entropy with information," Katherine N. Hayles notes, Shannon allowed for "entropy to be reconceptualized as the thermodynamic motor driving systems to self-organization rather than as the heat engine driving the world to universal heat death."[23] In this way, "chaos" changed from a sense of breakdown to a sense of complexity, unpredictability, and novelty.

Even this brief overview shows how malleable and far-reaching the scientific uses of entropy can be. Jeremy Campbell explains that entropy, "which began with investigations of something as objective and practical as the functioning of steam engines . . . gradually became so abstract it was subsumed by the theory of probability, and so general as to be applied to the universe as a whole."[24] Given the generative effects of the law on the human imagination, Campbell's extrapolation from steam engines to the entire universe is apt. The entropy law not only takes diverse scientific paths but also becomes a dynamic metaphor finding its way into disparate fields of inquiry. This plasticity can give rise to confusion and lack of precision; it is also what makes it a bountiful temporal metaphor. On the subatomic level, time does not operate in a forward-moving direction; rather, it operates in terms of probabilities: there, we find movement, change of place, vibration, but no movement *forward in time*. On the super-atomic level, however, time necessarily moves forward or toward increased entropy. This singular natural law can therefore be felt on the phenomenal level. Not only are human beings essentially temporal, but the experiences of torpor and breakdown are woven into our bodies and thus into our understanding of self. At the deepest level, the existential reality of entropics is constitutive of facticity and finitude.

THE METAPHOR OF ENTROPY

Although the entropy law was discovered relatively recently, it provided a term to retroactively understand phenomena that have always been of concern to human beings. Entropy as a metaphor brings to the foreground events that were always there but called by different appellations. This is the power of entropy's ubiquity and lawfulness: once found, it appears everywhere. Jorge Luis Borges speaks of a similar phenomenon in his short essay "Kafka and his Precursors." There, he describes a particular style belonging to Kafka that is far more common in literature than his writings alone, noting that personages as disparate as Zeno and Han Yu, to Kierkegaard and Browning, exemplify Kafka's peculiar genius while not necessarily resembling each other in manner, time, or theme. Borges' point in this brief essay highlights that without Kafka, it would not be possible to distinguish his particular voice in these earlier works because it simply wouldn't exist. "In each of these texts we find Kafka's idiosyncrasy to a greater or lesser degree, but if Kafka had never written a line, we would not perceive this quality; in other words, it would not exist."[25] One could not find what is "Kafkaesque" in earlier authors around the world had Kafka not written. But since he did, his style retroactively forms a lens through which to read other works. As Borges concludes, "the fact is that every writer *creates* his own precursors. His work modifies our conception of the past, as it will modify the future."[26] Kafka's themes can now be seen in thinkers reaching all the way back to Zeno's absurd paradoxes because his style illuminates what would otherwise remain hidden. In a similar way, the entropy law brings to the surface abundant themes of chaos, breakdown, slackening, and dissipation from before its discovery as law.

In his 1942 book, *World Hypotheses: Prolegomena to a Systematic Philosophy and a Complete Survey of Metaphysics*, Stephen Pepper conjectures that each great philosophical tradition in the West has a root metaphor that anchors and guides the vision promoted by a school of thought.[27] Arguing against logical positivism, Pepper repudiates the notion of truth outside of interpretation. Four metaphors (much like Thomas Kuhn's paradigms) vie for supremacy by claiming a totalizing theoretical vision of reality. Root metaphors claim elucidatory power over heterogeneous phenomena. There is nothing inherently *rational* in a chosen metaphor. Rather, success is based on its ability to serve as an explanatory model for emergent factual evidence.[28] Eric Zencey challenges Pepper's hypothesis that there are only four "root metaphors" in Western worldviews. In addition to the metaphors listed by Pepper (formism, mechanism, organicism, and contextualism), Zencey proposes that entropy is a useful and equally persuasive root metaphor.[29] The wide-ranging applicability of the entropic metaphor, particularly in the modern era, is central to Zencey's endorsement of its candidacy as a root metaphor. As with Borges' claim that once Kafka wrote, the Kafkaesque was evident throughout literature, so was the conceptual net of entropy illuminated by the discovery of the second law. What was already there but not specifically designated came to the foreground once the entropy law was widely known outside of scientific study. "The history of the idea of entropy," writes Zencey, "is a history not only of the scientific development of an idea, but also of the application of that idea in fields far removed from thermodynamics and information theory. It is a history of a root metaphor in search of structural corroboration."[30] Once that corroboration was established from the already existing studies, the metaphor took on sweeping explanatory powers. While entropy may not be as comprehensive as one of Pepper's root metaphors, Zencey correctly notes that it works exceedingly well as a guiding anchor of meaning and interpretation, particularly in present-day uses. Conceiving of entropy as a metaphor, in addition to being a scientific theory or "fact" about the workings of the universe, helps to clarify why it maintains such a hold on thinking and why it figures so centrally in my approach.

Zencey writes, "the second law has become embedded in our culture's collective imagination to a degree unusual for such physics esoterica," because of its profound explanatory power and conceptual malleability.[31] Developing these diverse engagements with entropics will involve utilizing key aspects of Zencey's project to chart the popularity of entropy as a metaphor. This does not mean, however, that the metaphor isn't unwieldy and often ill-defined. It is certainly commanding insofar as it can be applied to physics, economics, literature, and philosophy, but it is also somewhat perplexing pinning down what many of these disciplines actually mean in utilizing it. As soon as it steps outside of the measurement of heat or information, and into pseudo-measurements of various cultural and psychological phenomena that cannot be technically quantified, it is in danger of losing its conceptual exactitude. Be that as it may, this kind of "hypostatizing" is precisely what makes it such a far-reaching metaphor.[32] Zencey provides thirteen different formulations[33] that I fashion into three conglomerate ideas, with a fourth developed through understanding entropy as a force of creation. While all of these modes intertwine in the following chapters, each highlights select features of the following metaphorical expressions: homogenization, disorder, dissipation, and creation:

1. The first formulation of entropy is best understood as homogenization. This concept can be framed in terms of chaos (randomization, absolute undifferentiation, or complete uniformity). In all of these senses, chaos is understood as a lack of differing, discrete entities. This connotation of entropy is found not only in the scientific hypotheses of the chaotic beginning and ultimate end of the universe as such but can also be seen in

much early Greek thinking. Anaxagoras' cosmology, for example, begins with matter in undifferentiated combination, requiring the spontaneous act of Mind spinning to introduce differentiation and separation: chaos begins and possibly ends in homogeneity via a detour through multiplicity. The pull toward ultimate homogeneity and dedifferentiation can also be observed in Freudian psychoanalysis and Lévi-Straussean anthropology. Both thinkers were directly engaging the scientific formulation of entropy in the twentieth century, and their writings illustrate a marked emphasis on the fundamentally retrograde movement of life and culture and the unrelenting tendency of the mind and civilization's drive to monotony and stasis.

2. Entropy as dis (or counter) order. According to Martin Meisel, this is the notion of chaos "in its most general and traditional framing . . . the extreme of disorder, where all attributes assignable to order vanish. It is disorder made absolute."[34] Although this notion can be particularly irritating to scientists, it is perhaps the one most familiar in the phenomenological or experiential understanding of the term.[35] Zencey notes, at "its simplest level the second law decrees that things never fix themselves without inputs of energy, that things are easier to break than to fix, that order is more difficult to achieve than disorder."[36] Rather than the movement toward homeostasis of parts or molecules, here, the entropic functions as a way of naming the drive toward disarray. In common parlance, this is often what people mean when employing the word "entropy." This articulation leads inevitably to ruminations on death as the ultimate endgame of entropy's maneuverings. Aristotle's philosophy of nature is fundamentally teleological and anti-entropic. Yet, his notion of privation is an entropic concept in the sense of lack or imperfection. Challenges to rational order appear in German thinking in late modernity within the relationship between reason and purpose, nature, and materiality. Whether in Kant's philosophy (which tries to deny it) or Hegel's (which tries to sublate it into a higher spiritual truth), this aspect of entropy spills over into metaphors of decay and mortality, making it, in many ways, the most menacing and enthralling characteristic of the entropic metaphor. Here can be found many of the greatest, most archaic terrors: fears around age, irrationality, and confusion.

3. Building upon entropy as disorder, it can also signal a lack of energy available for work in a given system. Campbell notes that heat energy can be useful if it is contained in an orderly form: "It can drive machines, maintain life, produce a wealth of complex structures, both natural and artificial. In a disorderly form it can do none of these things."[37] Entropy can thus designate a lack of available energy *and* a measurement of a loss of energy, both of which indicate how much energy is *inaccessible*

for maintaining a system as a whole or specific elements within the system. Metaphors about inertia, slowing down, and energy shortfalls, although not necessarily "calculable," align with the original insights of Sadi Carnot and Clausius. They resonate with our own experiences of individual and worldwide fatigue and increasing environmental precariousness. When viewed from the perspective of life, the necessity for energy input required to sustain integrity (both organic and inorganic) and the staggering amount of energy "waste" produced as a byproduct becomes apparent. While some waste can be reincorporated, much is lost to the inevitable processes of decay and inaccessibility. The work of Beauvoir and Ball is particularly salient in showing how age and labor in the modern era become sites where humanity's inability to reconceive its relationship to entropism is glaringly and distressingly clear.

4. Finally, I add my own approach to the entropic, one rooted in the art and writings of Robert Smithson, Jane Bennett, and Friedrich Nietzsche, among others. Hesiodic Chaos, the firstborn of the gods, combines with Gaia and Eros to produce the entire Greek pantheon, thus showing the originary and generative power of entropic chaos. Entropy in this sense is primary and does not lead only to rust, rot, and ruin, but instead grounds creation and creativity. Entropy is also a site of emergence wherein we can conceive of new possibilities, even in the face (and because) of destruction. This formulation of the entropic metaphor is not grounded in pessimism, but rather in *entrepic* openness and respect. There is no life, no world, no universe without entropy. Shifting entropics away from ultimate heat death and toward the almost limitless explosions of forms counterbalances the experience of horror at decay and waste that leads to paralyzing inaction. It pivots instead toward care and reverence for life's inherent vulnerability and finitude.

Zencey observes that

> the entropy metaphor suggests that we live in a state of ontological anomie, that we are embattled residents of a universe that marches toward heat death, that all we accomplish is a temporary and local reversal of a natural disorder that awaits us and its as near at hand as the closest rusty tool, the nearest dilapidated building.[38]

Whereas this description captures a common feeling in entropic philosophy, it is only part of the picture. There is more to be cultivated from entropics. Chaos, disorder, and systemic breakdown may seem to extract vitality without adequate compensation, but these are also generative forces. Because, quite simply, without entropy, there is no life.

Artists and writers who tarry with the many themes of entropy are not worried about conceptual mixture and imprecision of scientific terminology. In charting the myriad ways that entropy functions in the cultural imagination, I build from Zencey's project to show the strength of the entropy metaphor in exploring past theories and contemporary practices. The second law began as a measurement of energy degradation in terms of usefulness for work. However, there are a number of corollary aspects that span a great deal of philosophical, social, psychological, and artistic territory.[39] Just as Borges introduces the retroactive discovery of Kafka in his predecessors, so can the entropic metaphor reveal a diversity of formulations and struggles providing comprehension in breakdown, dissolution, and, ultimately, creation. The entropy metaphor allows for a pliability not always open to science, boosting its form giving, generative, and creative capacity. Additionally, many of these presentations challenge Zencey's observation that "entropy is obviously pessimistic. Its use as a metaphor is a convenient shorthand for articulating a sense that things are running downhill, falling apart, getting worse."[40] It certainly is, all around us, getting worse, evoking seductive feelings of impotence and despair. But is this the only way to experience the entropic? Do we have to simply accept the end of the world as a given wrinkle in the ultimate conclusion of the universe as such? After all, in tandem with the second law is the first, wherein matter is neither created *nor destroyed*. So perhaps, this necessary sliding toward inevitable death is, from another perspective, an opening into something new. Even, I would stress, the very condition necessary for creation as such. Total entropy increases, but in that very movement, gives rise to all becoming. The slow death of the whole is, in fact, the life and generation of astounding local diversity on every conceivable level.

NOTES

1. Arthur Eddington, *The Nature of the Physical World* (New York: Macmillian, 1948), 74; cited in Isabelle Stengers and Ilya Prigogine, *Order Out of Chaos: Man's New Dialogue with Nature* (Boulder: Shambahala, 1984), 233.

2. Goethe, *Goethe's Faust*, trans. Walter Kaufmann (New York: Random House, 1990), 161. Martin Meisel observes that Mephistopheles, as a force of chaos, is the spring of action in *Faust*. Martin Meisel, *Chaos Imagined: Literature, Art, Science* (New York: Columbia University Press, 2016), 321–322.

3. The protagonist observes that the "world kept moving on; I alone was at a standstill." Haruki Murakami, *A Wild Sheep Chase*, trans. Alfred Birnbaum (New York: Vintage International, 2002), 8.

4. Ibid, 335.

5. Hideaki Yanagisawa, "Chaos Theoretical Explanation to Operating Time and Space in Literature: A Writer Shows a Chaos State Intentionally in a Novel and Gives Illusory Joy of Entropy Decreasing to Many Readers," SSRN, July 17, 2019, https://papers.ssrn.com/sol3/papers.cfm?abstract_id=3408257. Many thanks to Yoshie Hamanaka for translating this essay. Ronald Shusterman makes a more general claim that art itself is anti-entropic, "The Second Law of Thermodynamics stipulates that all transformations of a system produce entropy defined as a state of greater disorganisation and lesser energy (. . .) Metaphorically speaking, the work of art counters this movement towards disorganisation and stasis." Ronald Shusterman, "Anish Kapoor and the Anti-Entropy of Art," *Proceedings of the European Society for Aesthetics* 4 (2012): 482.

6. Entropy has to allow that there is a possibility that it can work in reverse, but the likelihood of this happening is so astronomically small as to be impossible. From a statistical viewpoint, it would be like tossing a coin and getting tails a million times in a row.

7. Nicholas Georgescu-Roegen, *The Entropy Law and the Economic Process* (Cambridge: Harvard University Press, 1971), 3. He elaborates that the "important fact is that the discovery of the Entropy Law brought the downfall of the mechanistic dogma of Classical physics which held that everything which happens in any phenomenal domain whatsoever consists of locomotion alone and, hence, there is not irrevocable change in nature" Ibid, xiii. Georgescu-Roegen's theory challenges economics built on classical mechanics and the principle of reversibility because it is incapable of seeing the negative environmental effects on the natural world.

8. Ilya Prigogine, "Time, Structure, and Fluctuations," *Science* 201, no. 4358 (1978): 778.

9. Mauro W. Barbosa de Almeida, "Symmetry and Entropy: Mathematical Metaphors in the Work of Levi-Strauss," *Current Anthropology* 31, no. 4 (1990): 373.

10. Georgescu-Roegen, *Entropy Law*, 129. Meisel explains that Hermann von Helmholtz (who is an influence on a number of thinkers studied in this book) divided the universe between heat that is no longer available and the diminishment of mechanical, electrical, and chemical force until equilibrium. Meisel, *Chaos Imagined*, 386.

11. More current research lends weight to this understanding of time's unidirectionality by noting that energy dispersal and object equilibrium result from "quantum entanglement," wherein "objects become quantum mechanically entangled with their surroundings." Natalie Wolchover, "New Quantum Theory Could Explain the Flow of Time," *Wired,* April 25, 2014, https://www.wired.com/2014/04/quantum-theory-flow-time/.

12. Despite this seemingly ironclad lawfulness of time's unidirectionality, Ilya Prigogine and Isabelle Stengers take up the argument between physicists of dynamics and thermodynamics, the former who accuse the latter of anthropomorphizing science to align with the human experience of time's futural directionality. Stengers and Prigogine, *Order Out of Chaos*. They further show how it is possible that, in open systems, the "dissipation of entropy is itself dissipated or temporarily reversed" thus producing information and structure. Patricia T. Clough, "The Affective Turn:

Political Economy, Biomedia and Bodies," *Theory, Culture & Society* 25, no. 1 (2008): 14.

13. Brian Greene, *Until the End of Time: Mind, Matter, and Our Search for Meaning in an Evolving Universe* (New York: Vintage Books, 2021), 18. Later Greene describes the "entropy two-step" as "any process in which the entropy of a system decreases because it shifts a more than compensating increase in entropy to the environment. The two-step ensures that even though entropy may decrease here it will increase there, securing the net entropic increase we expect." Ibid, 41.

14. "Entropy is an index of the relative amount of bound energy in an isolated structure or, more precisely, of how evenly the energy is distributed in such a structure. In other words, *high* entropy means a structure in which most or all energy is bound, and *low* entropy a structure in which the opposite is true" Georgescu-Roegen, *Entropy Law*, 5. Brian Greene describes this energy distinction as between high quality (low entropy) and low quality (high entropy). Greene, *End of Time*, 33.

15. Jeff Hester writes that a "low entropy state, says Boltzmann, is more ordered. A high entropy state is more disordered. It's easier to jumble things up than to go the other direction, which is why entropy always increases." Jeff Hester, "Entropy's Rainbow," *Astronomy* (October 2017): 16.

16. Luciana Terranova and Tiziana Parisi, "Emergence and Control in Genetic Engineering and Aritificial Life," *CTheory* (May 2000), https://journals.uvic.ca/index.php/ctheory/article/view/14604/5455.

17. Hester, "Entropy's Rainbow," 16. See also, Charles H. Bennett, "Demons, Engines and the Second Law," *Scientific American* 275, no. 5 (November 1987): 110.

18. Jeff Hester, "Entropy Redux," *Astronomy* (November 2017): 66. Philip Hefner notes that entropy opens up possibilities. He gives the example of the heat transfer between hot and cold that "makes it possible for more things to happen, more possibilities, and one of those possibilities is the formation of the life that is dependent on one sector of temperature that results from the transfer." Philip Hefner, "God and Chaos: The Demiurge Versus the Ungrund," *Zygon* 19, no. 4 (1984): 473. See also, Greene, *End of Time*, 55.

19. Georgescu-Roegen, *Entropy Law*, 187. See also, Almeida, "Symmetry and Entropy," 375. Maxwell's Demon remains an attractive hypothesis because the possibilities of reversing, or even maintaining entropy at a stable level, would abolish the need for oil, sunlight, and nuclear energy. Bennett, "Demons," 108.

20. Eric Zencey observes that "information" adds to the cognates of energy, which are low entropy, negentropy, information, and order. Eric Zencey, "Entropy as Root Metaphor" in *Beyond Two Cultures: Essays on Science, Technology, and Literature*, ed. Joseph W. Slade and Judith Yaross Lee (Ames: Iowa State University Press 1990), 194.

21. Allan Franklin and Paul M. Leavitt, "Borges and Entropy," *Review: Latin American Literature and Arts* (1975): 54.

22. Clough, "Affective Turn," 13.

23. Katherine N. Hayles, *How We Became Posthuman: Virtual Bodies in Cybernetics, Literature and Informatics* (Chicago: University of Chicago Press, 1999), 102.

24. Jeremy Campbell, "Observer and Object, Reader and Text: Some Parallel Themes in Modern Science and Literature," in *Beyond the Two Cultures: Essays on Science, Technology, and Literature*, ed. Joseph W. Slade and Judith Yaross Lee (Ames: Iowa State University Press, 1990), 25. In truth, the science of entropy is so complicated and diffuse that this presentation can only be cursory. For more detail, see, Meisel, *Chaos Imagined*, 379–389.

25. Jorge Luis Borges, "Kafka and His Precursors" in *Labyrinths: Selected Stories and Other Writings* (New Directions Publishing Corp, 1964), 178.

26. Ibid. Jeremy Campbell highlights this story in his description of how reader and text mutually create meaning in a way parallel to how quantum mechanics creates the meaning it seeks. Campbell, "Observer," 35. This quote also serves as the epigraph in Foucault's collection of essays and interviews. See, Michel Foucault, "Nietzsche, Genealogy, History," in *Language, Counter-Memory, Practice: Selected Essays and Interviews by Michel Foucault,* ed. Donald F. Bouchard, trans. Donald F. Bouchard and Sherry Simon (Ithaca: Cornell University Press, 1977), 139-64.

27. Stephen Pepper, *World Hypotheses: Prolegomena to a Systematic Philosophy and a Complete Survey of Metaphysics* (Berkeley: University of California Press, 1961).

28. A metaphor, in Pepper's sense, will become a successful root metaphor (i.e., it will elaborate a world theory) "if it is capable of serving as the foundation of an intellectual framework that can reconcile itself to whatever facts may be presented to it." Zencey, "Entropy as Root," 187. Emanuela Bianchi's notion of "tropology" is a concept that functions similarly to how I am using entropy. See, Emanuela Bianchi, *The Feminine Symptom: Aleatory Matter in the Aristotelian Cosmos* (New York: Fordham University Press, 2014).

29. Significantly, Zencey criticizes Pepper for his absolutism and insistence on the purity of the metaphors. Zencey, "Entropy as Root," 197. I am very much aligned with Zencey not only on the idea of entropy as a root metaphor but additionally that tracing it out must be multidisciplinary and historical.

30. Ibid, 191.

31. Eric Zencey, "Some Brief Speculations on the Popularity of Entropy as Metaphor," *The North American Review* 271, no. 3 (1986): 9.

32. Zencey, "Entropy as Root," 196.

33. Zencey lists the following reasons why entropy is popular as a metaphor: (1) entropy connotes disorder, (2) entropy is pessimistic, (3) entropy is vague, (4) entropy is utilized in calls for energy insulation, (5) entropy is aligned with energy, (6) entropy lends the authority of science to an idea, (7) entropy is a ubiquitous physical process, (8) entropy is a successful "mini-myth," (9) entropy is a law of nature visible in human relations, (10) entropy is what threatens order, (11) entropy is a talisman, (12) entropy reveals the human domination of nature, and (13) entropy allows for contradictory applications (Zencey 1986). In his analysis of the experiential meaning of entropy, Hefner lists his own five descriptions of entropy as: (1) dissipation/running down of energy, (2) degeneracy from previous order, (3) time's irreversible arrow, (4) chaotic disorderliness, and (5) alterations that make for possibility. Hefner, "God and Chaos," 471–474.

34. Meisel, *Chaos Imagined*, 31.
35. The problem with conceiving of entropy as disorder is that this is a highly relative term: "The idea of disorder arises in our minds every time we find an order that does not fit the particular purpose we have at that moment." Georgescu-Roegen, *Entropy Law*, 142. As Georgescu-Roegen suggests, it might be better to think of disorder in terms of "random order." Ibid.
36. Zencey, "Entropy as Root," 190.
37. Campbell, "Observer," 26.
38. Zencey, "Entropy as Root," 193.
39. Francesco Manacorda claims that this "'dissolution sentence' represents a topic whose universal applicability cuts through humanities and science, conflating biology, information theory, psychoanalysis and economics in a common ground and giving them a shared idiom." Francesco Manacorda, "Entropology: Monuments to Closed Systems," *Flash Art* (2005): 77.
40. Eric Zencey, *Virgin Forest* (Athens: University of Georgia Press, 1998), 21.

Chapter 2

Entropy in Ancient Greek Thought

> But why don't we always have it? Is it that time is not always irreversible? There are moments when you have the impression that you can do what you want, go forward or backward, that it has no importance; and then other times when you might say that the links have been tightened and, in that case, it's not a question of missing your turn because you could never start again.
>
> Jean-Paul Sartre, *Nausea*[1]

"The Last Question," Isaac Asimov's favorite short story by his own hand, tells the tale of seven generations of humanoid beings asking seven iterations of a centralized computer a single question. The Multivac, which begins as a tool for helping humans generate energy and achieve interstellar travel, eventually solves the problem of dwindling resources by showing how to harness the seemingly limitless power of the sun. Celebrating this (temporary) victory over entropy, two computer attendants, Lupov and Adell, meet to share a celebratory libation. The conversation quickly turns to whether or not the energy situation has been truly solved. For now, perhaps, but billions of years into the future, the energy will run out. Lupov observes:

> It all had a beginning in the original cosmic explosion, whatever that was, and it'll all have an end when all the stars run down. Some run down faster than others. Hell, the giants won't last a hundred million years. The sun will last twenty billion years and maybe the dwarfs will last a hundred billion for all the good they are. But just give us a trillion years and everything will be dark. Entropy has to increase to maximum, that's all.[2]

The impossibility of an endless renewable source of energy strikes the celebrants with dread. Adell, taken aback by the prospect of universal heat death, poses the question to the Multivac: "How can the net amount of entropy of the universe be massively decreased?" to which the Multivac, after a long period of silence, replies, "INSUFFICIENT DATA FOR MEANINGFUL ANSWER."[3] Even though the answer references a state of affairs billions of years into the future, it still unsettles the technicians asking, as does the incomplete reply given in response.

Generations of humans and computers come and go until finally, trillions of years into the future, humanity has fused with the "Cosmic AC" computer, the stars have all died out, the last consciousness has asked for the final time whether entropy can be reversed, and still, "insufficient data" comes as the response. Space and time end and nothing is left but the AC correlating all the data collected. Eventually, this hybrid human/AI consciousness persisting only to answer this single question learns that it is, in fact, possible to reverse the direction of entropy. Only, there is no one left with whom to share this. And so, the story ends with the AC commanding: "'LET THERE BE LIGHT!' And there was light."[4]

Asimov's story is both a philosophical and a theological meditation on the ultimate heat death of the universe. While the sun burning out billions of years into the future seems like a small concern in the face of present dwindling resources and waste accumulation, it still paints the universal picture (and certainly that of humanity) as one of ultimate demise. The two technicians are so concerned about the overwhelming nihilistic shadow cast by entropy that their question is about reversal, even as it will have no effect on their lives. Ultimately, the answer is yes: entropy's unidirectionality can be reversed. In order to be able to deliver this reply, the universe is born anew. The story captures a cosmic view that heat death is not the final destination but the beginning in an endless cycle of collapse and rebirth. While clearly besieged by energy drain and waning vitality, the cosmos is not ultimately headed toward frozen darkness. Or, at least if it is, its terminus will be the first moment of creation. Asimov's story presents a hypothesis that what appears as inevitable cessation is, from another perspective, the moment of cosmic birth. This notion of a cosmic regenerative cycle can be found in a number of ancient Greek philosophies as well.

Eric Zencey prudently notes that "in its focus on 'energy' . . . entropism bears a marked similarity in form to most pre-Socratic philosophies."[5] This claim reveals a particular culturally and temporally coded vein of thinking that I trace throughout this book. Chaos, disorder, darkness are not in themselves fearful. Thinking can respond in a variety of ways to these entropic forces, through excitement, enticement, or curiosity, not just fear. While not explicitly named as such, the entropic metaphor captures many strands of inquiry woven around the natural processes of change. Beginning with entropy in Greek thinking is strategic because early Greek thinkers are often preoccupied with these very ideas. The "Greeks," that fiercely contested group, often claimed as an origin for "Western" thinking, spark controversy about what counts as philosophy and who claims the origin.[6] Yet, there is a nomadic but important path traced in this book that finds many of the ideas of chaos, creation, and slackening in the works of Presocratic thinkers, Plato and Aristotle. These philosophers impact later philosophical, literary, and scientific traditions across the globe. Deep links connect ancient Greek modes of questioning into nature and the universe that funnel into the same questions the second law of thermodynamics sought to answer. The contemporary considerations in the final chapters make it fitting to begin from this fecund site.

The following investigations of the thought of Hesiod, Anaximander, Anaxagoras, Plato, and Aristotle do not provide an exhaustive study. Instead, I choose particular moments of entropic thinking in each that is illuminative of the struggle to come to terms with the disordering forces of chaos, temporality, and privation. Hesiod begins by showing chaos to be a generative yet threatening force that is both bounded and unbounded. Anaximander and Anaxagoras tarry with the indeterminate locus of creation and the ordering work of Mind. Plato's metaphysics is preoccupied with finding philosophical and theological mechanisms to prevent universal decay, and Aristotle maintains a kind of generative aspect of disorder, but only insofar as it is completely subordinated to form.

I do not treat entropy as a monolithic concept, nor as a single line of thinking, but rather a cluster of ideas and concepts for which the late-born term "entropy" serves as an umbrella.[7] Asking about the appearance of entropy before the nineteenth century requires a certain leniency in terminology that science will take millennia to name and determine. Nevertheless, a burgeoning awareness and engagement with entropic thinking suffuses Greek thought with its concerns for how to maintain perpetual becoming in the face of finitude. Whether viewed through Hesiod's description of the ascendency of the Olympian gods, the penalty of existence in Anaximander, the workings of Mind in Anaxagoras, or the power of Plato's divine craftsman and Aristotle's prime mover, the forces of chaos and nonbeing are shown to persistently trouble life. The battle centers on the desire to master, perhaps even defeat, the chaotic, formless, and degenerative machinations of a cosmos in flux.

I begin with Hesiod, whose poetry captures a kind of origin that comes to be *the* beginning for so many of the thinkers that follow. As Michel Foucault notes, this is because the origin "is associated with the gods, and its story is always sung as a theogony."[8] And so now we listen to how Hesiod sings the beginnings of the cosmos.

CHAOS AND DISORDER IN HESIOD

Given his iconic status in ancient Greek culture and his monumental influence on succeeding generations of poets and philosophers, there are few to compete with Hesiod's celebrated authority. His poetry describes the monumental struggle to master the forces of unruliness and disorder while also presenting a kind of originary, creative power to chaos. Both the *Theogony* and *Works and Days* are pointedly attuned to the presence of chaos and disorder, energies that demand to be disciplined. In the *Theogony*, Hesiod speaks of the rise of the Olympian gods and Zeus' imposition of authority and order over chaos and Kronos' lawlessness. Following his long praise of the muses and their powers of inspiration, he begins the poem proper by calling for the appropriate order for each thing that comes into being. "Chaos was born first and after her came Gaia the broad-breasted, the firm seat of all the immortals . . . and Eros, the fairest of the deathless gods."[9] While it is somewhat difficult to know what exactly Chaos as the first god would be, certainly Chaos, Gaia, and Eros remain the condition of possibility and generative forces for all future generations of living beings.

Martin Meisel explains that "the root of the word 'chaos' is the Greek verb stem *Xa*, meaning to yawn or to gape. It enters Western poetic and philosophic discourse in Hesiod's *Theogony*."[10] Andrew Gregory translates chaos as "chasm" insofar as it "can mean a gaping or yawning chasm, where the chasm is a limited space."[11] Yawning and gaping like the emptiness of an abyss, chaos is conceived as formlessness bounded by a kind of cosmic gateway. Chaos is also configured as a god of space, lacking distinct boundaries yet required for the generations of gods and monsters that struggle against and within the boundaries of order. While this god does not relate directly to the modern conception of chaos as disorder or randomness, the gaping and yawning chasm evokes a sense of boundlessness that calls to be ordered. This in turn speaks to an archaic omnipresence of foreboding disorder, pointing to the extent to which disorder and disorganization frame early Greek cosmology.

Further into the *Theogony*, Hesiod provides an elaborate description of the importance of oath-keeping among the gods, detailing the punishments for breaking vows as well as presenting the overview of the cosmos itself. The earth is a great disc at the center, surrounded by chaos. Outside of chaos, the sky and aither unfold at the topmost levels with Tartarus lying bottommost, exiled beyond the bronze limits of the earth. On this stage, the war plays itself out wherein older Titans are overthrown by the younger Olympians who achieve dominion through the justice of Zeus.[12] The Titans—those glorious, massive, outrageous divinities—ultimately lose and are cast out for eternity from the pantheon. The Titans' loss is accompanied by a banishment into the murky, windy, desolate realm of Tartarus. Hesiod describes the terrible journey of the defeated and expelled gods falling through the space of chaos to reach their final destination, doomed to spend eternity alive but powerless. Twice they plummet through chaos: ten days from heaven to earth and ten days from earth to Tartarus.[13] All of this, Hesiod explains, is the proper order brought by the domination of Zeus. When they leave the regimented realm of newly crowned Zeus, the Titans must plummet through the disordered, abyssal, chaotic space, entropically sapping their power and breaking down their godlike strength.

Like all of the old gods, Chaos' originally generative role is subsumed into the orderly universe governed by Zeus' justice. The power of formlessness—perhaps the very power to dissolve form—becomes the yawning, gaping chasms that surround the earth. These abysses function as the space necessary to keep heaven and Tartarus eternally separated, mediated by the earth upon which most divine and heroic drama occurs. While Chaos has been bounded and thus metaphorically held in check, it remains a haunting specter as the space through which the exiled Titans fell to banishment. Hesiod thereby reminds us that even though controlled by Olympian order, wild, archaic, and ineradicable powers remain integral to the eternal cosmic structure. Should the conditions of containment shift with a change of rule, they could be released back into the world with devastating force, perhaps producing a grand reordering. It would not be the first time that the gods' rule underwent a massive, historically defining shift. Hesiod reveals that entropic disorder is only ever temporarily contained, and the cosmos is always only provisionally stabilized.

In *Works and Days*, Hesiod tells of different times where pre-Olympian gods lived and ruled. Unlike Asimov's generations of humans and computers evolving into greater and more powerful beings, Hesiod sings of a kind of entropic *degeneration* of humans and gods. He speaks of a time of Cronus and a time of Zeus where the world operated according to vastly different natural and social laws. Cronus, the god of time, fathered a golden race of mortals who "lived like gods, carefree in their hearth, shielded from pain and misery. Helpless old age did not exist, and with limbs of unsagging vigor they enjoyed the delights of feasts, out of evil's reach."[14] Like gold, these beings did not rust, tarnish, or lose their integrity as they moved through time. Living like gods in peace and plenty, their bodies were strong and did not wane in strength. Hesiod offers no explanation why these golden children passed out of existence, only that a "sleeplike death subdued them," and the earth covered them.[15] The question lingers: if they do not experience age and declining bodily capacities, why would they ever succumb to a deathlike sleep? Perhaps they represent the anti-entropic desire to overcome old age and decline, even as these most perfect mortals still succumb to time.

Following the age of Cronus, disordered and ferocious races appear, unleashing uncontainable energies. Each race suffers from chaotic forces that upend rule and order, leading to destructive violence. Generation after generation of creatures arise, only to fall prey to foolishness, carnage, and death. The silver race is followed by bronze mortals who are vicious and powerful, bent on mutual destruction. Following this race's banishment to Hades, the fourth race, that of the demi-gods and Homeric heroes, arises only to succumb to reciprocal annihilation through warfare. Life exploded into multiple forms, only to meet brutal ends. The final age, that of contemporary humanity, is the fifth generation, the iron mortals. Unfortunately, "neither day nor night will give them rest as they waste away with toil and pain."[16] The iron-born will eventually fall into social and political chaos—disrespecting the affection between friends, families, and guests that is vital in the maintenance of societal harmony. It will be a time when "might will make right and shame will vanish."[17] The unjust will be rewarded while the good languish. At this point, divine Shame and Retribution will withdraw to Olympus, leaving behind a race of crooked and defenseless human beings. Unlike the ascendency of Olympian beauty and order charted in the *Theogony*, this awesome story of generations can be seen more as a tale of *de*generations. Even as gods work to preserve order and harmony, the machinations of entropic loss are inevitable as time relentlessly erodes life rather than refines it.

The bulk of *Works and Days* turns into Hesiod's advice to his wayward brother, Perses, on how to manage his life and property in the age of confusion where the gods of order have fled. Perses, the "great fool," needs a good talking-to as he seems to be lazy and disorganized—unsurprising given the general disarray of the iron age. Hesiod tells his brother that he can choose to have evil or good in his life, pleading "let there be order and measure in your own work"[18] by "observing due limit and timeliness in all your actions."[19] Advice on commerce, agriculture, marriage, and good citizenship centers around the idea that "For mortals order (εὐθημοσύνη) is best, disorder (κακοθημοσύνη) is worst."[20] Presumably, Perses needs substantial guidance to put his life and possessions in order, showing the tremendous pull of entropic forces in the corrupted age of humanity. What may have been simply a matter of living the natural order of life in the golden age has become, through degeneration, a powerful force of disorderliness requiring great energy to combat. Given how much of *Works and Days* is consumed by the issues of how to properly order life and property, it is clear that the disordering forces of chaos are impossible to entirely eliminate. Thus, there is a kind of urgency, and perhaps even futility, to the litany of guidelines Hesiod prescribes for Perses. The poet knows that ultimately his iron-born brother will succumb to the forces of entropy.

ENTROPIC PRECURSORS IN PRESOCRATIC PHILOSOPHY

While Hesiod's mythic poetry evokes the drama of the ongoing cosmic battle between order and disorder, the Presocratic philosopher, Anaximander, approaches the forces of chaos from a burgeoning philosophical framework emerging in the ancient Mediterranean. As opposed to chaos as a god or a realm, Anaximander speaks of the *apeiron* or the indefinite, indeterminate source from which things come into being and to which they necessarily return. Simplicius reports that in Anaximander, "the boundless (τὸ ἄπειρον)" is the existential source of all things.[21] As the site of genesis for all creation, it is also paradoxically the origin, or *arche*, of order as well. Whatever the boundless or indefinite *apeiron* is for Anaximander (which is difficult to ascertain definitively due to the ambiguity of the single surviving original quote), it functions as the guiding source from which everything that comes to be emerges and returns.

The *apeiron* moves and generates eternally, being identical to none of the elements themselves but rather constituting their vague source. Anything that comes to be from the *apeiron* must ultimately repay the cost of determinate existence insofar as each discrete entity that arises must ultimately perish: "according to what must be: for they give recompense and pay restitution to each other for their injustice according to the ordering of time."[22] Existence, as separation from the whole, brings with it the *necessity of destruction*. Time emerges as the process of separation, and all creation pays the penalty of time by rejoining the source.[23] While anything that comes to be must of necessity succumb to the entropic and perish, the *apeiron* is infinitely generative, thereby maintaining an eternally self-sustaining universe. According to Aristotle, the *apeiron* does not have a beginning but "seems to be the *arche* of the rest, and to contain all things and steer all things . . . and this is the divine. For it is deathless and indestructible."[24] Without any source or origin preceding it, the *apeiron* itself serves as the source of all generations. While everything that lives will die, the universe maintains itself as a kind of anti-entropic perpetual motion machine. Eternity wins over the degradations of time, and the *arche* remains untouched by the transformations that it generates. Only individual entities that emerge from the source truly degrade according to divine justice, thereby conquering entropy by their death and return. The eternal and ageless source of all is infinitely renewing and will never fall prey to entropic destruction.

While Anaximander posits the *apeiron* as the source of existence, Anaxagoras maintains a more complicated mixture of force and elements guided and ordered by the cosmic mind. To begin, all things that exist in the universe, from the infinitely large to the infinitely small, were together and *nous* (νοῦς), or Mind, was apart. "Together were all things, boundless (ἄπειρα) both in quantity and in smallness; for the small was boundless (ἄπειρον) too. And as all things were together nothing was manifest by reason of its smallness."[25] Mysteriously, *nous* begins to spin. In so doing, the great separation of things into what we know them to be was initiated, first slowly and then gaining momentum until spread throughout everything.[26]

Nous is a principle introducing motion and differentiation into primordial chaos.[27] It functions as a principle of order, taking material chaos and separating things into discrete entities through movement. While each thing expresses its character by virtue of a predominance of a certain kind of matter, everything also paradoxically remains in everything else in perpetuity. What predominates as flesh has trees, stars, planets, and bone within in it, just hidden from expression. The objects that populate the world of the senses exist in infinite duplications in the infinitely small and infinitely large as "all things have a share of everything."[28] As Michael M. Shaw explains,

> Anaxagoras has developed a conception of many instances of all sorts of things, including seeds, various qualities, and limitless human civilizations consisting of inhabited cities, manufactured works, and an earth with growing things, agriculture, a sun, etc. These compacted worlds must themselves include all such features, and so on to infinity, micro-and macrocosmically.[29]

The power of *nous* is thus so great that order is perfectly mirrored in the infinitely large and the infinitely small.

Anaxagoras' metaphysics offers an unusual twist to entropic philosophy. All matter and Mind are eternal: "no thing comes to be or passes away but is mixed together and dissociated from the things that are."[30] This insight aligns with the first law of thermodynamics and the conservation of matter. Yet, he posits an origin of motion, when *nous* begins to spin, which can be construed as the beginning of time itself. Unlike Eddington's arrow of time articulating entropic necessity, however, Anaxagoras conceives of no movement back to the originary cosmic homogeneity before mind's ordering power, only the continual, perpetual movement of mind and the endless separation of the primordial universal mixture. The universe exhibits eternal mixture and separation, never true generation and destruction so that the time of the world that begins in the infinite past will never come to an end in heat death.

Although Anaxagorean chaos is far from clear, entropic homogeneity finds a place in his philosophy. In *Philosophy in the Tragic Age of the Greeks*, Nietzsche writes that "there was a time and a condition of matter—regardless of whether of long or short duration—when *nous* had not yet influenced it, when matter was still inert. This is the period of Anaxagorean chaos."[31] Describing the seeds populating the cosmos (those infinitely small sources that contain all existing things), Anaxagoras "imagined as a total pell-mell of even the tiniest particles, the result of mixing, as though with mortar and pestle, all the elemental substances until they were like dust motes and could be stirred about in the chaos as though in a mixing-cup."[32] Nietzsche considers what could happen if the spinning were ceaselessly exerted on matter. While thermodynamic equilibrium seems to capture the beginnings, could it also be the conclusion as well? Would the spinning ultimately result in the creation of predominance to such an extent that nothing is able to interact with anything else? Heat death, in other words, resulting in an infinitely remote point in the future "when all the likes are gathered together and the primal essences lie side by side, undivided and in beautiful order, when each tiny particle has found its companions and its home, when the great peace enters the world after the great divisions and splits of the substances and no more split or divided material life."[33] At this point, *nous* will return to itself, no longer exerting influence or motion. Nietzsche's emphasis on this end as one of a peaceful, beautiful order, while not conducive to anything resembling human life, expresses a kind of cosmic harmony. To most, the infinitely expanding universe eventually running out of energy to sustain any kind of system—biological, geological, planetary, or atomic—feels terrifying, just as it does to Asimov's Lupov and Adell. But Nietzsche shows a vision of this as a universal accomplishment, a job well done, a time when Mind and matter repose, waiting for the process to randomly start all over again. The end prepares for the beginning, with an infinite tranquility in between. As the AC proclaims: let there be light.

For Anaxagoras, *nous* supplies the energy for combination, differentiation, unification, and work. Mind starts spinning and in so doing initiates the process of seeds separating into the various objects with which we are familiar. Through Mind's rotation, the universe ruptures into beautiful diversity. And while his worldview does not solve the problem of beginnings (How did *nous* begin spinning? *When* did *nous* begin spinning? What does the primordial universe look like before the separating out of rotary motion? Will separation ultimately usher in eternal homogeneity and repose?), it displays the workings of change, demanding a kind of order to arrange the universe into systems that emulate each other at all possible levels.

Anaximander and Anaxagoras offer two different responses to the destructive forces of degradation and decay that much later will come to be understood in terms of entropy. Anaximander's *apeiron* provides a limitless source of generation thus ensuring perpetual becoming. Anaxagoras' *nous* initiates continual and infinite separation that aims at a state of beauty and harmony that will possibly initiate a new beginning. Plato's philosophy picks up these ideas from his predecessors, seeking to explain change and time through various figures and processes that strive to bring disarray under the guidance of divine organization.

PLATO'S DIVINE ORDER

Anaxagoras' *nous*, understood as a principle of self-motion, is eternal, uncreated, and inexhaustible. Perhaps this draws Plato to directly reference Anaxagoras' philosophy in the fictionalized account of Socrates' last hours. Plato's philosophically rich and profoundly moving dialogue, *Phaedo*, makes the theme of the soul's immortality central to Socrates as he awaits the draught of poison that will end his life. The dialogue concludes with Socrates drinking hemlock, his body ultimately succumbing to death, thus positioning the soul's immortality as a fitting theme for his mourning friends to discuss.

In the first argument for immortality, Plato describes the generation of opposites, proposing a cycle of becoming in which just as the living die, so must the dead be reborn to complete an unending cycle of existence. Just as there is a process of falling asleep and waking up, there must be a process of dying and coming back to life. In arguing for this process, Socrates turns to one of his interlocutors and asks the question:

> If the two processes of becoming did not always balance each other as if they were going round in a circle, but generation proceeded from one point to its opposite in a straight line and it did not turn back again to the other opposite or take any turning, do you realize that all things would ultimately have the same form, be affected in the same way, and cease to become?[34]

Plato proclaims that becoming must be perfectly recurrent rather than unidirectional, which avoids a kind of universal entropic heat death. If life did not eternally come from death, just as death comes from life, everything would end up in the eternal sleep of Endymion; ultimately, everything would "have to be dead and nothing alive."[35] The interlocutors accept that the living *must* come to be from the dead in a ceaseless recurrence of coming to be. As elaborated below, Plato builds on this idea in the *Timaeus* and the *Statesman*, which offer two different myths of cyclic becoming, each providing a method to permanently stave off entropy: the former as a repeating cycle of revolutions, the latter through the reversal of time.

In another dialogue from roughly the same period as the *Phaedo*, Plato builds a city in speech in the *Republic*. Attempting to show how the city should be properly ordered and governed, he writes that philosophical natures are in love with the "learning which discloses to them something of the being that *is* always and does not wander about, driven by generation and decay."[36]

Painstakingly detailing the ideal city, he describes the qualities of the soldiers and guardians who will look after its care. The guardians, those most refined in body and soul, will monitor the children as they exercise and study in order to determine who among them will be chosen to guard and lead. They seek out those who will look after the integrity of the city as a whole, seeking to preserve the perfection modeled on the Good. Itself beyond being, the Good is the form of forms, that which shines knowability and existence on all the other timeless and perfect objects of intellection.[37] With such everlasting excellence as the archetype, and the most philosophical natures aligning the city's organization as closely as possible to this perfect standard, it appears that Plato has found a way to circumvent entropic decline on the social and political level. Yet, as he goes on to elaborate, nothing in the human or natural order escapes the grinding down of time and change.

Following seven books devoted to climbing the dialectical ladder up to the perfection of the Good, organizing the city in the best possible way so as to prevent degradation, political devolution turns out to be inevitable. After so much effort and energy has been expended to build multiple balustrades against decay, it nonetheless works its way into the city in the eighth book. While such a city would be difficult to change, it is not impervious "for everything that has come into being there is decay, not even a composition such as this will remain for all time."[38] Echoing the Hesiodic lamentation that the best of the mortals must necessarily give way to more violent and flawed generations, so must the best of cities give way to increasingly degraded political forms. In explaining why this decay inescapably occurs, Plato's voice becomes a kind of poetic lament on the fact that nature is mixed into all human accomplishments. As such, no matter how finely tuned the observation and education of children, the arranging of sexual pairings, and the overall project of eugenics, sometimes couplings will produce imperfect offspring. Despite the tremendous exertion to banish disorder through ordering, chance and contingency cannot be permanently prevented from entering the city. This insight will ultimately lead Plato to argue that society cannot maintain perfection, but the universe as a whole can.

Referencing the Hesiodic races of gold, silver, bronze, and iron, Plato speaks of what happens when the purity of the metals is not maintained. A kind of "chaotic mixing" of the different natures engenders an unsalvageable "unlikeness and inharmonious irregularity."[39] The different regimes devolve from the ideal organization, leading ultimately to tyranny, which is likened to a kind of "disease" that grows and festers. Disease, in the final move from democracy to tyranny, appears as an excess—one that can be seen in seasons, plants, bodies, and regimes. Understood as systemic breakdown, disease is inevitable, ushering in decline and ultimately complete social collapse.[40] However, Plato's ideal world, generally understood as the timeless and ageless realm of the forms, provides a powerful counterforce to the entropic decay of nature. While physical, psychic, and social diseases permeate existence, ensuring that all things that come to be will inevitably decay, the forms after which they are modeled always *are* suffering neither change nor death. Much like Anaximander's *apeiron*, Plato's forms act as an eternal source from which generation continuously emanates without being in any way altered by this generative power. However much entropic decline dominates nature, the forms ensure a perpetual wellspring of existence. However, for perfect order to prevail, the divine craftsman who looks to the forms as models of the universe will be necessary.

The *Timaeus* is a cosmological dialogue supposedly taking place the day after the discussion in the *Republic*, moving from the order of the city to the order of the universe. This dialogue picks up the concern with the immortality of the soul and the apprehension about staving off universal decay seen in both the *Phaedo* and the *Republic*.[41] The dialogue brings out the ways in which the entropic poses a threat, all the while maintaining faith that universal order triumphs through divine intervention. This ambitious piece of cosmology offers an explication of a deific principle that actively orders a primordial material chaos, one that calls to be ordered because of its inherent entropic tendencies.

The dialogue opens with the observation that the fourth interlocutor, who had been present the day before, is absent due to illness.[42] Already, in the opening lines, the entropic appears in the form of sickness, a sign of the disordering material principle that returns much later in the discussion. When Timaeus takes center stage following the dialogue's prelude, he begins to present his hypothesis on the workings of the cosmos. Timaeus explains that "of all the things that have come to be, our universe is the most beautiful, and of causes the craftsman is the most excellent. This, then, is how it has come to be: it is a work of craft, modeled after that which is changeless and is grasped by a rational account, that is, by wisdom."[43] The cosmos is created by the divine artisan made specifically to ward off entropic decay. Plato elaborates that the god, like Hesiod's poet, "believed that order was in every way better than disorder."[44] Motivated to make the most beautifully ordered cosmos, the god constructs its body out of the four elements. This body, "having come together into a unity with itself [. . .] could not be undone by anyone but the one who had bound it together."[45] The deity thus not only creates the universe but does so in such a manner that he alone is the only one who can undo his artifact. Functioning directly as the only force able to ward off entropy and serving as the keeper of elemental order and harmony, the god keeps nature continuously becoming, like a clockmaker constantly winding their clock. Or, perhaps more accurately, like a clockmaker who makes a perpetual motion timepiece that cannot be stopped other than through the maker's direct interference.

Timaeus claims that the material world is merely a copy of the invisible and eternal world that serves as its model. The demiurge creates the universe as a living animal endowed with intelligence and soul in order to make it as close to the invisible formal perfection upon which it is fashioned. Since the invisible realm suffers no creation, change, and destruction, the artisan strives to produce a creation that will maintain itself in perpetuity. Composed out of the four elements, the body of the world is harmonious and enduring. This living creature, spherical in shape, is so close to perfection that it does not suffer disease and old age because there is nothing outside of its singular body to invade it from without. Without an outside, its waste is its food, and it revolves in a circle, as this is the most perfect motion.[46] Timaeus explains that the universe must be a living whole with nothing outside or leftover without external or internal threatens to its integrity.[47]

This material creature, eternally enduring without waste or need, serves as a model of anti-entropic accomplishment. The perfect creature made by the flawless god, Timaeus forms an impeccably contained, energy-conserving universe. The second law commands that low entropy fuel necessarily degrades into high entropy waste, yet Plato's universe recycles itself, without additional energy. The craftsman is an eternally living thing, functioning as a kind of divine Maxwellian demon warding off entropy in perpetuity. This god is in some way reminiscent of the eternally enduring and creative *apeiron* in Anaximander, except taking the shape of an actual being rather than a vague, indefinite source. The god orders the eternal chaotic material into both a world body and a world soul.[48] Chaos as a principle of material disorder thus requires the direct power of divinity to put it into working order and to keep it that way.

Timaeus interrupts his lengthy discussion noting that a true account of the universe's creation requires a description of the errant cause. This cause, the *chora* (χώρα) is space, rudimentarily conceived. Hearkening to the yawning abyss of Hesiod's chaos, the *chora* serves as the "place" of the universe. This explanation, due to its subject matter, can only be probable but helps to formulate the condition of the universe before the ordering work of an artisan god and the creation of time itself. Before this act of invention, the elements exist in a kind of receptacle, the "nurse" of generation itself. The *chora*'s nature allows it to take on the impressions of what it contains, without ever becoming permanently altered. Like a perfume base that must itself remain odorless, the *chora* lacks its own form but serves as an invisible and formless receptacle for creation. This nurse of becoming contains all matter, moved unevenly by the four elements, in turn moving them, as with the winnowing of grain.[49] While only accessible by a kind of "bastard reasoning," Plato's account presents the tension between the forces of disorder and order. As Hesiod's Olympians eventually banish—but do not ultimately destroy—chaos, Plato's artisan god, must form the disparate elements through divine work. But the irregular motion of the *chora* that contains them can never be fully subdued.

After a protracted pontification on the constitution of the elements, Timaeus addresses the form and function of flesh. He carefully goes through the parts of the body, the major organs, the processes of respiration, ingestion, and so on in order to show how creatures are both like the divine nature after which they are modeled and unlike it because of their materiality. Turning specifically to the nature of age and disease, he explains how the triangles composing the body are worn down due to lifelong conflict between them. Children are made up of tightly fitted triangles, but these clash with many adversaries over time.[50] Old age consequently results from the material elements wearing down through the grinding and clashing of various internal and external systems. While the universe exists in perpetuity from the constant presence of the artisan, the individual creatures within it come to be and pass away according to their nature.

Timaeus observes that death by old age is best, a time when the triangles that fix the soul to the body become so loose that the soul flies away with joy, released from its geometric prison. Disease is a violation of material sameness and proportion, resulting from a disorder of the elements. In the succeeding analyses, Timaeus charts the numerous diseases and corruptions that are produced by the all-out war between the elements. Disorder exemplifies the fundamental character of maladies as a confusion between elements, systems, organs, blood, bile, and phlegm. Of course, the battle can only be fought for so long. Eventually, disease or old age will loosen the triangles of order for good. As Hegel will echo in the following chapter's discussions of the animal organism, Plato notes that "every disease has a certain makeup that in a way resembles the natural make-up of living things" and an individual in a species "is born with its allotted span of life, barring unavoidable accidents."[51] Try though it might to extend life beyond its time through medicines and treatments, the result will almost always exacerbate the condition and hasten death. As with Anaximander, all natural and political life pays the penalty of existence, even as the cosmos continues eternally. Plato thus succeeds in showing both the threat and inevitability of natural decay, as well as its salvation through the eternal workings of the divine.

Bringing together the ideas of immortality, degeneration, and a universe that wards off destruction through the intelligent creation of cyclical patterns, Plato reworks the Hesiodic tale of the generations of gods and human beings in his dialogue, the *Statesman*.[52] Retelling the myth of the ages of the metals, he writes of a time of Cronus and a time of Zeus, illustrating the necessity for a good leader to keep the city in order. Socrates and an unnamed Eleatic Stranger begin their conversation, picking up from the previous day's discussions (recounted in the *Sophist*) in order to paint an accurate portrait of the statesman—who they are, what they do, and over whom they are to rule. Failing in their initial attempt to separate the proper domain of the statesman, the interlocutors begin again, traveling a different road that takes a rather surprising turn. Offering to provide some amusement, the Stranger announces that a story must be inserted into the discussion. It is, to be sure, a very odd story, introduced in order to correct an earlier error in the conversation. A fascinating, yet convoluted and confusing tale, the myth told by the Stranger requires a reorientation of thinking, much like the bastard form of reasoning required to gain access into thinking the *chora*.

Directing Socrates to listen to his tale as would a child, the *Stranger* embarks upon a story about order and the natural principles of disorder that must be held in check. Like the story from the *Timaeus*, the *Stranger* explains that the universe is a living creature, endowed with intelligence by the creator. Because of its material nature, it necessarily changes, significantly, toward increasing disarray without the guidance of the god to keep it in line. This is because "absolute and perpetual immutability is a property of only the most divine things of all, and body does not belong to this class."[53] Whereas Timaeus' god appears to achieve an almost complete victory over disorder, the Stranger's tale takes a different turn. During this myth, Plato describes two distinct times: the age of Cronus and the age of Zeus. The former depicts a time when the god steers and guides the cosmos and human beings; the latter speaks of the time when humans are left to their own devices and must rule themselves.[54] As humanity currently dwells in the age of Zeus, the goal is to find a state that most closely imitates the age of Cronus. When the god travels with the universe, all is in order; however, when he lets it go, "of its own accord it turns backward in the opposite direction, since it is a living creature and is endowed with intelligence by him who fashioned it in the beginning."[55] Since the universe has a "bodily nature," it necessarily undergoes change. Because it is divine, it moves in a circular motion, but insofar as it is bodily, it can go both forward and backward, depending on whether Cronus is actively steering the cosmos or has withdrawn. Through this unique cycle, Plato presents a different ordering than the one described in the *Timaeus*.

When the divine departs, leaving the universe to its own nature, the latter undergoes retrograde movement, going "backwards through countless ages."[56] While human beings may be living in a time of forward circular movement, there was (and will be again) an event of cosmic reversal. When this age of Cronus returns, time ceases its forward motion, begins to go backward, causing mortal creatures to become younger until they disappear altogether. When the god releases control of the helm and withdraws to his outlook, "fate and innate desire made the earth turn backward."[57] While it is not entirely clear why the helmsman steps away, or what that means regarding the ultimate direction of the universe, it is not unlike winding a music box and having the music play (only in this case, backward). Those buried in the earth return to life and all the animals and people live without states or family, perfectly ordered, tended by Cronus.

Eventually, a powerful collision occurs, the beginning and end rush apart, resulting in a massive universal cataclysm. Once calm descends, the world exercises care and order over itself, following the teachings of the creator. Despite its motivation to maintain self-rule, the material element, as part of its primeval chaotic nature, is

> infected with great disorder before the attainment of the existing orderly universe. From its Composer, the universe has received only good things; but from its previous condition it retains in itself and creates in the animals all the elements of harshness and injustice which have their origin in the heavens.[58]

The material element that *preexists* the ordering of the creator god brings not only the menace of disorder but also causes harshness, evil, and injustice. When Cronus is present, goodness spreads throughout, but when separated from his creature, a growing chaos ensues.[59] Left without the guiding, ordering influence of the great pilot, the universe flounders, beset by trouble and confusion, sinking "in the boundless (ἄπειρον) sea of diversity."[60] Upon witnessing the precarious state of his beloved creature, the helmsman steps in once again, setting the world in order and restoring its agelessness and immortality. This cosmically epic and confusing myth describes a kind of perpetual motion machine, but one different from the self-contained universe of the *Timaeus*. In it we find another Maxwellian demon sorting the retrograde forces of the universe to prevent entropic victory.

It is not unreasonable to view the two competing forces—the perfection of the god who brings order and immortality to the universe in cyclic fashion and the imperfection of the material element which pulls the universe toward disorder, injustice, and ruin—as ancient representations of the first and second laws of thermodynamics. While the systems are distinct, the *Statesman* and the *Timaeus* agree on this precise point: matter and energy are eternally preserved and merely undergo different kinds of organization and disarray. In the *Timaeus*, the god is eternally present, keeping his creation free from decay and death. In the *Statesman*, the conservation and eternity of energy are guaranteed by the existence of the god who comes in at the moment of maximum disorder and rights the cosmic ship. As soon as the god withdraws, the workings of entropy are unleashed—slowly at first but increasing as time and forgetfulness spread. In addition, the entropic forces affect local human systems more drastically than they do the cosmos.[61] Human society is in dire straits once the deity departs. Such a state necessitates gods such as Prometheus, Athena, and Hephaestus to provide art, agriculture, and technological wisdom to prevent the eradication of humanity. Whereas the second law demands that entropy *always* increases, Plato's pilot rushes in as a *deus ex machina* at the last moments, rescuing the cosmos from maximum disorder, restoring goodness and orderliness. God "took again his place as its helmsman, reversed whatever had become unsound and unsettled in the previous period when the world was left to itself, set the world in order, restored it and made it immortal and ageless."[62] For whatever reason, the god once again withdraws and allows the entire process to repeat, presumably, ad infinitum. Plato's Stranger portrays a universe where matter tends toward ever-increasing entropy without any possible reversal. Plato's demon-god ensures, however, that this will never be the case.

These depictions illustrate how Plato's cosmos must consider the chaotic natural forces that are necessarily a part of the world of becoming. Both the best city in the *Republic* and the eternal universe in the *Timaeus* and the *Statesman* are modeled after the timeless forms, and in so doing, work to keep entropic forces at bay. While the city cannot maintain itself indefinitely, Plato's two versions of the universe's creation and stewardship can. The *Statesman* and the *Timaeus* agree that the universe requires some sort of cycle to achieve immortality and ward off deterioration, thereby showing Plato's abiding concern with how the universe is best ordered for the sake of warding off destruction.

ARISTOTLE'S UNCREATED UNIVERSE

This chapter's various themes—chaos, the indefinite, Mind, the Good, god—paint a variegated portrait of the early Greek poetic and philosophical attempt to understand and contain the irrational, formless, and destructive workings of entropy. Aristotle surfaces as a crystallization of these struggles with the brash confidence of one who believes he has emerged victorious in their banishment. Plato's philosophy moves in the direction of securing the universe's existence by modeling it after timeless, invisible perfection, adding the stewardship of divinity to keep it ordered and good. Aristotle walks a step further, taking up the task of securing the universe from the threat of entropic temporality, subduing disorder through the subordination of privation to form, and taking the divine craftsman out of the picture entirely through the assertion of an eternal, uncreated cosmos, and a perfect, and perfectly detached divinity. His notion of privation may prove to be the greatest challenge to order of any of the forces and figures heretofore studied, thus requiring its containment by form. In addition, his uncreated and eternal universe provides by far the mightiest blockade against entropy yet encountered. An examination of *Physics* Book I and *Metaphysics* Book XII shows how Aristotle's formulation most clearly situates the Greek philosophical understanding of the disorder as subordinate to an organizing principle or system.

In *Physics* Book I, Aristotle tackles the Parmenidean problem of explaining change and generation. Parmenides maintains that if what is is, and what is not is not, then there is no accounting for coming to be.[63] How can black hair turn white? How can a child that was not, come into existence? While the question of any living thing's generation requires a sense of substratum as matter (that which remains constant through change), qualitative change requires a sense of substratum as substance (the individually existing organism) through which all change occurs. Aristotle finds that a conception of "complex" change is required to account for these transformations. All change is complex, so any change in a single living thing requires an understanding of "coming to be" as a movement between contraries through an individual substance. "Everything comes to be from both subject and form,"[64] according to Aristotle, which can be illustrated through the example of the contraries of the musical and the unmusical, or the white and the not-white. Being unmusical or not-white is not something positive but rather the paradoxical presence of what *cannot*, in itself, appear. Since essential nonbeing is impossible, Aristotle's notion of privation belongs to a substance as an accidental property, manifesting as a noticeable *lack* of a potentially positive characteristic. For example, privation paradoxically "appears" as a lack of color or a lack of knowledge.

A substance is the subject that persists through most changes. With regard to the substance itself, the subject is the primary underlying matter of the thing, and the form consists of a pair of opposites understood as form (εἶδος) and privation (στέρησις). Everything that comes to be is thus composed of matter and the form that the matter takes. In the example of the musical and unmusical,

> there is, on the one hand, something which comes to be, and again something which becomes that—the latter in two senses, either the subject or the opposite. By the opposite I mean the unmusical, by the subject [person]; and similarly I call the absence of shape or form or order the opposite, and the bronze or stone or gold the subject.[65]

Here, Aristotle distinguishes between the two sources of complex change: (1) the underlying substratum and (2) that which is *the opposite of the form*, determining that all oppositions can be reduced to this most general conception of the contraries. According to his view, the primary contraries for all natural things are form (what the thing *is*, its essence, or its nature) and *privation*, and nothing besides.[66]

Aristotle identifies privation as the *absence of shape, form, or order*. The absence of shape (ἀσχημοσύνην) means a want, or lack, of form.[67] In the example of the unmusical person as opposed to the musical one, he clarifies that "unmusical" is not something positive, but rather the manifestation of a lack. While this may seem to be a relatively safe position to maintain, Aristotle puts forward a truly radical idea insofar as an Aristotelian substance, understood as the essence of a living body, comes to be from the *not-being* (μὴ ὄν) of privation.[68] This notion—that the essence of life comes from not-being—posits a complete contradiction, because what is *not* simply *cannot be*. Privation, like any property (such as being nonmusical or not-white) is only accidental to matter. Privation is thus like an appearance of the unwieldy chaos of the visible world to which Plato's demiurge brought divine order. While form is the actual principle, Aristotle's philosophy still sets itself the task of accounting for the appearance of—and ultimately control over—lack. Without absence gnawing at the edges of form, change would be impossible, and Parmenides' vision of an unchanging universe would prove victorious. With the notion of complex change, however, Aristotle can account for "accidental nonbeing" coming into existence as form. He agrees,

> that nothing can be said without qualification to come from what is not. But nevertheless, we maintain that a thing may come to be from what is not in a qualified sense, i.e., accidentally. *For a thing comes to be from the privation (τῆς στερήσεως), which in its own nature is something which is not*.[69]

Thus, in one and the same move, Aristotle simultaneously makes lack and absence appear, just as he moves to contain it within the primary power of form.

Stereisis means the deprivation, negation, or lack of a thing. Because of the metaphysical priority of form to substance, privation, as form's contrary is "in its own nature something which is not."[70] In *Physics I*, privation and form serve together (with the substratum) as the first principles of substance.[71] Under this shadow, entropic decay must be a *loss* of a prior order, or the possibility of a higher order's emergence. Thus, for Aristotle, privation can only be predatory, never primary or actively causal, in any given entity. It merely serves as a source from which an active and living being emerges. Privation (as anti-form or the decay of form) thus appears as an unseemly, confused, disordered loss of form, but *never qua privation itself*. On this view, privation and disorganization threaten to dismantle any organized system, manifesting as threat par excellence. Form designates what the thing is, its essence.

Privation names the presence of absence. Privation is *not*, meaning, *it would be pure nonbeing*.[72]

In discussing privation as the contrary of form, Aristotle makes the provocative claim that the former may often seem as if it were a "bad actor" (*kakapoion*) insofar as it seems to be an agent of nonexistence. He proposes this because privation is the opposite principle of form, which is "divine, good, and desirable."[73] Thus, *because* form is divine and good, the contrary to form may *appear* to be bad, "an evil agent" of nonexistence.[74] While he does not label the many ways in which this may be the case, the notion of privation indicates the dangerous entropic principle with which all of the Greek thinkers so far studied must contend. Privation serves as an umbrella concept, naming that which is not (death), that which inhibits or disrupts form (dissolution, decay), and that which opposes differentiation (homogenization).

Matter is of such a nature that it can lack or express form. While entirely unformed materials such as wood and bronze cannot exist except in theory, Aristotle provides a glimpse of the material cause as that which is necessary for all composite beings but will always be secondary in importance.[75] A substance comes into being through matter desiring and yearning for form. The catch, however, is that matter desires only being, never privation.[76] In the creation of substances, matter turns away from privation and toward form. Aristotle thus overcomes the entropic forces of breakdown and formlessness through materiality's desire, and even preference for, form over privation.[77] In a vision of struggle from disordering privation to ordering form, matter desires form *because* matter contains the principle of privation *and eternally wants* to move into the better state.

Notable in Aristotle's discussion of matter and privation in *Physics* is his deep commitments to the primacy of form as well as his cognizance of the unreal reality of lack—something that is largely absent from his predecessors. The life of all substances is one where material lack desires formal completion only to inevitably be once again overcome by lack. Despite the supremacy of the formal principle, the individual living thing perishes from the privation that is inextricably a part of its nature. The individual may die, but the perpetual persistence of form fosters generation of new life from out of privative matter for eternity.[78] The entropic concept of privation is necessary for the generation of all substances but will never overturn the perfect functioning of the universe. Aristotle's prime mover will ensure the necessity of this.

Privation's menace could prove to be too great to contain, were it not for the uncreated universe and god ensuring harmony. In Book XII of the *Metaphysics*, Aristotle asserts that there must be an eternal and unmovable substance because without one, "all things are destructible."[79] His cosmos requires that movement not come into nor pass out of being and that time neither begins nor ends. Abhorring the entropic origins proposed by certain predecessors (such as Hesiod or Anaxagoras) where "the universe would have been generated from *Night* or from the *togetherness of all things*, or from nonbeing," Aristotle instead posits an eternal universe, coming from and going nowhere but always in its own perfect state.[80] Rejecting the emergence of creation from the night, or the indefinite, or the nothingness of nonbeing, he offers his alternative to the cause of existence in the figure of the prime mover. Aristotle argues that "the first heavens must be eternal. There is therefore also something which moves them. And since that which is moved and moves is intermediate, there is a mover which moves without being moved, being eternal, substance, and actuality."[81] The prime mover solves the problem of true creation *ex nihilo*. Banishing the entropic once and for all, Aristotle argues that there must be a substance that is immaterial, pure actuality, and therefore *entirely without privation*. He, therefore, describes a god that stands as a guardian of life and guarantor against ultimate destruction, but also one which does not do anything other than think of its own perfection. The universe always was and will be. No origin in Mind suddenly spinning or an indefinite vortex need be sought. No divine maker to construct and maintain order need be invented. The universe is, and always will be, and his self-thinking god has no direct agential role in this other than being the eternally perfect object of desire. Unlike Plato, Aristotle's god does not literally take the chaotic matter already in the universe and form it into an artifact based on eternal truth. Nor does Aristotle's god actively oversee the universe in its circular or cyclic undulations. Rather, Book XII of the *Metaphysics* speaks of god as eternal and uncreated—a perfect intellectual being, without body, that the heavens themselves desire.[82] Through massive envelopment of the cosmic problems of his predecessors, Aristotle thus ensures that there will be no ultimate heat death, but only the calm assurance that what was will always be, eternally perfect in its perpetually secured existence.

Here the vast and byzantine journey through early Greek thinking comes to an end. What begins with the yawning chasm of Hesiodic chaos, the space through which gods fall and that limits the realms of heaven and earth, culminates in Aristotle's uncreated and wholly fixed universe. The entropic metaphor weaves throughout all these stories through visions of chaos, disorder, materiality, and lack. While this narrative of gods and forms comes to be dominant in the battle to confine entropy, let us not forget the other thread spoken by Homer and Sophocles—the story of the *entrepic* not as a battle against the threats of disorder and dissolution but one of care and reverence in the face of death. The *entrepic* counter-narrative will face increasing silence in the following chapters, only to reemerge later in the praise of different ways of conceiving the chaos, matter, creation, and finitude. But it is always there.

NOTES

1. Jean-Paul Sartre, *Nausea,* trans. Lloyd Alexander (New York: New Directions Publishing Corporation, 1964), 57.
2. Isaac Asimov, "The Last Question," *Science Fiction Quarterly* (November 1956), Accessed May 3, 2021, http://www.gdctangmarg.com/Photos/04_02_2001_35_54Sem%20II_Asimov.pdf.
3. Ibid.
4. Ibid.
5. Zencey, "Entropy as Root," 194.
6. I have no interest in asserting the origins of philosophy to lie in Greek thinking and maintain that I offer one thread, not *the* thread of the history of ideas on entropic phenomena. For an astute analysis of the exclusions of world philosophy from the philosophical canon see, Peter K. J. Park, *Africa, Asia, and the History of Philosophy: Racism in the Formation of the Philosophical Canon, 1730–1830* (Albany: State University of New York Press, 2014).
7. Perhaps my approach is closer to what Nietzsche and Foucault would call genealogical, which identifies "the accident, the minute deviations—or conversely, the complete reversals—the errors, the false appraisals, and the faulty calculations that gave birth to those things that continue to exist and have value for us." Michel Foucault, "Nietzsche, Genealogy, History," in *Language, Counter-Memory, Practice: Selected Essays and Interviews by Michel Foucault,* ed. Donald F. Bouchard, trans. Donald F. Bouchard and Sherry Simon (Ithaca: Cornell University Press, 1977), 146.
8. Ibid, 143.
9. Hesiod, *Theogony,* 115–120.
10. Meisel, *Chaos Imagined,* 48.
11. Andrew Gregory, *Ancient Greek Cosmogony* (London: Bristol Classical Press, 2007).
12. Apostolos N. Athanassakis, "Introduction," in *Theogony, Works and Days, Shield,* by Hesiod, trans. Apostolos N. Athanassakis, 1st ed. (Baltimore: Johns Hopkins University Press, 1983), 8.
13. Hesiod, *Theogony,* 715–730.
14. Hesiod, *Works and Days,* 114–116.
15. Ibid, 117.
16. Ibid, 176–177.
17. Ibid, 192.
18. Ibid, 306.
19. Ibid, 694.
20. Ibid, 472.
21. Anaximander, Fr. A9, in *The Texts of Early Greek Philosophy Greek Philosophy,* trans. Daniel W. Graham (Cambridge: Cambridge University Press, 2010). While generally taken to mean without limit, indefinite, and inexhaustible, τὸ ἄπειρον comes to include "spherical" or "round" insofar as the circumference of a circle has no necessary beginning or end point. Kurt Pritzl, "Anaximander's 'Apeiron' and the Arrangement of Time" in *Early Greek Philosophy: The Presocratics and*

the Emergence of Reason, ed. Joe McCoy (Washington: The Catholic University of America Press, 2013), 26.

22. Anaximander, *Texts of Early Greek Philosophy*, Fr. A9.

23. Pritzl writes, time "is the judge making assessment of injustice and enforcing the payment of penalty and retribution." Pritzl, "Anaximander's apeiron," 32.

24. Anaximander, Fr. B1, in *A Presocratics Reader: Selected Fragments and Testimonia*, ed. Patricia Curd, trans. Richard D. Mckirihan and Patricia Curd (Indianapolis: Hackett Publishing Company, 2011). There is debate over whether this is a full fragment or is part testimony.

25. Anaximander, *Texts of Early Greek Philosophy*, Fr. B1.

26. This describes a primordial condition of mixture and homogenization, serving as a precursor to what Boltzmann later comes to understand about entropy as a movement of homogenous distribution. However, whereas Anaxagoras describes a homogeneous state at the beginning of things (before *nous* introduces motion), Boltzmann will claim as the final consequence of all motion toward randomness.

27. Friedrich Nietzsche, *Philosophy in the Tragic Age of the Greeks*, ed. and trans. Marianne Cowan (Washington, DC: Regnery Publishing, 1962), 101.

28. Anaxagoras, *Presocratics Reader*, Fr. B6. See also, Anaxagoras, *Presocratics Reader*, Fr. B4.

29. Michael M. Shaw, "Parataxis in Anaxagoras: Seeds and Worlds in Fragment B4a," *Epoché: A Journal for the History of Philosophy* (2017): 282.

30. Anaxagoras, *Presocratics Reader*, Fr. B17.

31. Nietzsche, *Tragic Age*, 101.

32. Ibid, 102.

33. Ibid, 107.

34. Plato, "Phaedo," in *Five Dialogues*, trans. G.M.A. Grube, ed. John M. Cooper (Indianapolis: Hackett Publishing Company, 1981), 72a-b.

35. Ibid, 72d.

36. Plato, the *Republic*, ed. and trans. Allan Bloom (Basic Books, 1991), 6.485b.

37. Ibid, 6.509b.

38. Ibid, 8.546a.

39. Ibid, 8.547a.

40. For a discussion on how Plato links injustice to disease in the *Republic* see, Sara Brill, *Plato on the Limits of Human Life* (Bloomington: Indiana University Press, 2013), 111–114.

41. As Philip Hefner observes that "the philosophical and mythic roots of this negative feeling toward the fruits of the second law can be illuminated by Plato's explanation of the creation of the world" in the *Timaeus*. Hefner, "God and Chaos," 471–474.

42. Plato, *Timaeus* in *Plato: Complete Works*, 17a.

43. Ibid, 29a.

44. Ibid, 30a.

45. Ibid, 32c.

46. Ibid, 33b-c.

47. "That is why [the god] concluded that he should fashion the world as a single whole, composed of all wholes, complete and free of old age and disease" Ibid, 33a. Timaeus continues to explain that soul infuses and envelopes creation. Ibid, 36e. This formulation can be seen as a response to Anaxagoras, who does not guarantee the eternity of time.

48. Plato explains: "as the model was an everlasting Living Thing, he set himself to bringing this universe to completion in such a way that it, too, would have that character to the extent that it was possible. Now it was the Living Thing's nature to be eternal, but it isn't possible to bestow eternity fully upon anything that is begotten. And so he began to think of making a moving image of eternity: at the same time as he brought order to the universe, he would make an eternal image, moving according to number, of eternity remaining in unity. This number, of course, is what we now call 'time.'" Ibid, 37d. The dualism of necessity and intellect allows Plato to subordinate disorder, decay, irregularity, and other entropic forces into a perpetual cycle governed by intelligence.

49. Ibid, 52e. Timaeus distinguishes two causes: intelligence and necessity (the *chora* will be the third, the errant cause): "we must describe both types of causes, distinguishing those which possess understanding and thus fashion what is beautiful and good from those which, when deserted by intelligence, produce only haphazard and disorderly effects every time." Ibid, 46e.

50. Ibid, 81d.

51. Ibid, 89b-c.

52. Plato addresses this theme in the *Timaeus* as well. Plato, *Timaeus*, 40e–41a.

53. Plato, the *Statesman* in the *Statesman, Philebus, Ion,* ed. and trans. W. R. Lamb (Cambridge: Loeb Classical Library, 2006), 269d. For an excellent collection of essays on the *Statesman*, see, John Sallis, ed., *Plato's Statesman: Dialectic, Myth, and Politics* (Albany: SUNY Press, 2017).

54. See also *The Laws* where Plato says that the "lesson is that we should make every effort to imitate the life men are said to have led under Cronus; we should run our public and our private life, our homes and our cities, in obedience to what little spark of immortality lies in us." Plato, *The Laws* in *Plato: Complete Works*, 713e–714a.

55. Plato, *Statesman*, 269c.

56. Ibid, 270a.

57. Ibid, 272e.

58. Ibid, 273c.

59. Plato explains that "the ancient condition of disorder prevailed more and more and towards the end of time reached its height." Ibid, 273d.

60. Ibid. Christoph Horn translates this passage as the cosmos being "dissolved in the bottomless abyss of unlikeness." Christoph Horn, "Why Two Epochs of Human History? On the Myth of The Statesman," in *Plato and Myth: Studies on the Use and Status of Platonic Myths*, eds. Pierre Destrée, Francisco J. Gonzalez, and Catherine Collobert (Leiden: Brill, 2012), 411.

61. Horn notes that "it seems plausible to assume that human living conditions took a sudden turn for the worse when the God withdrew, whereas the rational,

divinely instructed cosmos was merely subject to a slow process of decline." Horn, "On the Myth," 410.

62. Plato, the *Statesman*, 273e.
63. Aristotle, *Physics*, trans. R. P. Hardie and R. K. Gay, in *The Complete Works of Aristotle*, vol. 1, ed. Jonathan Barnes (Princeton: Princeton University Press, 1984), 191a25-30.
64. Ibid, 190b20.
65. Ibid, 190b10-17.
66. Specifically, "one is the form or the definition; then further there is its contrary, the privation." Ibid, 191a14.
67. Aristotle also uses privation to mean the principle *opposite* to that of form. Aristotle, *Physics*, 190b12-15.
68. Ibid, 191b15-16.
69. Ibid, 191b15-16 (italics my own).
70. Ibid, 191b16.
71. In *Physics II.1*, he notes, "privation too, is in a way a form." Ibid, 193b19-20.
72. Matter has privation as a property only accidentally. Ibid, 191a9–191a12.
73. Aristotle, *Physics*, 192a16.
74. Ibid, 192a15.
75. To be clear, while a material substratum can manifest either form or privation, privation is understood as part of the formal cause (as the opposite of form to be precise) and not at all as the material substratum.
76. See, Michael M. Shaw, "Unqualified Generation in Aristotle's Natural Philosophy," ed. S. J. William Wians and Gary M. Gurtler, *Proceedings of the Boston Area Colloquium in Ancient Philosophy* (Leiden: Brill, 2014), 77–106.
77. For a discussion of matter as more than lack of form, see Chapter Three in *Aristotle on the Matter of Form*. Adriel Trott, *Aristotle on the Matter of Form: A Feminist Metaphysics of Generation* (Edinburgh: University of Edinburgh Press, 2019).
78. For more on this, see, Shaw, "Unqualified Generation."
79. Aristotle, *Metaphysics*, trans. W. D. Ross, in *The Complete Works of Aristotle*, vol. 2, 1071b5.
80. Aristotle, *Metaphysics*, 1072a19-20. Hesiod and Anaxagoras, among others, are likely intended here.
81. Ibid, 1072a21-27.
82. Ibid, 1072b1-4.

Chapter 3

Entropy in German Philosophies of Nature

We have drawn far-reaching conclusions from the hypothesis that all living substance is bound to die from internal causes.
Sigmund Freud, Beyond the Pleasure Principle[1]

"Menoetius" fighting son . . . the carrion blowflies
will settle into his wounds, gouged deep by the bronze,
worms will breed and seethe, defile the man's corpse—
his life's ripped out—his flesh may rot to nothing'
But glistening-footed Thetis reassured him:
"O my child, wipe these worries from your mind.
I'll find a way to protect him from those swarms,
The vicious flies that devour men who fall in battle.
He could lie there dead till a year has run its course
and his flesh still stand firm, even fresher than now . . ."
Homer, The Iliad[2]

Thomas Pynchon's short story, "Entropy," opens with a quote from Henry Miller's novel, *Tropic of Cancer*:

Boris has just given me a summary of his views. He is weather prophet. The weather will continue bad, he says. There will be more calamities, more death, more despair. Not the slightest indication of a change anywhere. . . . We must get into step, a lockstep toward the prison of death. There is no escape. The weather will not change.

This ominous epigraph foretells of an ensuing calm, not in terms of peace, but in terms of death. Set in 1957, Pynchon's story describes overlapping parties, peoples, intoxicants, and life. The action vacillates between the decline to heat death in one apartment and the chaos of an ongoing party in another. In the former, a man named Callisto wakes up to the third day of gently cradling a dying bird to his body. His apartment is described as a hermetically sealed hothouse, "a tiny enclave of regularity in the city's chaos, alien to the vagaries of the weather, of national politics, of any civil disorder."[3] It is an anti-entropic island, maintained by ecological balance between plant, avian, and human life. While momentarily offering a vision of self-perpetuating and contained existence, it ultimately fails to maintain an impossible equilibrium.

As the bird quietly inches toward expiration, Callisto mulls over the workings of thermodynamics, love, and power. Pitting the heat death of the universe—a time when form and motion cease in a cosmic homogeneity—against the fluctuations of meteorology which reassuringly staves off this most monstrous possibility, Callisto frets about an incredible yet ominous portent: the temperature outside has not moved from a frigid 37 degrees Fahrenheit for three days straight. He is concerned that rather than entropic stasis waiting patiently billions of years in the future, it could perhaps be right now.

A middle-aged man clearly undergoing his own embodied and intellectual awareness of decline, Callisto has a shrewd understanding of the laws of thermodynamics. In essence they boil down to: "you can't win, things are going to get worse before they get better, who says they're going to get better."[4] Only theoretical systems and engines can be perfectly efficient, as Clausius, Gibbs, and Boltzmann had taught him.[5] The terrible knowledge of the movement toward stasis causes him to struggle against allowing this knowledge to turn into a pessimistic fatalism.

The little bird's immanent death only becomes known to Callisto through an interruption—energy coming from another apartment makes its way into the closed system of his own. At that point, "he became aware of the faltering" of the bird's heartbeat that, within minutes, "ticked a graceful diminuendo down at last into stillness."[6] The sadness hangs heavily over Callisto as he is distraught at the failure of heat from his body to communicate life to the now still bird. Like the cold outdoor temperature, the bird's frozen heartbeat discloses that heat death is already here. In a dramatic enactment of this finality, Callisto's partner, Aubade, rushes to the window, smashing it with her fists, ultimately sitting with him on the bed to

> wait with him until the moment of equilibrium was reached, when 37 degrees Fahrenheit should prevail both outside and inside, and forever, and the hovering,

curious dominant of their separate lives should resolve into a tonic of darkness and the final absence of all motion.[7]

"Entropy" conveys a sense of nature as a system that cannot possibly maintain itself in perpetuity. Ultimately, Callisto cannot transmit the heat from his body to the bird. This miscarriage leads to a vision of nature carrying within itself an essential, irreversible sickness. Rather than Plato's vision of an eternal cycle of death and rebirth, the dead remain dead, and everything moves toward inertia in Pynchon's story. The temperature outside of the apartment is static, and the natural world cannot jump-start production of more heat and energy. Pynchon describes the ultimate victory of cold motionlessness over dynamic acceleration.

The natural world exhibits an inevitable and ineluctable tendency in material entities to decay. Entropic philosophy takes this tendency to be omnipresent and unassailable. The following studies explore possible responses to this fundamental feature of all life. While the laws of thermodynamics postdate the Germans discussed, the ideas of decay, slackening, disease, and death contribute to entropic philosophy in important and constitutive ways before the law's discovery. The Greeks demonstrated a concern for and struggle with chaos and destruction and so too do the philosophers studied in this chapter. The concern with degeneration returns in all three thinkers, but the way in which they manage it dovetails and diverges from the Greeks.

Immanuel Kant, F. W. J. Schelling, and G. W. F. Hegel can be seen as responding to some of the core concerns raised by the ancient Greek thinkers discussed in the previous chapter. In particular, how does philosophy contend with the creation and maintenance of the world since it is infused with evidence of destruction and death? Scientific concerns and empirical observation played a role in the structure of Greek theories on the origin and conclusion of the universe. As with the previous discussion on Greek thinking, this chapter does not survey all major treatments of nature in late modern German thought. Rather, I highlight an entropic theme of chaos as an unruly natural threat that gets carried over into these later philosophical treatments. Kant positions chaos outside of nature's purposiveness, Schelling treats natural chaos as a legitimate ground of God, and Hegel develops a philosophy of nature whose premise is the domination and spiritualization of the disorderly elements of natural life.

Much German philosophies of the eighteenth and nineteenth centuries moved away from early modern conceptions of nature as distinct from and even opposed to human rationality. These views take seriously what is irrational (or prerational) in the natural world and how it is connected to the human spirit. In *The Critique of Pure Reason*, Kant famously makes knowledge of nature as it is in itself inaccessible, relegating knowledge to how nature appears to rational cognition. In *The Critique of Judgment*, Kant returns to nature to explore the possibility that there may be an underlying link between it and freedom. Here, Kant introduces judgments of purposiveness, which hypothesize a place for rational life in nature. Although impossible to prove, it appears *as if* nature is oriented toward the nurturing and flourishing of rational life. Kant turns to the purposivity of nature as he discerns its apparent chaos and inhospitableness to humanity as a genuine threat to reason and morality: if nature will not accommodate the ends that reason demands, the moral law itself is void. Responding to the Kantian dilemma, Schelling takes up nature on its own terms more earnestly, considering it to be a real ground for existence working with and against God's eternal perfection. Schelling makes absolute the *a priori* union of reason and nature that Kant only suggests. Following an overview of some of the ways that Kant and Schelling highlight and problematize nature, I turn to a more focused study of Hegel's *Philosophy of Nature*, where the battle between spiritual rationality and chaotic materiality wages all the way through the life and death of the animal organism.

THE PROBLEM OF NATURE IN KANT AND SCHELLING

This book's focus on the human experience of entropics makes Kant's perspective a fitting place to begin the present investigation. A philosopher of progress, he presents one of the brightest flashes of the European Enlightenment as it reaches its apex, balancing precariously before its downward turn into late modernity (a theme developed in the following chapter). Therefore, considerations of decline and dissolution appear mostly as hints, through cracks in the architecture of human reason. The third book in his critical project, *The Critique of Judgment*, captures the human experience of nature without extending this experience beyond rational cognition. This has the effect of tempering the anthropocentric audacity so often woven into many natural philosophies and brings in a perspective on entropics that makes no claim on the world as it is in itself but only insofar as it appears to us.

The Critique of Judgment offers a discussion of aesthetic judgments of taste as well as teleological judgments of nature. While science judges its objects in terms of mechanism, living beings appear to humans both mechanistically *and* in terms of final purposes. Rational beings don't simply observe the laws of cause and effect in nature or ask how to incorporate objects into use; they additionally ask what something is *for* and *why* it exists. In trying to address these differing judgments, the *Critique of Judgment* stands as a final piece of the puzzle bringing together the claims of reason and the recalcitrant otherness of the natural world. Kant set up a seemingly unbridgeable divide in the first two *Critiques*. Practical reason demands the establishment of a moral world order. The faculty of the understanding portrays nature as at best unhelpful in this and at worst obdurately opposed. If this bifurcated reality speaks the truth of the world, then it is irrational to pursue moral ends as they are unwelcome and unrealizable in nature. This conclusion leads to theoretical failure and practical despair. However, the third *Critique* shows a dimension of human life—reflection and judgment—where nature is amenable, even affirmational of human freedom. Kant's critical project consequently ends not in an antinomial stalemate but rather in hope.[8]

For Kant, we come to think nature analogically to a causality that works in terms of purposes. Human beings approach nature as if it were organized teleologically, that is, in terms of final ends. As is the case with aesthetic judgment, teleological judgment is reflective and not determinative. In other words, the concept of purpose cannot be applied to the heterogeneity of the natural world as it appears, yet judgment produces the notion reflectively that nature appears *as if* it were in fact designed purposively. Despite displaying chaos and disorder, nature *seems* to harmonize with our rational faculties such that humanity is not only at home in the world but is in fact the highest purpose of it.[9]

The principle governing organized beings dictates that every part is both a purpose and a means and in "such a product nothing is gratuitous, purposeless, or to be attributed to blind natural mechanism."[10] The concept of an organism is one in which everything fits, and each part is both cause and effect of every other. Perhaps organisms, for as long as they exist, can be conceived as finite-perpetual motion machines, producing and produced by all of the parts of which they consist. The idea that there could be a gratuitous element with no apparent end in an organism is, quite simply, irrational. Put in entropic terms, a wholly purposeless organ or part would signal material chaos concealed in the constitution of the organism. Earlier, in the "Idea for Universal History with a Cosmopolitan Intent," Kant states this idea succinctly: "In the teleological theory of nature, an organ that is not intended to be used, an organization that does not achieve its end, is a contradiction."[11] Furthermore, he continues, "if we stray away from that fundamental principle, we no longer have a lawful but an aimlessly playing nature and hopeless chance takes the place of reason's guiding thread."[12] Kant rejects randomness by underscoring the ways in which organisms would contradict their purpose if they were to admit of a chaotic aimlessness in their form or activity.

In developing his conception of teleological judgments, Kant describes an internal purposiveness of organisms, as well as an external purposiveness about the relation of all things in nature to one another. The internal purposiveness of individual organisms maintains structural integrity, while external purposiveness explains how one thing in nature serves another as a means and a purpose. The combination of internal and external purposiveness reveals an awesome system where the human being ultimately finds a *place*—even a place of "favor" in the cosmos—"just as if nature had erected and decorated its splendid stage quite expressly with that aim."[13] Rational beings are even entitled to go beyond mere mechanism to reflect on a possible immaterial cause and order of the natural world and the human place within it. Cognizing nature *as if* it were created by a supersensible being for the purpose of engaging and expanding rational life situates humanity in creation as the "ultimate purpose of nature here on earth, the purpose by reference to which all other natural things constitute a system of purposes."[14]

Yet, despite insisting on human specialness from the perspective of teleological judgment, Kant realizes that nature's destructive powers do not always cooperate with final purposes. Sometimes nature lies in wait, ready to cast rational order into the chasm of the inorganic. While nature appears to human being as if suited to rational and moral ends, from the side of nature's determinacy, it

> is very far from having adopted him as its special darling and benefitted him in preference to the other animals, but has in fact spared him no more than any other animal from its destructive workings: plague, famine, flood, frost, or attacks from other animals large or small, and so on.[15]

From the position of the natural world, nothing indicates that rational beings are exempt from powerful, destructive forces. Moreover, humanity also does not spare itself from wreckage as "man himself does all he can to work for the destruction of his own species."[16] What may appear as a harmoniously organized world providing habitats to foster and support organic beings and systems actually shows signs of inhospitality upon closer investigation.

> Land and sea contain memorials of mighty devastations that long ago befell them and all creatures living on or in them. Indeed, their entire structure, the strata of the land and the boundaries of the sea, look quite like the product of savage, all-powerful forces of a nature working in a state of chaos.[17]

Geological evidence from the eruptions of violent, world-shaping elemental forces provokes an uneasy worry that everything could be the result of an "unintentional mechanism" rather than a rational plan. This line of thinking causes Kant to ponder whether or not the evidence of natural destruction challenges the centrality of rationality as nature's ultimate purpose.

Even though human beings think according to purposes and can thus alter the course of the natural world, they are no more special than a single blade of grass or a titanic wave of ocean water from nature's perspective. Kant solves this predicament by asserting that teleological judgment is merely reflective. While the understanding of the *Critique of Pure Reason* demanded the study of nature's appearance according to natural necessity, reflective teleological judgment considers the world as a system of purposes with rational life as its aim. As Kant muses, "without man all of creation would be a mere wasteland, gratuitous and without a final purpose."[18] However, if nature is *not* purposive, then humanity has no right to feel any sense of belonging. While Kant's critical project rescues him from having to definitively solve this dilemma one way or another, it is clear that chaos is not entirely eradicable from the system.

Nature, it turns out, may haphazardly help reason achieve moral purpose, but the natural and human world throw up roadblocks incessantly thwarting action. To illustrate this point, Kant posits the dilemma facing a moral atheist, such as Spinoza (who denies an intentional God and with it, purposiveness). While someone like Spinoza may expect nature to conform to contingent plans now and again, moral atheists cannot expect the harmonization of their reason and morality to conform to an immortal god or soul. Rather, "Deceit, violence, and envy will always be rife around him."[19] Kant argues that moral beings who yet reject the proof of God's existence face the horrors of existence without the palliative promise of a higher order:

> no matter how worthy of happiness they may be, nature, which pays no attention to that, will still subject them to all the evils of deprivation, disease, and untimely death, just like all the other animals on the earth. And they will stay subjected to these evils always, until one vast tomb engulfs them one and all (honest or not, that makes no difference here) and hurls them, who managed to believe they were the final purpose of creation, *back into the abyss of the purposeless chaos of matter from which they were taken.*[20]

Such a thought—that there may be no moral world-author—is rare in Kantian thinking. This possibility seems so dark that Kant devotes no more than this brief passage to contemplating it, concluding that morality would have to be rejected by such a good-hearted atheist. Instead, the solution to the chaotic threats plaguing all naturally organized beings is to assume a supersensible substrate of existence, "the existence of a moral author of the world, i.e., the existence of a God" to make it bearable.[21] Otherwise, there is no escaping the conclusion that life is ultimately meaningless and all that awaits rational beings is the unthinking, roiling chaos of nature's destructive forces. This prospect drives a good deal of Kant's later thinking on religion, history, taste, and teleology because he deeply desires to have nature correlate with human morality.²² Yet, nature's chaos is very difficult to purge from even the most rational desire.

Questioning Kant, what if rational life is not the ultimate end of nature? What would it mean to focus on the "abyss of the purposeless chaos of matter" from which life emerges and to which it will return? What if belonging to the world means *not* assuming a supersensible safety net? Kantian assumptions certainly provide metaphysical comfort about reason and nature, but they also encourage flights into the illusory and an elision of the very real issues with which entropic philosophy must contend: disorder, breakdown, and death. If rational life is not the *telos* but rather one of infinite manifestations of universal chaos, the desire for a supersensible guarantor should be jettisoned and the blooming pandemonium of the here and now embraced.

Edging closer to these possibilities within the abyss of chaotic matter, Schelling adopts the formulation of nature as an organism.²³ While Kant's *Critique of Judgment* delves into the teleological structures of nature's appearance, Schelling is widely recognized as the first German idealist to treat *Naturphilosophie* seriously on its own terms. While he published an impressive amount on the relationship between nature and thought, I focus primarily on the *Freiheitsschrift* to show the entropic strands connecting the Kantian and Hegelian treatments of nature. Kant's philosophy makes no claims about the natural world in itself, but his belief that rational life is the highest purpose relegates the natural forces of chaos to the margins of concern. Attempting to give not only a real place to good and evil but also a reality to nature primeval with God, Schelling names an originary chaos that eternally resists and provokes the domination of God and mind. In "The Essence of Human Freedom," he writes that "following the eternal act of self-revelation, all is rule, order, and form in the world as we now see it. But the ruleless still lies in the ground as if it could break through once again, and nowhere does it appear as though order and form were original, but rather *as if something initially ruleless had been brought to order*."²⁴ Schelling's chaotic origin is the darkness preceding the light of God, a creaturely gloom that all natural beings inherit by virtue of coming into existence, and one that not only cannot be banished but which forms the warp and weft of all life.

What is provocative from an entropic orientation is the priority of this ruleless ground functioning as the dark space from which all things must be born and into which they return. While this creaturely darkness impels rational beings to strive for the good, it has a concrete reality that cannot simply be erased by God's love. Evoking the natural philosophy of the Greek thinkers who inspire his thinking, Schelling speaks of the ground as an "original longing [that] moves presentiently like an undulating, surging sea, similar to Plato's matter, following a dark, uncertain law, incapable of forming something lasting by itself," yet rousing the ordering principle of light and divine perfection.[25] Schelling, unlike Kant, has no problem in conceiving of chaos as primordial and exceeding order's grasp, yet as simultaneously necessary to the emergence and inspiration of God's light and human freedom.

As material bodies work against motion and vivacity, this recalcitrance calls forth the opposing activities of order and light. Using the theories of Leibniz and Kepler, Schelling writes about how bodies slow because of the "tendency towards inertia that is innate in matter and peculiar to it, i.e., in the inner limitation or imperfection of matter. But it should be noted that inertia itself cannot be thought of as mere privation, but is something positive indeed."[26] Schelling here describes matter as essentially inertial and imperfect. Yet, unlike Aristotle's concept of privation as the quizzical appearance of nonbeing, Schelling posits this inertial force as a positive aspect of materiality—a natural chaotic principle that is the appearance of evil. The longing that lacks understanding pulls human creatures to the elemental and material, to something like that state existing before the Platonic ordering of the demiurge.[27] But this yearning is precisely the spur that drives human freedom to assert itself and to choose lightness over dark. Since human beings are the only ones for whom the question of good and evil is meaningful, only they must contend with material inertia and the gloomy longing to return to cosmic chaos.[28]

Developing his ideas regarding the ground, Schelling retells the myth of the metallic generations of humans previously taken up by Hesiod and Plato. He writes of a primeval past, a time of blessed ignorance followed by an age of gods and heroes and the ascendency of nature. But all is not serene during the heroic age since nature's chaotic darkness is omnipresent. Diverging from Hesiod and Plato's telling, Schelling explains that,

> because the essence of the ground can never engender true and perfect unity by itself, the time comes when all this glory dissolved, the beautiful body of the previous world decays as from a terrible disease, and finally chaos enters again.[29]

As the forces of chaos gain supremacy over the successive generations of human beings, the ground asserts dominance thereby filling the world with evil. Schelling's primary concern centers on the possibility of evil in the human will, but in so doing reveals the ineradicability of material chaos and its disordering tendencies. Because of this, Schelling's philosophy of nature discovers an ineliminable "sadness clinging to all finite life."[30] Yet, this evil, emerging at the height of the natural ground's dominion, exists in order to call the coming light of God's goodness, love, and order. The melancholy infused throughout finitude allows entropic forces to appear as a natural necessity rather than a site of denial, even as its purpose is to serve as God's inseparable ground to be eternally overcome by his love and light.

HEGEL'S *PHILOSOPHY OF NATURE*

I now turn to Hegel as a corollary to Kant's optimism and Schelling's melancholy, not because he avoids the refuge of purpose and belonging, or because he gives a space for natural chaos to exist as necessary to God's goodness.[31] Rather, Hegel's philosophy offers a portrait of the capriciousness of nature's irrationality through emphasizing that all natural life is destined for death. Hegel's philosophy of nature also gives a voice to the sad inertia of the natural world, but his entire project is devoted to overcoming the menace of nature's contingency by sacrificing it to spiritualization. Left to itself, nature is at the mercy of disarray, disease, and, ultimately, extinction. The entropic eventually expends the vitality of the system, necessitating the final, spectacular moment of nature's self-sacrifice to God. Nature's death in the service of Spirit's birth underscores the extreme lengths to which philosophers will go to elide the magnitude of entropic inevitability. The theme of nature's essential incapacity to maintain eternal life is a core component of Hegel's *Naturphilosophie*. While organic (specifically animal) life is the highest production of the natural world, this great achievement, like Callisto's bird, is infected with an inborn seed of death. Without the eternal life of Spirit born from the ashes of the self-sacrifice of nature, Hegel's world would end up very much like the perpetual 37 degrees of Pynchon's story.

Schelling's scathing criticism of Hegel's philosophy of nature may or may not have contributed to its relatively poor reception over the centuries. Certainly, *The Philosophy of Nature* is an odd book, sandwiched between the minor *Logic* and the *Philosophy of Mind*, the second of his three-part encyclopedic system. A combination of systematic idealistic philosophy and empirical science, *The Philosophy of Nature* forms a vital component of Hegel's philosophical system as a whole, despite its idiosyncratic message.

The Philosophy of Nature shines light on the entropic pull of the natural world against the human and divine impulses. Instead of accepting the limitations of human cognition set forth in Kant's curtailment of knowing and metaphysics, Hegel views Kant's undertaking as stopping short in the ultimate attainment of truth. The antinomial results of the critical project become a necessary preparatory stage in the fulfillment of truth itself, rather than a strict limit on knowing. Nature as it is in itself remains wholly inaccessible to Kant, whereas Hegel describes nature as the externalization of Spirit/mind/ God. Hegel's entire system is built upon Spirit externalizing itself as nature and subsequently spiritualizing, idealizing, and mastering it. Nature appears as the other to mind, as mind lost in disordered chaos but also as implicitly rational and knowable since it is, in the end, only Spirit alienated from itself. Hegel's nature does not exist of its own accord and is thus unlike Schelling's conception of nature as ground. Nature is therefore never more than the externalization of Spirit, there only to be overcome. Nature's disorder must undergo rational ordering with mind dominating the entropic tendencies of matter and life. Anything else would leave open the possibility of decay and death achieving a perverse victory over God.

Deeply influenced by the concept of life discussed in Kant's *Critique of Judgment*, Hegel maintains the idea of Kantian natural purposiveness to ultimately harmonize the disorder of the natural world with the ordering principles of Spirit.[32] Mechanism fails to account for the most important natural development: organic life. Nature is the externalized concept, therefore unfree and irrational. Hegel characterizes nature as apartness (*Außereinander*), infinite separateness (*unendlichen Vereinzelung*), and externality (*Äußerlichkeit*). The determinations of the concept lack the self-subsisting unity of the spiritual subject and instead "have the show of an *indifferent subsistence* and *isolation* in regard to each other."[33] Nature is nothing more than alienated Spirit, created for the ultimate purpose of Spirit losing itself in its other so as to get itself back, knowing itself *as and in its other*. For Hegel, the

> study of nature is thus the liberation of Spirit in her, for Spirit is present in her in so far as it is in relation, not with an Other, but with itself. This is also the liberation of Nature; implicitly she is Reason, but it is through Spirit that Reason as such first emerges from Nature into existence.[34]

In Hegel's system, God creates nature so as to spiritualize it, thus making it divine. Much like Aristotle's discussion of matter as desiring form in the *Physics*, Hegel conceives of the natural world desiring the spiritualization of the divine. There exists an inner yearning for holy ordering within every rock, tree, and animal.

The irrational and contingent appearance of nature thus eventually gives way to the freedom and self-determination of Spirit. Spirit's journey of liberation requires a movement beginning in abstract space and time and ending with the highest production of nature: the living animal organism. The organism's superiority—specifically the freely mobile animal—lies in its ability to *maintain* itself through the play of contradictions running throughout the natural world. All of nature is oriented around the creation of "a being which is capable of containing and enduring its own contradiction" or is a *subject*, even if only in inchoate form.[35] Entropic philosophy highlights Hegel's focus on nature's lack of self-organization and susceptibility to disturbance.

Inevitably, even the animal organism falls to the forces of externality, those irrational claims on unity leading to breakdown of self-subsisting entities.[36]

"Nature," Hegel explains at the beginning of *The Philosophy of Nature*, is

> the Idea in the form of *otherness*. Since therefore the Idea is the negative of itself, or is *external to itself*, Nature is not merely external in relation to this Idea (and to its subjective existence Spirit); the truth is rather that *externality* (*Äußerlichkeit*) constitutes the specific character in which Nature, as Nature, exists.[37]

Spirit is precisely the movement of self-expulsion for the purposes of coming to know fully what it is. Material nature lacks the inherent relationality of the ideal concept, and therefore natural things exist in isolation from each other, related only by the work of mind which must excavate their inherent belongingness. Nature is not free, for here, as with Schelling's ground, contingency rules. Nature remains an unresolved and unresolvable (at least by its own efforts) riddle and contradiction.[38] As such, nature is unstable and unpredictable, even inertial, and this essential determination follows every shape of its development. Nature is characteristically defined by a fundamental positedness, degradation, unreason, and "impotence" (*Ohnmacht*). Its reality has meaning only as othered, positioned outside of Spirit, lacking internal conceptual consistency or the fully realized concreteness of the idea.[39] Nature is therefore enmeshed in "imperfection," "confusion," "degeneration," and inadequacy,[40] which must be overcome by mind knowing it theoretically and practically in a series of progressive stages. Plato's *Timaeus* worked to subdue the entropic chaos of matter through direct intervention of the demiurge's act of creation and stewardship. While Hegel does not speak of a creator god in this way, his natural philosophy must invoke the divine in order to master and ultimately overcome the entropic forces inherent in nature's irrationality.

The opening sections of *The Philosophy of Nature* presents glimpses of the entropic. In the division of the project, Hegel clarifies that nature's otherness first appears in its immediacy as "mutual outsidedness" and "infinite separatedness." Space and time are the first antitheses to emerge which is nature in its purest abstraction and most extreme externality. Space, expressed as the inert "side-by-sidedness" (*Nebeneinander*), forms the ground for the objects and systems that operate within it. In its pure immediacy, however, nature contains no difference, just pure, continuous asunderness (*Außereinander*). Such a characterization points to the way in which the natural world—from stones to stars to mammals—must contend with the absolute physical separation of beings and entities. The total separation and lack of a center forms the most universal and abstract aspect of nature itself.[41] Although for Hegel, each successive stage will sublate this first immediacy into itself (thereby overcoming the initial division) the entropic pull of parts away from each other remains an essential, ineradicable element of the natural world in each of its developmental stages. A grounding chaos therefore characterizes nature in each successive level. Although order will achieve victory over disorder, separation remains an essential component within the entire natural world, thus displaying entropic forces that cannot be overcome without the domination of nature by Spirit.

Following the treatment of space, Hegel remarks that the first negation of externality is time. The negative unity of time describes the very heart of finitude: "time itself is the *becoming*, this coming-to-be and passing away. The *actually existent abstraction, Chronos*, from whom everything is born and by whom its offspring is destroyed."[42] Temporality is to be what it is not and not to be what it is. Becoming is this pure vanishing of the moment. Only Spirit is eternal and only the finite perishes.[43] This truth follows Hegel's analysis throughout *The Philosophy of Nature*. Whether geometrical, cosmological, environmental, or bodily, every natural system is finite and ultimately vanishes.[44]

Hegel sublates space and time into matter and motion. Here is where we find the real flaw of the natural world: matter's unity is only ideal, having its gravitational center outside of itself. This decentering means that anything material is unable to achieve subjective unity.[45] This move recalls Schelling's conception of matter exhibiting a tendency toward inertia, lack of unity and essential imperfection. Matter's failure to achieve unity is because its center is not a spiritual center but instead lies outside of it as a force acting upon it from without. Therefore, matter is "eternally condemned" to long for unity, resulting in the "most unhappy *nisus*."[46] As the synthesis of space and time, matter produces a movement that pulls away from a center. Hegel succinctly notes elsewhere in *The Philosophy of History* that "the nature of Spirit may be understood by a glance at its direct opposite—*Matter*. As the essence of Matter is Gravity, so, on the other hand, we may affirm that the substance, the essence of Spirit is Freedom."[47] In other words, the lightness of Spirit as self-determining freedom is best understood in distinction from the weight of matter as pure determinacy. Matter is real: "the palpable and tangible, what offers resistance," yet it is so in opposition to the unfettered essence of Spirit.[48] Because it is the identity of space (as immediate asunderness) and time (as negativity), matter is composite, impenetrable, and resistant. Materiality's essential defectiveness therefore lies in the inability of attaining self-perpetuating inwardness.[49] Matter unites space, time, place, and motion in their chaotic interplay; without material chaos, there would be no becoming and no life. But at the same time, this chaos is an oppositional force to the eternal unity and simplicity of Spirit. Essentially, matter teaches a negative lesson opposing spiritual freedom. Only that which has reason and intellect is capable of true being-for-self, self-determination, and ensouled existence.

The first appearance of matter comes in the form of inert bodies which exist through movement and cessation exerted by something outside of themselves. As Hegel explains, the "finitude of the body, i.e., its inadequacy to its concept, consists here in this: as matter, the body is only the *abstract*, immediate unity of time and space."[50] The inertness of material bodies comes from the lack of internal, spontaneous motion from within. While it may sound odd to formulate gravity as matter's external center, it makes sense if gravity is understood as a force acting *upon* not *within* matter. While gravity can never give internal unity to matter, it does serve as a goal that matter ceaselessly desires, not unlike matter desiring form in Aristotle's metaphysics. An entropic reading focuses attention on how materiality prevents free subjectivity and eternal stability because it is always uncentered. Matter is a persistently impeding force that infects Nature's externality and grounds its essential dependence.[51] While not overemphasizing the first stages of development, I want to highlight some conclusions that can be drawn from the opening movements of *The Philosophy of Nature*: (1) nature's essence as externality contaminates all matter, and by extension every material entity; (2) nature lacks the unifying center of the concept and is consequently vulnerable to the predations of decay; and (3) matter has its center (gravity) as an ideal outside of itself, for which it longs, but that remains impossible to realize. In essence, matter and thus *all* natural systems are defined by the burden of finitude.

Because of materiality, every finite thing is subject to decay, slackening, or organic death.[52] From this truth, entropics become most evident in the discussion of life in the final sections of *The Philosophy of Nature*. The entirety of Hegel's philosophy of nature moves toward the discussion of life and, in particular, animal life. The animal is "the microcosm, the center of Nature, which has achieved an existence for itself in which the whole of inorganic nature is recapitulated and idealized."[53] Just as Kant spoke of the organism's purposiveness wherein every part is cause and effect of every other part, so too for Hegel, animal life is a system of reciprocal ends and means. The organism converts "its own members into a nonorganic nature, into *means*, lives on itself and produces its own self, i.e., this same totality of articulated members, so that each member is reciprocally end and means, maintains itself through the other members and is in opposition to them."[54] The animal is constantly borrowing energy and materials from the environment, cycling these through its body, and reproducing the same processes internally. In this way, the organism preserves itself by turning its parts into means for self-preservation. Much like Kant, who finds natural purpose only when (1) parts depend on their relationship to the whole for their functioning and (2) the parts of the thing form a unity because they are reciprocally the cause and effect of each other,⁵⁵ Hegel insists that preservation requires this kind of circular, inherently self-sufficient process. All systems require energy for maintenance and the animal is no different insofar as "each member draws on the others for its own needs."⁵⁶ The organism engages the nonorganic in order to maintain its integrity. By doing this, it has a *feeling* of self, persevering in its time and unique environment for a bit, until it eventually succumbs to death.

The multiple activities taking place to sustain the organism's inviolability do not produce a harmonious, frictionless, organic machine. Rather, as the animal has recapitulated into itself all of the earlier stages of nature (such as space, time, gravity, matter, etc.), each part of its body is in a state of discord with the others insofar as the parts and organs are distinct. These differences allow for structural soundness, but like Timaeus' bodily triangles, the tension and threat of collapse is ever present. Imbalance, evident in disease or starvation, results from an overdrawing of energy from one part by another, causing disruption and ultimately destroying the organism. Hegel describes an organism existing only insofar as it can maintain the balance of difference and energy until its destruction. Furlotte writes that the entire natural cycle recapitulated in the animal reveals "the radical instability and insufficiency of material nature to completely realize conceptual, subjective structuration of the sort realised in the domain of spirit."⁵⁷ Despite this instability, the animal organism exhibits limited capability for self-maintenance and environmental adaptation as long as it persists, which is why it is the jewel of nature in Hegel's system.

The animal as an individual structure does not only operate with its internal parts converting and borrowing energy from each other but also as a singular entity in a relationship with the larger environment. There thus arises a contradiction between the organism and the environment in which it lives, consumes, and reproduces. Admittedly, Hegel has an unusual way of describing how animals are formed by the sublation of earlier abstract shapes of nature. Space, time, and gravity are incorporated into the more concrete developments of inorganic entities, and ultimately plants and animals. Animal life only exists through the assimilation and utilization of all the previous natural stages. Because nature is externalized Spirit, the nestings of the most undeveloped into the most developed cannot be shorn of their inherent movement toward disorder. Death is present in every living creature from the moment of its inception as the tension between matter and its gravitational center portends. The impotence of nature

> subjects not only the development of individuals to external contingencies—the developed animal (and especially man) can exhibit monstrosities—but even the genera are completely subject to the changes of the external, universal life of Nature, the vicissitudes of which are shared by the life of the animal, whose life,

consequently, is only an alternation of health and disease. The environment of external contingency contains factors which are almost wholly alien; it exercises a perpetual violence and threat of dangers on the animal's feeling which is an *insecure, anxious,* and *unhappy* one.[58]

Hegel makes several critical qualifications in the preceding quote. First, he underscores the essential impotence of nature; second, nature's various forms are affected through and through by contingency insofar as they are prey to forces over which they have no ability to predict or control. The most damaging of these can be seen in living organisms (particularly animals) displaying a wide array of imperfections, confusions of form, and, as Hegel terms them, "monstrosities." The animal's environment is suffused by violence from decentered, imperfect materiality; its anxiety is a consequence of life being beset by external forces of environment and internal forces of lack and sickness that pull it apart and ultimately destroy it. The natural world is thus thoroughly saturated by the entropic forces that lead to breakdown and death. Just as Aristotle's notion of privation provides an understanding of annihilation yet proves necessary for the existence of any living substance, so is death present in all life in Hegel's natural philosophy, as both its opposite, yet necessary condition.

The genus is superior to the individual creature in Hegel's system, producing a strain necessary for the existence of the individual as an individual but also ultimately responsible for the individual's undoing.[59] How something surrenders to material chaos and lifeless externality ultimately depends on what causes systemic breakdown. For example, organisms get sick from an irresolvable conflict between the organic and the inorganic. Disease [*Krankheit*] is the animal's entanglement "with a nonorganic power" wherein either an organ or a system is put into opposition with the unity of the whole organism.[60] Just as Plato's *Timaeus* speaks of death and disease resulting from triangular disorders within the body, Hegel claims that disease causes the breaking apart, breaking down, disruption, and waning of the self-subsisting whole: "In disease, the animal is entangled with *a nonorganic power* and is held fast in one of its particular systems or organs in opposition to the unity of its vitality."[61] Ultimately leading to the death of the organism, disease emerges when one of the systems or parts of the animal breaks away and dominates or antagonizes the rest. What would be a fluid exchange of energy between parts and systems maintaining the health of the organism becomes a disharmony when the flow is interrupted. Because the organism carries the inorganic within it (space, time, matter, and gravity), a disproportionality forms between the inner ability of the organism to self-maintain and the external stimuli of the environment overwhelming its borders. In short, disease is the direct result of the forces of differentiation and separation.

Disease signals the essential inadequacy of a finite particular to embody the universal, which is why in the end, it must be sublated into its truth. Without subjectivity and inner cohesion, matter pulls the organism apart.

Hegel acknowledges that organisms can certainly recover from specific diseases, but such recovery is merely a temporary forestalling of the inescapable fate of decline into death. Even if death by violence or disease is evaded, eventually the organism is no longer capable of maintaining itself *as* a system. "The process of life," Hegel writes, "has become the *inertia* of *habit*; it is in this way that the animal brings about its own destruction."[62] If the organism avoids death by violence or disease, it eventually falls into rigid old age, life persisting only through the monotony of bodily habits. The dynamism of life gives way to waning, habitual torpor. The unavoidable slowing down and the lack of organic innovation becomes the conservative repetition of routines. The organism becomes an empty repetition of vital processes which ultimately lead to its waning and death.

The inert elemental eventually overtakes life. Only Spirit can withstand this entropic movement. In fact, Hegel writes of the organism that "the disparity between its finitude and universality" is the *"original disease* and the inborn *germ of death*, and [the] cancellation [*Aufheben*] of this disparity is itself the *accomplishment of this destiny.*"[63] The finite existing entity and the universality of the concept that forms its essence are the *original* disease, "cured" only when the animal dies and returns to the chaotic elemental. Such words are reminiscent of Anaximander's claim that all that comes to be from the *apeiron* must pay the penalty for existence by returning to it. Death in Hegel's philosophy results from removing the disparity between the spiritual source and the individual creature.

Reading Hegel's thought through an entropic scope brings into view the inescapable movements of finite systems influencing and borrowing from each other. Matter, gravity, space, and time create the structures of finitude because nature's essence is externality. The inherent lack of a spiritual center produces relentless forces that pull apart individual material beings. Living and maintaining structure can only ever be temporary, and all systems will eventually succumb to inevitable inactivity. For Hegel, the individual dies so that the universal may be eternal. In this way, he continues in the tradition of Plato and Aristotle who acknowledge the entropic at the individual level of those entities that come into and pass out of existence but reject it on the cosmic level where order and perfection eternally stave off decline. Presenting a grand movement between unity and disunity Hegel depicts a sort of mortal clock where the inorganic ultimately achieves dominance in the individual by becoming an unstoppable force of division. Perhaps this is why the organism—even the highest and best—must ultimately die for the true life of Spirit to emerge.

And so it ends: with the emergence of Spirit from the dead husk of petrified nature. The expelled, alien visage of spirit returns to itself through the sublation of natural existence. All along, it seems, what really defines externality and drives the movement of Spirit to overcome self-alienation are the entropic structures of time, space, matter, and gravity that form the ground of finitude and materiality. Because nature is essentially externality (which is entirely bound up with the chaos of a materiality that cannot be fully contained or eradicated), Spirit must overcome this entropic threat through sublating it into a higher form, and neutralizing death through spiritualization.

All three thinkers studied here offer different approaches to the human relation to the incipient chaos of the natural world by evoking specters of death, disorder, and chaos to inform and challenge their philosophical systems. Kant, Schelling, and Hegel write about the various ways that the natural world presents itself to rational beings. Kant's discussion of natural purposiveness shows human being at home in the world, even if no determinate judgment can be made about this natural hospitality. While nature cannot be said to be organized by God for the purposes of human life to flourish, it nonetheless appears as if it were in fact so. Chaos lurks in the wings but ultimately is kept at bay by nature's hypothetical, rational, supersensible substrate. Schelling's nature, as an antagonist to the force of divine love, offers a real, substantial ground for material chaos. The natural ground is essential to God's existence and activity. Hegel's philosophy of nature presents a systematic understanding of the implications of nature as alienated, externalized Spirit, lost in the world of things and forces. Only nature's self-sacrifice can overcome the pervasive forces of disunity and disorder that beset all natural things. In all three philosophers, the material chaos of the natural world remains in the interstices of the rational, divine order, just as it does in their ancient Greek predecessors.

The following chapter takes up these manifestations of death explicitly in Freudian psychoanalysis and Lévi-Straussean anthropology where entropy is the great leveler of diversity in culture and psychic life. The vivacity that bursts into art, philosophy, science, and political organization cannot continue indefinitely. Rather, these authors will show how the quickening that brings both natural and spiritual life is dominated by a slackening that leads to cultural and psychological decay.

NOTES

1. Freud, *Pleasure Principls*, 53.
2. Homer, *Iliad,* 19.35–40.
3. Thomas Pynchon, "Entropy," in *Slow Learner: Early Stories* (New York: Little, Brown and Company, 1985), 83–84.

4. Ibid, 87.

5. Pynchon is the first to admit that entropy is a difficult concept to get one's head around. He writes, "Since I wrote this story I have kept trying to understand entropy, but my grasp becomes less sure the more I read." Ibid, 14. Pynchon also thematized entropy in his novels, *The Crying of Lot* 49 (1965) and *Gravity's Rainbow* (1973).

6. Ibid, 97.

7. Ibid, 98. Aubade's act of window-smashing challenges Callisto's misplaced desire to maintain an anti-entropic enclave. In so doing, "she elects to allow disorder to penetrate a closed system—because either way the system will decay. Too much order leads to stagnation; too little results in disintegration." Joseph Slade, "Entropy and Other Calamities," in *Pynchon: A Collection of Critical Essays*, ed. Edward Mendelson (Upper Saddle River: Prentice-Hall, 1978), 80.

8. See Chapter One of Kristi Sweet's, *Kant on Freedom, Nature, and Judgment: The Territory of the Third Critique*, forthcoming with Cambridge University Press for an extended analysis of this philosophical claim.

9. Immanuel Kant, *The Critique of Judgment*, trans. Werner S. Pluhar (Indianapolis: Hackett Publishing Company, 1987), 253.

10. Ibid, 255.

11. Immanuel Kant, "Idea for a Universal History with a Cosmopolitan Intent," in *Perpetual Peace and Other Essays*, trans. Ted Humphrey (Indianapolis: Hackett Publishing Company, 1983), 30.

12. Ibid.

13. Kant, *Critique of Judgment*, 260.

14. Ibid, 317.

15. Ibid, 318.

16. Ibid.

17. Ibid, 315.

18. Ibid, 331.

19. Ibid, 342.

20. Ibid (italics my own).

21. Ibid. Although we can never determinately say that there is a God (a supersensible intentional creator of the world according to purposes), we can say that "cognizing the inner possibility of many natural things is quite unthinkable to us and is beyond our grasp unless we think of it, and of the world as such, as a product of an intelligent cause." Ibid, 282. Kierkegaard will later pose the problem: "If a human being did not have an eternal consciousness, if underlying everything there were only a wild, fermenting power that writhing in dark passions produced everything, be it significant or insignificant, if a vast never appeased emptiness hid beneath everything, what would life be then but despair?" Søren Kierkegaard, *Fear and Trembling and Repetition*, ed. and trans. Howard V. Hong and Edna H. Hong (Princeton: Princeton University Press, 1983), 15.

22. Sweet, *Kant on Freedom*.

23. Andrew Bowie, trans. "Introduction," in *On the History of Modern Philosophy*, ed. F. W. J. von Schelling (Cambridge: Cambridge University Press, 1994), 9.

24. F. W. J. von Schelling, "Philosophical Investigations into the Essence of Human Freedom and Related Matters" in *Philosophy of German Idealism*, ed. Ernst Behler (New York: Continuum, 2003), 238 (italics my own). Wes Furlotte contrasts the barrenness of Hegel's philosophy of nature with the dynamism of Schelling's. Wes Furlotte, *The Problem of Nature in Hegel's Final System* (Edinburgh: Edinburgh University Press, 2018), 37.

25. Schelling, "Philosophical Investigations," 239.

26. Ibid, 247.

27. Schelling clarifies that "all evil strives to return to chaos, i.e., to that state in which the initial center was not yet subordinated to light. It is an upsurging of the centers of yet unintelligent longing." Ibid, 250.

28. This gloomy longing is akin to the allure of the death drive in Freud as discussed in the following chapter.

29. Schelling, "Philosophical Investigations," 254.

30. Ibid, 270.

31. It warrants mentioning that Schelling finds Hegel's move from logic to nature to be tortured because "nature *in general* is for him nothing but the agony of the concept." Schelling, *History of Modern Philosophy,* 153.

32. For more discussion on this, see, Adrian Johnston, "The Voiding of Weak Nature," *Graduate Faculty Philosophy Journal* 33, no. 1 (2012): 103–157.

33. G. W. F. Hegel, Philosophy *of Nature: Being Part Two of the Encyclopaedia of the Philosophical Sciences*, trans. A. V. Miller (Oxford: Clarendon Press, 1970), 17.

34. Ibid, 13. The overwhelming feminization of nature in Hegel's philosophy cannot be ignored as it has repercussions throughout the entire system. While adequately addressing this would go too far afield in the present study, I take it up explicitly in other works. See, Shannon Mussett, "Death and Sacrifice in Hegel's Philosophy of Nature," *Epoché,* ed. Nancy Tuana 22, no. 1 (2017): 119–134, and Shannon Mussett, "Life and Sexual Difference in Hegel and Beauvoir," *Journal of Speculative Philosophy* 31, no. 3 (2017): 396–408.

35. Hegel, *Philosophy of Nature*, 385.

36. This is why Hegel tells us that although the life is the highest level attained by nature, it is still flawed because all life "is at the mercy of the unreason of externality, and the living creature is throughout its whole life entangled with other alien existences." Ibid, 17. I mostly agree with Adrian Johnston's reading that there we are wrong to read Hegel's absolute idealism as "an insatiable, monad-like mega-Mind devouring and digesting the entire expanse of non-mental being without leftovers." Johnston, "Weak Nature," 117. Yet, these remainders, most evident in forces of chaos, disorder, materiality, and contingency, are the obsession of Spirit's activity. Even if it fails, Spirit still desires to incorporate nature's externality in all of its manifestations.

37. Hegel, *Philosophy of Nature*, 13–14. Hegel defines externality in the *Zusatz* to section 254 as "Heres" that exist side by side. See, Ibid, 29. Raoni Padui explains that there is something fundamentally irrational that belongs to nature, and we must "understand this resistance or externality not as a logical mismatch between concepts and the infinite manifold, but as a quality of nature itself." Raoni Padui, "Hegel's

Ontological Pluralism: Rethinking the Distinction Between Natur and Geist," *The Review of Metaphysics* 67 (2013): 136.

38. Hegel, *Philosophy of Nature*, 17. For a discussion of the two uses of contingency (dependence and conditionality/irrationality and chance) see Padui, "The Necessity of Contingency and the Powerlessness of Nature: Hegel's Two Senses of Contingency," *Idealistic Studies* 40, no. 3 (2010): 243–255.

39. Hegel, *Philosophy of Nature*, 23.

40. Ibid, 416. Much literature deals with what is at stake in this positioning of nature in Hegel's philosophy that I am not able address in my focus on the entropic metaphor. For more specific research in this area, see Terry Pinkard, "Speculative Naturphilosophie and the Development of the Empirical Sciences," in *Continental Philosophy of Science*, ed. Gary Gutting (Maldan: Blackwell Publishing, 2008); Johnston, "Weak Nature"; Stephen Houlgate, ed. *Hegel and the Philosophy of Nature* (Albany: SUNY Press, 1998); Alison Stone, *Petrified Intelligence: Nature in Hegel's Philosophy* (Albany: SUNY Press, 2005); Sebastian Rand, "The Importance and Relevance of Hegel's Philosophy of Nature," *The Review of Metaphysics* 61 (2007): 379–400; Padui, "Hegel's Ontological Pluralism"; Padui, "Necessity of Contingency."

41. As Furlotte elaborates, "spatiality is a chaotic impotence . . . Hegelian nature, quite literally, begins in absence, in that which, in a crucial sense, is not actuality." Furlotte, *Problem of Nature*, 33.

42. Hegel, *Philosophy of Nature*, 34. Time is negativity itself or, "the negative unity of self-externality." Ibid.

43. Hegel writes, "only the natural, therefore, is subject to time in so far as it is finite; the True, on the other hand, the Idea, Spirit, is *eternal*." Ibid, 35. Hegel furthers that "time is only this abstraction of destruction." Ibid, 36. Furlotte frames it thus: "the chaotically violent nature of temporality" consumes its own momentary children like Chronos devouring his offspring. Furlotte, *Problem of Nature*, 41.

44. Hegel asserts that "all finite things are temporal, because sooner or later they are subject to change." Hegel, *Philosophy of Nature*, 36.

45. The gravity in matter is "the confession of the nullity of the self-externality of matter in its being-for-self, of its lack of self-subsistence, of its contradiction." Ibid, 46. Hegel's discussion of matter emerges out of Kant's formulation of matter as the force of attraction and repulsion. See, Gerd Buchdahl, "Hegel on the Interaction Between Science and Philosophy," in *Hegel and Newtonianism*, ed. M. J. Petry (Dordrecht: Kluwer Academic Publishers, 1993), 64–66, and Pinkard, "Speculative Naturphilosophie," 27.

46. Hegel, *Philosophy of Nature*, 46. This unhappy nisus recalls the melancholy of finite life in Schelling.

47. G. W. F. Hegel, *The Philosophy of History*, trans. J. Sibree (Amherst, NY: Prometheus Books, 1991), 17.

48. Hegel, *Philosophy of Nature*, 44.

49. Furlotte, *Problem of Nature*, 43. Chapter 6 will ultimately challenge this conception of matter as one that fights against rather than within the forces of entropy. What Hegel shows us is that the impenetrability and foreignness of matter has a long-standing history that informs the entropic metaphor.

50. Hegel, *Philosophy of Nature*, 48.

51. Hegel writes "this resistance which the body encounters in its contingent motion belongs, of course, to the necessary manifestation of its lack of self-subsistent being." Ibid, 53.

52. For example, the organism, "is always on the point of passing over into the chemical process: oxygen, hydrogen, salt, are always about to appear, but are always again sublated and only at death or in disease is the chemical process able to prevail." Ibid, 274.

53. Ibid, 356.

54. Ibid, 377.

55. See Kant, *Critique of Judgment*, 252.

56. Hegel, *Philosophy of Nature*, 378.

57. Furlotte, *Problem of Nature*, 26.

58. Hegel, *Philosophy of Nature*, 416–417.

59. The genus is superior to the individual even as it attains existence through the individual organism, but the "genus preserves itself only through the destruction of the individuals who, in the process of generation, fulfill their destiny and, in so far as they have no higher destiny, in this process meet their death." Hegel, *Philosophy of Nature*, 414.

60. Ibid, 440.

61. Ibid (italics my own). Disease appears when any of the living systems or organs comes "into conflict with the inorganic power (*Potenz*), establishes itself in isolation and persists in its particular activity against the activity of the whole." Ibid, 428. Later he says that "In disease, the animal is entangled with a nonorganic power and is held fast in one of its particular systems or organs in opposition to the unity of its vitality." Ibid, 440. I also deal with this issue of disease and death in Mussett, "Death and Sacrifice."

62. Ibid.

63. Ibid, G. W. F. Hegel, *Hauptwerke in sechs bänden*, vol. 6. (Hamburg: Felix Meiner Verlag, 1992), 375 (translation modified, italics my own).

Chapter 4

Leveling Modernity

Entropy in Freud and Lévi-Strauss

> To cruelly paraphrase Martin Luther King, the arc of history is long, but it bends toward catastrophic annihilation.
> Barbara Ehrenreich, *Natural Causes*[1]

A profound, timely, but seductively pessimistic novel, Philip K. Dick's *Martian Time Slip* explores time, decay, and the breakdown of human civilization. The twilight of the species becomes evident throughout the work, despite the fact that human beings have developed the ability to colonize Mars. Importing the brokenness of the Earth into the new planet, the Martian colonists move within their world in various degrees of denial, many of them through mental illnesses that have proliferated in response to species fatigue.

Martian Time Slip tells a time and mind-bending story about a failing Earth colony on a desiccated planet. Arnie Kott, the petty president of a local water company, shows his power by squandering the most precious resource on Mars. He wallows in steam baths that "had been constructed so as not preserve the run-off. The water drained out onto the hot sand and disappeared forever."[2] Kott is the quintessential "Earthling"—intentionally ignorant, selfish, conniving, and, most importantly, wasteful. His story is one of desire to have more than one should, to deliberately take from others scarce means and even scarcer pleasures.

In his desire to get the scoop on an anticipated business deal before the UN buys seemingly worthless lands for development (lands, most significantly, that house the last remaining outposts of the indigenous inhabitants on the verge of total annihilation from colonization), Kott recruits the services of a nonverbal autistic boy whom he believes can see into the future. This boy, Manfred Steiner, can in fact see into the future, but his visions manifest pure terror and hostility. He experiences the world as a horrific blooming of decay at hyper speeds: "The environment around him is so accelerated that he cannot cope with it, in fact he is unable to perceive it properly."[3] His withdrawal from the world results from an inability to recognize anything thriving in its appropriate form. Instead, he sees only the organic and inorganic structures of the world decaying into rot and death, a kind of analog to the decay and rot of the human species. Kott believes he can use the boy's skills to make money off the UN land sale because Manfred can glimpse the massive dormitory building project yet to be built. But unknown to Kott, Manfred can only view it in its state of tragic dilapidation. Through Manfred's eyes, the Earth's ruin is transferred to Mars, leading to a lifeless and broken future.

Unable to speak, Manfred remains a silent witness to the horrors of entropic decay which he calls "gubbish." He constantly moves in a harrowing future, a "world where gubbish ruled, and he had no voice."[4] Dominated by the entropic to the point where all creativity and creation—all complex structures—necessarily lose their integrity, Manfred perceives only putrefaction. Staring out over a landscape where the massive apartment complexes have yet to be built, he sketches what will come: "The buildings were old, sagging with age. Their foundations showed great cracks radiating upward. Windows were broken. And what looked like stiff tall weeds grew in the land around. It was a scene of ruin and despair, and of a ponderous, timeless, inertial heaviness."[5] Manfred lives a microcosm of the ruin toward which the Martian colonists and native *Bleekmen* are inevitably spinning. As a result, the entropic (what Dick names the "inertial") is a site of abjection and revulsion. In this story, Dick portrays a movement of a great leveling of human civilization and discrete structures. Rather than a future filled with novelty and potential, the future decays into a homogenous, wrecked wasteland.

Dick's vision of Martian collapse proves to be merely the mirror image of Earth's inability to face entropy's inevitability. Both Sigmund Freud and Claude Lévi-Strauss directly engage this formulation of entropic movement toward destruction through discussions of complex structural breakdown into homogeneity. Approaching this development from psychoanalysis and anthropology underscores how the entropic metaphor cannot simply be claimed by any particular branch of thinking.[6] It rebuffs any attempt of containment, which is why it is such a fecund prism through which to unite seemingly disparate fields of study. This chapter focuses on these two thinkers because they voice the entropic metaphor in particularly pointed ways. The more boisterous claim of entropics—that systems fall apart without additional energy—is only one way the second law asserts itself. The unremitting movement of all difference to sameness is another. The sliding toward thermodynamic leveling not only figures in physics but helps to explain the relentlessly draining aspects of psychic and social life. Just as Dick's Mars depicts the degradation of minds and societies in their failure to escape torpor, so Freud and Lévi-Strauss explore the inevitability of inertia as captured by the death drive. Human psychology and society can be understood as systems composed of fluid edges facilitating exchanges of internal and external energies. What becomes obvious is that the interchanges are not self-sustaining or perpetually renewing, but rather require constant influxes of energy in order to persist. Studying psychology and society reveals in striking clarity that these energies are limited and unrenewable.

A stark portrayal of homogenization and simplification emerges in the Freudian death drive and Lévi-Straussean entropology. Both write of great movements toward cultural and biological quiescence as they pertain to the individual human psyche and society as a whole. Weaving a tale of life emerging from and desiring a return to the stillness of inorganic (therefore simple) existence, Freud traces the largely unconscious desire to cease existing altogether. This narrative requires that human psychology take seriously its own participation in the death drive and its seductive retrograde appeal. Lévi-Strauss outlines the devolution of human society away from difference and multiplicity toward sameness and homogeneity, bearing witness to colonialism and capitalism's razing of difference. Reading them together provides insight into how individuals and civilizations present profoundly regressive, entropic movements.

FREUDIAN ENTROPICS

In a remarkably poignant 1915 piece titled "On Transience," Freud tells the story of a summer walk in the countryside with a "taciturn friend" and a "young but already famous poet."[7] Most likely accompanied by Ranier Maria Rilke and Lou Andreas Salome, he marvels at how the poet felt no joy in the natural beauty all around them because with winter, it would all be gone. This despondency spreads to all things naturally and artistically beautiful because ultimately nothing beautiful can last. The beautiful is, as Freud notes, prone to decay, and this can give rise to two possible responses: the pessimism of the young poet in refusing to enjoy the moment or the resistance to this resigned posture taken by the good doctor accompanying him. Freud rebels against the poet's mourning of what has not yet passed by declaring in an Aristotelian pose that that which is beautiful for a day is no less beautiful than that which is beautiful forever:[8]

> A flower that blossoms only for a single night does not seem to us on that account less lovely. Nor can I understand any better why the beauty and perfection of a

work of art or of an intellectual achievement should lose its worth because of its temporal limitation. A time may indeed come when the pictures and statues which we admire to-day will crumble to dust, or a race of men may follow us who no longer understand the works of our poets and thinkers, or a geological epoch may even arrive when all animate life upon the earth ceases.[9]

There may indeed come a time when all life disappears from the earth, but mourning impermanence should not be the final word on the matter. Although Freud's remarks are largely made in order to discuss his burgeoning theory of mourning and melancholia, the short piece is bookended by the observations of the poet and the devastating fallout of the First World War. The War, Freud continues,

destroyed not only the beauty of the countrysides through which it passed and the works of art which it met with on its path but it also shattered our pride in the achievements of our civilization, our admiration for many philosophers and artists and our hopes of a final triumph over the differences between nations and races. It tarnished the lofty impartiality of our science, it revealed our instincts [*Triebleben*] in all their nakedness and let loose the evil spirits within us which we thought had been tamed for ever by centuries of continuous education by the noblest minds.[10]

Although the devastating work of war annihilates not only the transient beauty of nature but also many great artistic, scientific, and cultural achievements, Freud maintains that their ephemerality does not diminish their worth. In fact, fleetingness only enhances their value. The destruction of beauty is inevitable, but as glimpsed in the earlier discussions of the *entrepic* turning in Homer and Sophocles, a more life-affirming posture may be one in which this is embraced rather than lamented. All things born and created ultimately crumble and the arrow of time ceaselessly flies forward. In short, everything, from meadows, to stones, to cathedrals and scientific theories, dies. Yet, the impossibility of eternal duration only heightens the preciousness and precariousness of these finite productions and systems.

Later in his life, Freud's theoretical works brim with fascinating hypotheses on a drive manifest deep within the very structures of organic life. This drive, beyond the libido, explains the dark tendencies toward destruction and devastation so knotted into the lifeblood and creative impulses of human beings. Beginning with *Beyond the Pleasure Principle* (1919), he develops an almost sinister counterpoint to *Eros* in the form of the death drive (*Thanatos*). The silent, counterforce to (and master over) libidinal unification and preservation strives to return organic life to the fantasy of the inert, undisturbed status of the inorganic. This movement, running against the noisy maneuverings of organic accord, turns out to be the oldest and in many ways, most powerful drive, illuminating an entropic bent toward equilibrium rather than evolutionary complexity. The drive for stasis shows human psychology to be filled by an unconscious yearning for stillness or, what it ultimately amounts to, death.

Freud opens up a distinct line of questioning that is born from asking into the origins of privation and chaos. Much of his theoretical opus centers on the libido, or the primary living force of binding, unifying, and creating life. Unsatisfied with the erotic drive as the ultimate explanation of certain psychological outliers (such as the compulsion to repeat unpleasurable actions or memories, the overwhelmingly destructive forces of aggression, and the surprisingly conservative character of instinctual life), Freud sought a different cause. What he discovered was something else, something more primal than the libido.[11] Eros (a god appearing before in Hesiod's cosmology) manifests in Freud with a primary purpose directed to uniting individuals, families, peoples, nations, and humankind itself.[12] Thanatos, however, serves no obvious unifying or socializing role, thus posing the single greatest threat to all life.

In *Beyond the Pleasure Principle*, Freud makes explicit how deeply he was affected by the ways in which the sciences (medical, physiological, biological, and physical) bolster many of his fundamental insights into human psychology. By tethering the psychological to the scientific, he sought to validate his theories beyond psychoanalytic practice and theory. Jessica Tran The (et al.) shows how Freud's theory of the death drive is not a late development but can be found in nascent form in his discussions of the "principle of inertia" in "A Project for a Scientific Psychology (1895)." The authors claim that this association is directly tethered to the entropy law and Hermann von Helmholtz's school of physics. The principle of inertia aligns with the second law of thermodynamics "according to which the world tends toward an annihilation of the differences that produce effects, in a search for a state of equilibrium."[13] In other words, the advance toward homogenous equipoise, which is the equivalent of the organism's death, can be traced from the early discussions of the principle of inertia all the way through to the late discovery of the movement toward the inorganic expressed in the death drive. Insofar as it is the initiative toward equilibrium, the death drive is essentially entropic. If this is the case, then life in Freud "would be destruction itself, compensated at each moment by the process of creation. In this respect, life could no longer be defined as that which resists destruction, or the increasing entropy of the universe."[14] Destruction would reign supreme in Freud's theory, with stable systems as only temporary epiphenomena, rather than the primary universal telos. This is because life is not what resists destruction but what is in fact produced by it.

Not only influenced by Helmholtz's school, Freud additionally finds confirmation of the existence and operation of the death drive in Gustav

Fechner's principle of stability. All life moves in the direction of lowering excitation and inertia in Fechner's work; in fact actively *desiring* this.[15] Fechner, a physicist turned philosopher and experimental psychologist, created a scientific framework that becomes useful for Freudian psychoanalysis. Fechner formulated the Weber-Fechner law which quantifies the perception of change of a stimulus. Building upon the notions of organic stimulation, Freud was able to anchor his emerging theory of the death drive scientifically.[16] As elaborated by Gregory Zilboorg:

> Freud never gave up his belief—I am tempted to say faith—that the parallel he drew between Fechner's ideas in physics and his own in human psychology was not really a parallel but an actual proof that his concept of the mental apparatus and its energy was actually the same as Helmholtz' and Fechner's ideas about physical energy. To this faith he clung to the last expressing the hope that some day the whole complexity of human reactions and relations could be reduced to some as yet undiscovered physico-chemical reactions.[17]

Much like the conception of the laboring body as a machine addressed in the following chapter, Freud views human psychology driven by the same laws governing the increase and decrease of energies and drives. He saw himself solidifying psychoanalysis as a science wholly in line with the scientific theories emerging out of the nineteenth and twentieth centuries. As Jacques Lacan notes,

> Contrary to what has been trumped up about a supposed break on Freud's part with the scientism of his time, (. . .) it was this very scientism—which one might designate by its allegiance to the ideals of Brücke, themselves passed down from Helmholtz and Du Bois-Reymond's pact to reduce physiology, and the mental functions considered to be included therein, to the mathematically determined terms of thermodynamics (the latter having attained virtual completion during their lifetimes)—that led Freud, as his writings show, to pave the way that shall forever bear his name.[18]

As Lacan and Zilboorg both emphasize, Freud was profoundly invested in contemporary scientific developments, particularly as entwined in the laws of thermodynamics. While the libidinal impulses to unite and procreate dominate his earlier formulations, the appearance of a tendency that works silently against these Darwinian goals cannot be understood without considering scientific advancements in thermodynamics. Particularly, Freud shows how the entropy law infuses the language describing the organism's motivations and strategies to deal with pleasure and unpleasure. Building from Fechner's studies, Freud comes to view pleasure not as the result of increased excitation, but rather resulting from diminution—evident in sexual fulfillment, digestive satiation, and all states where a release of unpleasurable buildup leads to bodily calm.

Following a different current of development, one that moves away from diminution, Darwinian evolution maintains progression of species from the simple to the more diverse and complex.[19] While Darwinism is not teleological, Elizabeth Grosz explains, evolution "is a fundamentally open-ended system that pushes toward a future with no real direction, no promise of any particular result, no guarantee of progress or improvement, but with every indication of inherent proliferation and transformation."[20] For his part, Fechner explores a different tendency than this drive toward proliferation and transformation working on and in life on this planet and the universe as such. Rudolf Arnheim observes that "unconvinced and indeed repelled by the Darwinian notion of the survival of the fittest, Fechner conceived of the original state of all being as that of a comprehensive primordial creature" held together by gravity and containing a chaotic fertility.[21] Fechner's "Principle of Stability" reframes the second law of thermodynamics by asserting constant systemic change until the achievement of global stability, at which point all alteration ceases from within and can only come about from without.[22] The primordial universal creature is entropic, yet composed of innumerable smaller systems borrowing and loaning finite quantities of energy until change ceases altogether through the achievement of total stasis.

Fechner's *Some Ideas on the Creation and Development History of Organisms (Einige Ideen zur Schöpfungs und Entwicklungsgeschichte der Organismen)* investigates the value of Darwinian evolutionary theory, as well as of the relationship between the inorganic and organic worlds. In chapter eleven of this truly beguiling text, he draws a comparison between the inorganic and the organic, insofar as the inorganic world more directly tends toward stability.[23] Conjuring a vision of eternal standstill, Fechner says that stability is a condition where further change is no longer possible. He names death (the movement of the organic into the inorganic) as proof of the tendency since nothing hinders the demise of finite living beings.[24] Unlike Plato and Aristotle, who conjure divine figures to stave off ultimate demise, Fechner's universal creature moves uninterruptedly to expiration.

Fechner elaborates in the supplement to chapter eleven of *Some Ideas* (quoted by Freud at length) that pleasure and unpleasure obey the same principle of stability, such that pleasure increases to the extent that it approaches stability and unpleasure increases to the extent that it approaches instability. At the end of the essay, he suggests that pleasure is the condition for attaining steadiness, whereas pain is deviation from it. Claiming that Fechner's view "coincides in all essentials with the one that has been forced upon us by psycho-analytic work," Freud adopts the notion of pleasure as reduction in tension in *Beyond the Pleasure Principle*.[25] According to Grosz, Freud uses Fechner's constancy principle to argue that the organism

> attempts to keep the quantity of energy or excitation as low as possible, not so low as to "wind down," to approach death, but low enough not to "overstimulate" the organism, causing it to seek all sorts of inappropriate outlets to vent the excessive energy that would otherwise accumulate. There is an entropic principle internally directing the organism towards simplicity and quiescence, impelling it gradually towards death.[26]

For much of Freud's works, the pleasure principle motivates most human actions. While this may initially appear counterintuitive (insofar as much human activity requires a great deal of unpleasure), organisms consistently strive for pleasure via the circuitous demands of the reality principle. What we really want, we cannot have, so we make do with more or less inadequate substitutions. The experience of discharging unpleasurable buildup through libidinal release requires submission to the demands of the external world. Since unmediated satisfaction of desires and needs is impossible, redirection, repression, and sublimation are necessary alternatives. Substitutive satisfaction is as good as it gets. Yet even the reality principle insufficiently explains certain phenomena that simply do not obey the pleasure principle, no matter how many detours drives take. The reality principle demands the achievement of socially acceptable (or at least not socially damaging) pleasure. And yet, antisocial forces persist, both toward ourselves and toward others, that may appear at first glance to be expressions of libido, but upon closer inspection, express something else entirely.

In his analysis of numerous veterans returning from the horrors of World War I, Freud noticed that many had repetitive dreams of their experiences. Even nightmares, for Freud, can be expressions of the pleasure principle insofar as the experience of our fears can release us from the painful buildup of our conscious and unconscious anticipation of them. Discussed primarily in terms of what later came to be called post-traumatic stress disorder, Freud's "traumatic neurosis" charts the macabre tendency causing people to repeat the most harrowing events of their lives without any real catharsis from these repetitions. People who have experienced a trauma—in particular, one for which they were unprepared or ill-prepared—often exhibit a compulsion to repeat negative distress without any pleasurable benefits.[27] Significantly, the compulsion to repeat evokes a past that dominates the present, determines the future, and, in addition, repeats events that do not provide pleasure and never did. Freud finds evident in certain repetitive actions, memories, and dreams, something "more primitive, more elementary, more instinctual [*triebhafter*] than the pleasure principle which it over-rides."[28] Although it seems to be the expression of nothing more than self-inflicted torture, the compulsion to repeat is actually a fantasmatic desire to return to a mythical, primal state of complete contentment.

Freud prepares his readers for what might appear to be far-fetched conjecture but is in fact a deep meditation on the meaning and functioning of this principle. He speculates on the origins of consciousness developing from the simplest life forms, themselves emergent from the inorganic world. Unlike most Greek conceptions that posit a kind of life inherent in matter (that must be controlled or formed, as in Aristotle's distinction between form and privation in chapter 2), Freud argues that organic existence is forced into being through relentless prodding by the external environment. Unlike Hegel's assertion of nature as alienated spirit, Freud's life is an accident, first appearing in its simplest form and very quickly dying. Eventually, the simplest unicellular vesicle maintains a brief existence despite the antagonisms of external stimuli through the development of a dead covering protecting its internal integrity from the outside world. In its earliest configuration, life appears as a simple system maintaining itself through protection against and exchange with the external environment.

As organisms develop greater complexity, those urges originating from "within" the boundary of the dead cortical layer must be discharged into the environment or they will cause the demise of the organism.[29] These drives take on greater force as they seek expression, requiring more elaborate schemes to facilitate release into the external world. Rather than organic life striving to complicate, diversify, and prolong itself, the organism (whether simple or complex) is compelled into existence. As a result, life doesn't seek to endure; instead, it actually strives to expire. Life, even for the simplest forms, is brutal and best hastily escaped, built as it is upon the terrible, tragic wisdom of Silenus: "What is best of all is utterly beyond your reach: not to be born, not to *be*, to be *nothing*. But the second best for you is—to die soon."[30] Since retroactive prevention of existence is impossible, the organism instead craves death as quickly as possible. Life is nothing more than the path organisms are compelled to follow to nonbeing.

The compulsion to repeat unpleasurable experiences thus reveals something more original or, rather, *beyond* the pleasure principle. Freud's "discovery" of a universal, retrograde drive reveals

> *an urge inherent in organic life to restore an earlier state of things* which the living entity has been obliged to abandon under the pressure of external disturbing forces; that is, it is a kind of organic elasticity, or, to put it another way, the expression of the inertia inherent in organic life.[31]

An entropic perspective clearly gives rise to this provocative hypothesis of a fundamentally conservative, even *backward* reaching drive. Change, differentiation, and development are not internally imposed upon an organism but are externally enforced. Unlike Aristotle's claims that change and differentiation found within animate life illustrate the soul expressing its *internal* striving, Freud hypothesizes that initially change comes from without. If given a say in the matter, no living thing would alter or adapt (or even exist at all) but is rather forced by the world to do so. Life seeks to restore an earlier state of affairs by any path, one wherein energy and excitation are reduced to calm. This sliding toward dissipation and desire for death is in line with a key aspect of the entropy law. The environment thus foists energy upon the organism, forcing it to push back against its inherently entropic tendencies.[32] Without the addition of external vitality, the organism would pursue the quickest path it could toward homogenization rather than complication. Life is the detour that inorganicity takes on its way back to itself. For Freud, the true origin and aim of life is death.[33] Or, the origin and aim of life is a state of maximum entropy understood as utmost calm and complete simplicity.

When Freud ascertains the regressive character of instincts in *Beyond the Pleasure Principle*, he challenges the notion of organic (and ultimately social) progress toward betterment, even perfection, rejecting it as an unsupportable "illusion." Ironically, as Karyn Ball notes, he "transfigures the laws of conservation and entropy into the psychophysical asymptotes of a preternatural urge to devolve into an inorganic, stimuli-free state as the ultimate defense against entropy."[34] Organic systems mimic the inorganic more than they deviate from them as all of them tend toward decay into simpler, undisturbed forms. Life is that which evades and even directly opposes the law of entropy but only temporarily, and never on a universal, systemic level.[35] If life increases entropy, it only makes sense that it has a deep kinship with the death drive. Even the pleasure principle, which unifies for Freud, is merely a function in the service of "the most universal endeavor of all living substance—namely to return to the quiescence of the inorganic world."[36] Freud indeed paints a deeply entropic picture of life on earth.

Anthropocentric bias fools human beings into believing in a unique form of progress outside the framework of the rest of nature. Although Eros works to preserve the organism, protecting it from external threats of annihilation through unification and the internal buildup of unpleasurable tension, it does so only in the service of the drive toward stasis, allowing for a temporal elongation of life only so that the organism can take its unique pathway to death. Much like Hegel's description of the organism's own "inborn seed of death," discussed in the previous chapter, finite organisms are systems that, left to their own devices, succumb to entropy. How could it be any different than the rest of the natural world? The death drive, as a movement toward the primordial, elemental, chaos, dominates the relationship between the unifying libidinal energies of Eros and energy input from the external world.

In *Civilization and Its Discontents*, Freud restates his belief that

> besides the instinct to preserve living substance and to join it into ever larger units, there must exist another, contrary instinct seeking to dissolve those units and to bring them back to their primaeval, inorganic state. That is to say, as well as Eros there [is] an instinct of death.[37]

These two instincts, which mutually oppose each other—one seeking unification, one seeking dissolution—are the very antagonistic forces responsible for life.[38] The struggle between unification and destruction may lead to an uncertain future, but the more primal and powerful inertial instinct seems to point to the inevitable defeat of Eros by Thanatos. Civilization (*Kultur*) supposedly separates humans from nature, protecting against the threat of nature's chaotic predations as well as allowing communal living without mutual destruction. Civilization is thus Eros' greatest achievement even as it is under constant siege by individual frailty, natural disaster, and reciprocally desired harm. The energy of the great system of "civilization" will be expended in the struggle against the archaic pull of the second law of thermodynamics, and humanity will be unable to withstand it. Civilization is not immune and ultimately falls to entropy, as Lévi-Strauss explores below.

It is important to recognize that the death drive is not simply another instance of the entropy law but rather a human psychical mechanism that expresses entropic truths. Although the discussions in his later theoretical works can sound highly metaphysical, Freud is ever devoted to constructing a narrative bringing psychoanalytical insights in line with the natural sciences. In his desire to make the psychoanalytic interpretation of the origins and processes of life scientifically verifiable, he incorporates the thought of the scientists who most clearly mirror his own. Even though he has been taken to task for his use (or misuse) of nineteenth-century biology and physics to organize his views surrounding the origin and functioning of the human psyche, his descriptions are rich with entropic metaphors that provide a pointed language for the shared human experience of the inertial. Freud argues that life seeks to maintain the minimum amount of energy and to undergo as little excitation as possible. Like Fechner's universal entropic organism, Freudian life inevitably succumbs to the empty repetitions of habit and termination. Life will always be successful in removing internal and external excitations altogether because it is dominated by this originary drive. Thus, the dissipation of energy from the system leads to the (heat) death of the organism, which itself is a version in miniature of the workings of the universe as a whole.

LÉVI-STRAUSSEAN ENTROPICS

The conclusion of *Tristes Tropiques*, Lévi-Strauss' profound and byzantine work of theoretical field anthropology, surmises that modern anthropology would be better named as "entropology." He coins this term out of the belief that anthropology really only studies societies in decline. What was once a world full of myriad cultures, languages, and geographically distinct places has been increasingly leveled by the practices of colonialism and capitalism. Anthropology, as entropology, prevents the kind of denialist delay of entropics, which only results in the constant anxiety about a future death without motivating present action. Entropology refocuses to the fact that entropy is *now*. Much like Manfred Steiner's vision of future Martian buildings as nothing more than complete structural breakdown, Lévi-Strauss sees the future devastation as a present phenomenon. Like Freud before him, Lévi-Strauss provides insight into concrete and lived forces working against differentiation, progression, and advancement. And, like Freud, he hones in on civilization's heart of darkness. He asks that, rather than romanticize the death drive's rapaciousness in the machine of contemporary civilization, humanity instead mourn the end of the world that has already come and gone.[39] While his view, like Dick's, may not foster a sense of optimism (or even hope for the future) taking entropics seriously helps to break pathological attachments to the very structures, processes, and practices that lead humanity to the path of destruction in the first place. Such reorientation can at best mitigate entropic forces, but never avoid or contain them entirely.

Lévi-Strauss aspires to unite social and natural sciences in his own discipline of structural anthropology. This form of anthropology blends aspects of biology, psychology, and sociology in an interdisciplinary study of specific cultures with a mind to unlocking the largely unconscious, universally shared structures permeating all societies. Different in tone and delivery from many of his other works, *Tristes Tropiques* is at once a travel account, an anthropological study of societies in various stages of development, and a devastating philosophical critique of capitalist and colonialist exacerbation of world decline. The lyricism, detail, heterogeneity, and poignant sadness mark it as a singular product of its time and place. Part of Jean Malauri's *Terre Humaine* series, it was written and organized in a feverish frenzy over many years and eventually published in 1955. In this work, Lévi-Strauss moves through various voices and frameworks (autobiography, philosophy, anthropology, travelogue) offering no single way to capture what exactly he is doing. Its piecemeal approach, far from weakening his observations, makes them more provocative, as they present entropic decline from distinctive and interlocking styles, without promising a unity of message.

Lévi-Strauss sought the most basic, unconscious structures of the mind that all people, in whatever stage of development, share. Whether in advanced capitalist France or among the Nambikwara living with few material possessions, human beings share structures such as kinship, religion, mythology, and food preparation. He believes studying the simplest social groups illuminates the basic relations that undergird *all* cultures. Much of Lévi-Strauss' works, such as *The Elementary Structures of Kinship*, *Mythologies*, and *Tristes Tropiques*, focus on cross-cultural, invariant forms (such as within kinship systems or myths). Despite the universality of these structures, they display fundamental irreversibility insofar as they can die out or transform into different forms. While human beings may be able to set up various mechanisms to forestall entropy (taboos, marriage rules, customs, territories), the machine inevitably breaks down as no myth, no rule, no place lasts forever. No form of community, family, or sociality can keep humanity safe and thriving in perpetuity. While the unconscious structures that produce these cultural concretions remain fixed, the realities themselves transform immediately upon practice. Breakdown and decline therefore necessarily permeate all concrete cultural practices without exception.

Tristes Tropiques observes the great devastation brought upon the indigenous cultures as a result of contact with the colonizing world's voracious appetite for development and resources. Even as he struggles to capture a snapshot of unmolested human society, Lévi-Strauss is surrounded by evidence of Western infection and the production of what Frantz Fanon calls the "colonized subject."[40] Cultural differences progressively fall into degradation and assimilation as a result of capitalist expansionism. The truly unique, largely subsistence societies he observes are in various stages of identity loss, disease, alcoholism, and existential melancholy. Barbara Ehrenreich calls this the "fatal malaise," and argues that it serves as the background of Lévi-Strauss' reflections in *Triste Tropiques*: "decimated native cultures, stripped of customs, rituals, or traditional means of subsistence, left listless and dispirited by their encounter with the West."[41] Although he manages to find many tribes living in simple societies, he is deeply aware of the fact that these groups suffer irreversible obliteration from the encroachment of modernization. Entropology portrays the historical sadness at the razing of culture and the failure to sustain diversity as these unique societies dwindle into annexation and death.

Sensitive to his own European orientation that places him as a permanent outsider to the cultures he observes (such as the Caduveo, Bororo, and Nambikwara), he notes his deficiencies when it comes to interacting and documenting these small human collectives. Early in the book, long before we hear the details of the various tribes with whom he lives and works, he laments the loss permeating his journey into the unknown. Original encounters with truly exceptional and foreign societies are no longer possible. In fact, it has been impossible for hundreds of years. In the service of profit-making and cultural and religious conversion, the merciless work of colonialization has succeeded in destroying the lands and practices of indigenous peoples from the moment of first contact. This is the legacy of the West—to destroy what it finds, level differences, and pollute what was once pristine in the relentless march toward global domination. While at first appearing as a drive toward progress, this march is itself a product of entropic forces pushing toward inertia and homogenization. Western civilization simultaneously denies and accelerates this devastating practice of leveling everything it touches. Lévi-Strauss observes:

> Now that the Polynesian islands have been smothered in concrete and turned into aircraft carriers solidly anchored in the southern seas, when the whole of Asia is beginning to look like a dingy suburb, when shanty-towns are spreading across Africa, when civil and military aircraft blight the primeval innocence of the American or Melanesian forests even before destroying their virginity, what else can the so-called escapism of travelling do than confront us with the more unfortunate aspects of our history? Our great Western civilization, which has created the marvels we now enjoy, has only succeeded in producing them at the cost of corresponding ills. . . . The first thing we see as we travel round the world is our own filth, thrown into the face of mankind.[42]

Everything that marks technological and financial progress reveals itself to be a part of a global machine of waste production and cultural destruction. The entropic perspective magnifies the staggering amount of irrecuperable garbage vomited by capitalism onto real people and places.[43] The energy exploited by colonialism to create extravagant lifestyles steamrolls cultures, producing high-entropy, unrecyclable waste. Great human diversity (as well as biodiversity) is being wiped out with alarming speed and efficiency, replaced by a gray homogeneity of people and landscapes. The loss of biodiversity corresponds to the loss of cultural diversity such that Lévi-Strauss believes modernity is left only to bear witness to the destruction.[44] Western practice does not primarily work toward novelty and creativity, but is rather an engine running on the monstrous, tragic, and inevitable forces of entropy, breaking down differences and flattening peoples and places.

Technological and colonial expansion requires massive expenditures of energy to develop and maintain, which they do by drawing those energies from other systems, such as the land and labor of indigenous cultures and natural resources. In one sense, Western "progress" seems to run *counter* to entropy insofar as it expands and multiplies, working its way into every available niche across the globe. Rather than fall apart, it increases in power through the proliferation of its presence. However, in another sense, entropology provides a fully global perspective on technological development and the violence of colonialization as clearly hastening the heat death of the shared world. Certainly, systems borrow energy from each other; however, the energy that fuels these systems is geographically and materially finite. Lévi-Strauss saw what is even more frighteningly obvious now: humanity intentionally accelerates its own radical demise. The sealing of the world into one global community inhibits novelty from contact with the unfamiliar, even as contact often destroys what is most beautiful about world diversity. Eventually, there will be no energy left to feed the machines of culture and progress and human society will exist no more. The silence and quietude of the grave will come all too soon as humanity hastens toward nothingness. He writes:

> The world began without man and will end without [him]. The institutions, morals and customs that I shall have spent my life noting down and trying to understand are the transient efflorescence of a creation in relation to which they have no meaning. . . . [Man] himself appears as perhaps the most effective agent working towards the disintegration of the original order of things and hurrying on powerfully organized matter towards ever greater inertia, an inertia which one day will be final.[45]

Human beings, with their great conceitedness and self-centeredness, believe themselves to be immune to the forces of entropy; however, as Lévi-Strauss observes, humanity is merely a flash in the pan and a terribly destructive one at that. The bustling, hurried, frantic desire to survive and thrive on Earth reveals humanity as a force of decomposition, dismantling complexity like termites devouring rotten logs on the forest floor. We tend to think of ourselves as exceptional, and in some ways, we are. But not for the reasons that we like to think. He continues:

> From the time when he first began to breathe and eat, up to the invention of atomic and thermonuclear devices, by way of the discovery of fire—and except when he has been engaged in self-reproduction—what else has man done except blithely break down billions of structures and reduce them to a state in which they are no longer capable of integration?[46]

Lévi-Strauss captures the way in which humanity excels at taking low-entropy energy and producing irredeemable high-entropy waste. Yet its denial of waste and destruction are symptomatic of the knowledge that entropy and death are inevitable.

Critics accuse Lévi-Strauss of cultural relativism in *Tristes Tropiques*,[47] but he maintains throughout this work that every society has its advantages and disadvantages, with certain members enjoying greater privileges and social inequity a fundamental fact. However, this does not mean that every society is equal to every other one. Rather than disparaging the idea of progress, he writes in *Structural Anthropology*:

> I should like to see progress transferred from the rank of a universal category of human development to that of a particular mode of existence, characteristic of our own society—and perhaps of several others—whenever that society reaches the stage of self-awareness.[48]

He continues powerfully:

> A society can live, act, and be transformed, and still avoid becoming intoxicated with the conviction that all the societies which preceded it during tens of millenniums did nothing more than prepare the ground for *its* advent, that all its contemporaries—even those at the antipodes—are diligently striving to overtake it, and that the societies which will succeed it until the end of time ought to be mainly concerned with following in its path.[49]

Lévi-Strauss likens such an unearned and unwarranted position of superiority to maintaining a geocentric vision of the universe with humanity as the greatest creation therein. Such a position assumes that the world and its riches exist only to be used by and for a certain kind of society, regardless of the billions of other living beings that must share finite resources.

Humans tend to find the most immediate as the truest, and the farthest in time and space less so. However, we are deeply embedded in history, and losing sight of that entrenchment thoughtlessly speeds our collapse. History provides an ethical demand: duty to fellow humans, duty to knowledge, and duty to the physical world itself. Nevertheless, given the human agential role in world inertia and destruction, this demand becomes difficult to hear in the cacophony of destruction. Echoing Freud's melancholic poet, all fine accomplishments—from agriculture to urbanization, the greatest works of art, science, and literature, and the technology created to drive them all—will eventually be swallowed into general chaos. While it is tempting to see civilization as a kind of complex machine capable of providing salvation given time and diligence, such a view is mistaken. Ultimately, most (if not all) civilizations feed upon low-entropy fuel and spit out high-entropy waste. Continuing, Lévi-Strauss writes, "civilization, taken as a whole, can be described as an extraordinarily complex mechanism, which we might be tempted to see as offering an opportunity of survival for the human world, if its function were not to produce what physicists call entropy, that is inertia."[50] Such entropic effects call forth the inertial heaviness of the dilapidated buildings awaiting the future of Dick's Martian landscape and its last indigenous inhabitants. This steamrolling tendency leads to Lévi-Strauss' profound proclamation that anthropology "could with advantage be changed into 'entropology,' as the name of the discipline concerned with the study of the highest manifestations of this process of disintegration."[51]

The conclusion of *Triste Tropiques* is depressing. Although Lévi-Strauss does his best to dissociate these astounding acts of destruction from individual persons, he yet notes that the "rainbow of human cultures" will eventually sink "into the void created by our frenzy."[52] This leaves only the brief reprieve of "arresting the process," interrupting and *"unhitching"* from the mad whirl hurtling toward destruction. How is this possible amid the chaos? For Lévi-Strauss, perhaps only in those brief moments where we contemplate a mineral, smell a lily, or share a look with a cat. In the end, although lovely, this does not appear to offer any kind of enduring optimism or hope. The forward march of entropic decline—thoughtlessly adopted and accelerated by modern humanity's unchecked greed and myopia—produces a kind of isolated individualism and paralyzing passivity. Since it cannot be stopped, it can only be witnessed. Rather than transforming ways of thinking and acting, at best we are left with recording the slow heat death of the world.

This chapter explored an aspect of entropics in Freud and Lévi-Strauss to show how entropy, now named and known as a scientific law, becomes directly and intentionally used as a theoretical framework to understand human psychology and society. While the science of entropy is clearly present in Freud's desire to provide a scientific basis for his psychoanalytic theories and Lévi-Strauss' coinage of "entropology," it largely functions as a metaphoric concept signaling the pull of decline, death, and homogenization. The death drive, at work in both Freudian psychoanalysis and entropology, constantly threatens (and paradoxically provides a motive force for) much human action and production. The fatalism at the heart of both theories is supported by the inevitable and unstoppable workings of the entropy law itself. In many ways, Freud and Lévi-Strauss emerge as the pinnacle of entropic philosophy, showing the profoundly nihilistic and cynical undertones in much Western thinking. In both theories, time merely tracks the movement toward homogeneity and quiescence. Human beings may think themselves unique, outside of the workings of the rest of nature, feeling proud and smug in cultural production and expansion. Nevertheless, these misconceptions are byproducts of entropic denial rather than great achievements of spirit. No culture, innovation, or god will save us from decline. The unrelenting desire to return to the inorganic works constantly in cultural practices, *especially* in those cultures that are in the most acute denial.

Undoubtedly, a pallor of pessimism, like the Schellingian melancholy spread over all finite life, hangs over the discussion of these theorists. The death drive is admittedly terrifying to think through: how could positing the goal of life as death *not* cause an abysmal deflation of the world?[53] Yet, in their pessimism, they encourage different ways of thinking by sounding the alarm of the danger of unchecked aggression and cultural expansion. The disavowal of optimism puts to rest once and for all the delusion that we can cheat death or that our hands are clean. However, confronting the powerful forces of death's presence and effects removes many of the deceptions of progress, whereas simply denying death only hastens misery, violence, and the very demise we seek to escape. In a similar vein, Lévi-Strauss' naked criticism of supposedly "advanced" societies challenges delusions of superiority by acknowledging the addiction to entropy's acceleration. The failure to recognize the death-cult worship of waste production, unnecessary expansion, and cultural erasure is nothing short of global suicide. While decline and waste are inevitable, no law states that they must be foolishly hastened. Society only maintains some stability through temporarily arresting and negotiating with entropy.[54]

Ultimately, I call for a reorientation toward the *entrepic* which hearkens back to the insights gleaned from Homer and Sophocles and encourages a turn toward care ethics at the conclusion of this study. While no system can be eternally maintained, we must imagine a world where energy borrowing allows for the increase rather than decrease of human and environmental diversity through reverence and care. A society that works with, rather than in denial of entropy, would not be an Edenic paradise, but one that requires the sacrifice of almost all products and practices that are currently in place: disposable, mass-produced goods, commercial travel, factory and industrial farming, wasteful housing—the list goes on. Nonetheless, to simply bar the possibilities for change allows death the devastating and tragic last word.

The following chapter explores one important way that the failure to work within entropic limitations has caused profound harm in contemporary American society. It offers itself as only one of hundreds of possible case studies in the phenomenon of simultaneously denying and accelerating (or alternatively, accelerating by denying) entropy developed in this chapter. The machine of capitalist culture has a shattering impact on almost everyone, but in particular, on the most materially and socially vulnerable populations. Building from the leveling and accelerating tendencies described in Freud and Lévi-Strauss, I now move to study the laboring elderly in the United States as their marginalization, exploitation, and abuse lay bare the multiple problems confronting the modern world's relationship to entropics.

NOTES

1. Barbara Ehrenreich, *Natural Causes: An Epidemic of Wellness, the Certainty of Dying, and Killing Ourselves to Live Longer* (New York: Twelve, 2018), 196.

2. Philip K. Dick, *Martian Time Slip* (New York: Vintage Books, 1995), 15.
3. Ibid, 44.
4. Ibid, 130.
5. Ibid, 143.
6. Lévi-Strauss and Freud were at heart, interdisciplinary thinkers. Freud was trained by biologists, physiologists, psychologists, and medical doctors, and his writings contain many direct references to literature and philosophy. Lévi-Strauss' structural anthropology (itself influenced by Freudian psychoanalysis) also links to multiple disciplines. As Lévi-Strauss writes in *Triste Tropiques*: "Between Marxism and psychoanalysis, which are social sciences—one orientated toward society, the other toward the individual—and geology, which is a physical science—but which has also fostered and nurtured history both by its method and its aim—anthropology spontaneously establishes its domain." Claude Lévi-Strauss, *Tristes tropiques*, trans. John Weightman and Doreen Weightman (New York: Penguin Press, 2012), 58. Although Lévi-Strauss admits an uneasy relationship to philosophy, he studied it as a student at the *Sorbonne* before changing directions to anthropology.
7. Sigmund Freud, "On Transcience," in *The Standard Edition of the Complete Psychological Works of Sigmund Freud*, trans. and ed. James Strachey (London: The Hogarth Press, 1999), 305.
8. Aristotle, *The Nicomachean Ethics*, ed. and trans. Martin Ostwald (Upper Saddle River, NJ: Prentice Hall, 1962), 1096b.
9. Freud, "On Transience," 306.
10. Ibid, 307.
11. Freud finds "besides the instinct to preserve living substance and to join it into ever larger units, there must exist another, contrary instinct seeking to dissolve those units and to bring them back to their primeval, inorganic state. That is to say, as well as Eros there was an instinct of death." Freud, *Pleasure Principle*, 77.
12. Ibid, 82.
13. Jessica Tran The et al., "From the Principle of Inertia to the Death Drive: The Influence of the Second Law of Thermodynamics on the Freudian Theory of the Psychical Apparatus," *Frontiers in Psychology* 11 (February 2020): 5.
14. Ibid, 7.
15. Freud was also influenced by Fechner's *"Principle of Pleasure,"* however, whereas "Fechner wrote of the tendency of the mind to keep a state of approximate stability, Freud spoke of the tendency to keep an approximately constant level of stability. From Freud's point of view, pleasure occurs when excessive stimulation decreases and unpleasure when the level of stimulation is increased above certain limits." Mark S. Micale, *Beyond the Unconscious: Essays of Henri F. Ellenberger in the History of Psychiatry* (Princeton: Princeton University Press, 2016), 102. Freud was thus more concerned with the self-protective motivations of organisms and the drive toward stability and homeostasis. Ibid.
16. Fechner is most famous for the discovery of the "psychophysical basic law" which provides a mathematical formulation measuring the relation between stimulus and sensation. Ibid, 96. Elizabeth Grosz criticizes Freud, arguing that "in deriving the death drive from Fechner's 'constancy principle,' Freud conflates it with the principle

of inertia, and it is only through such a confusion that he 'scientifically' legitimates the postulation of the death drive." Elizabeth Grosz, "Darwin and Feminism: Preliminary Investigations for a Possible Alliance," in *Material Feminisms*, eds. Stacy Alaimo and Susan Hekman (Bloomington: Indiana University Press, 2008), 89.

17. Gregory Zilboorg, "Introduction," in *Beyond the Pleasure Principle*, by Sigmund Freud, trans. James Strachey (New York: W. W. Norton & Company, 1959), xxviii–xxix.

18. Jacques Lacan, *Science and Truth*, ed. and trans. Bruce Fink (New York: W. W. Norton & Company, 2006), 728. Ernst Wilhelm von Brücke was Freud's teacher of physiology and anatomy for many years and had a profound influence on his thinking. Freud remained convinced that the laws of physics exerted the same influence on inorganic as well as living beings. Helmholtz was foundational in the idea of entropism as a tendency leading eventually to the heat death of the universe.

19. Contrary to dissolution, evolution supports the idea of "progress or at least increasing articulation rather than degradation of energy." Rudolf Arnheim, *Entropy and Art: An Essay on Disorder and Order* (Berkeley: University of California Press, 1971), 33. It should be noted that Darwin's *Origin of the Species* (1809) recognizes a high degree of chance in nature and rejects the idea that time's irreversibility necessarily implies progress.

20. Grosz, "Darwinism and Feminism," 38. Darwin's future points forward to an opening up into "diversification, or bifurcation of the latencies of the present, which provide a kind of ballast for the induction of a future different but not detached from the past and present." Ibid, 43. This diversification is why Grosz finds a fecund site in Darwin for feminism and political discourse in general.

21. Arnheim, *Entropy and Art*, 36.

22. Ibid, 37.

23. "The organic kingdom is subject to development in the sense of this principle in solidarity with the inorganic [Das organische Reich unterliegt dem Entwicklungsgange im Sinne dieses Prinzips solidarisch mit dem anorganischen]." Gustav Fechner, *Einige Ideen zur Schöpfungs und Entwicklungsgeschichte der Organismen* [*Some Ideas on the Creation and Development History of Organisms*] (Leipzig: Breitkopf und Härtel, 1873), https://www.projekt-gutenberg.org/fechner/schoepfg/schoepfg.html (my translation).

24. Like species forms, everything in the universe tends toward stability. Fechner believes that the thorough application of this principle must also consider "the psychic side of existence [*die psychische Seite der Existenz*]," which is itself partially conscious and partially unconscious. Fechner, *Creation and Development*.

25. Freud, *Pleasure Principle*, 5. Freud returns to Fechner's principle of constancy in *The Ego and the Id*, where he claims that this principle governs life which "consists of a continuous descent towards death." Sigmund Freud, *The Ego and the Id* (New York: W. W. Norton and Company, 1960), 46.

26. Grosz, "Darwinism and Feminism," 291. The desire of matter for form discussed in Aristotle's *Physics* is the opposite of this claim. In Aristotle, matter is impelled toward, rather than away from life.

27. Freud explains that the "compulsion to repeat also recalls from the past experiences which include no possibility of pleasure, and which can never, even long ago, have brought satisfaction even to instinctual impulses which have since been repressed." Freud, *Pleasure Principle*, 21. Catherine Malabou challenges the move to go beyond the pleasure principle in Freud because it is impossible to characterize the form of the death drive. Rather, Malabou argues that there are only two different occurrences of pleasure. Catherine Malabou, "Plasticity and Elasticity in Freud's 'Beyond the Pleasure Principle,'" *Parallax* 15, no. 2 (2009): 47.

28. Freud, *Pleasure Principle*, 25.

29. Freud defines these urges as "the representatives of all the forces originating in the interior of the body and transmitted to the mental apparatus." Ibid, 40.

30. Friedrich Nietzsche, *The Birth of Tragedy and the Case Against Wagner*, trans. Walter Kaufmann (New York: Vintage Books, 1967), 42.

31. Freud, *Pleasure Principle*, 43.

32. Another way to look at this might be that a living organism maintains its highly ordered structure "by sucking low entropy from the environment so as to compensate for the entropic degradation to which it is continuously subject." Georgescu-Roegen, *Entropy Law*, 192. There is thus "nothing wrong in saying that life is characterized by the struggle against the entropic degradation of mere matter." Ibid.

33. The only challengers to this phenomenon for Freud can be found in the germ cells which are the true life instincts seeking temporary immortality through progress and development. Freud, *Pleasure Principle*, 48–49.

34. Karyn Ball, "Losing Steam After Marx and Freud," *Angelaki* 20, no. 3 (2015): 60.

35. Nicholas Georgescu-Roegen frames the relation between life and entropy in the following way: "Living being can evade the entropic degradation of its own structure only. It cannot prevent the increase of the entropy of the whole system, consisting of its structure and its environment. On the contrary, from all we can tell now, the presence of life causes the entropy of a system to increase faster than it otherwise would." Georgescu-Roegen, *Entropy Law*, 11.

36. Freud, *Pleasure Principle*, 76.

37. Sigmund Freud, *Civilization and Its Discontents*, ed. and trans. James Strachey (New York: W. W Norton & Company, 1961), 77.

38. Here Freud quotes Goethe's *Faust* and Mephistopheles as the spirit that negates. Freud, *Discontents*, 80.

39. Nathan Gorelick writes, "consider that other great prophet and poet of modernity, Claude Lévi-Strauss, particularly his 1955 memoir *Tristes Tropiques*, a text which in fact is less memoir than work of mourning. No matter how far and wide his travels or the purported exoticism of his informants, inevitably the great anthropologist finds only the ruins of what had been or, at best, cultures irreversibly corrupted by what is called progress, which, like the death drive motoring it, can itself move in but one direction. He finds not cultures but the living corpses of culture, animated and puppeteered by their own slow death, driven toward the inertia that results from the elimination of all difference." Nathan Gorelick, "Psychoanalysis at the End of

the World" in *Lacan and the Environment*, ed. Clint Burnham and Paul Kingsbury (London: Palgrave Macmillan, 2021), 6.

40. Frantz Fanon, *Black Skin, White Masks,* trans. Richard Philcox (New York: Grove Press, 2008), 78. The colonized subject is also the main theme of *The Wretched of the Earth* where Fanon speaks about how the colonialist oppressor "creates the spiral of domination, exploitation and looting." Frantz Fanon, *The Wretched of the Earth,* ed. and trans. Richard Philcox (New York: Grove Press, 2004), 14.

41. Ehrenreich, *Natural Causes*, 108.

42. Lévi-Strauss, *Tristes tropiques*, 38.

43. On this very point, Fanon writes "the colonialist makes history and he knows it. . . . The history he writes is therefore not the history of the country he is despoiling, but the history of his own nation's looting, raping, and starving to death." Fanon, *Wretched*, 15.

44. Such an image recalls Walter Benjamin's interpretation of Paul Klee's 1920 *Angelus Novus* painting, which shows "an angel looking as though he is about to move away from something he is fixedly contemplating. His eyes are staring, his mouth is open, his wings are spread. This is how one pictures the angel of history. His face is turned toward the past. Where we perceive a chain of events, he sees one single catastrophe which keeps piling wreckage upon wreckage and hurls it in front of his feet. The angel would like to stay, awaken the dead, and make whole what has been smashed. But a storm is blowing from Paradise; it has got caught in his wings with such violence that the angel can no longer close them. The storm irresistibly propels him into the future to which his back is turned, while the pile of debris before him grows skyward. This storm is what we call progress." Walter Benjamin, "Theses on the Philosophy of History" in *Illuminations*, trans. Harry Zohn (New York: Schocken, 1969), 249.

45. Lévi-Strauss, *Tristes tropiques*, 413.

46. Ibid.

47. In addition to the metaphorical and sometimes sloppy use of linguistics and mathematics in his anthropology in general, see Terrence Turner, "On Structure and Entropy: Theoretical Pastiche and the Contradictions of 'Structuralism,'" *Current Anthropology* 31, no. 5 (1990): 563–568.

48. Claude Lévi-Strauss, *Structural Anthropology*, trans. Clair Jacobson and Brooke Grundfest Schoepf (New York: Basic Books, 1963), 335.

49. Ibid, 336.

50. Lévi-Strauss, *Tristes tropiques*, 413.

51. Ibid, 414.

52. Ibid, 413.

53. See James A. Godley, "Infinite Grief: Freud, Hegel, and Lacan on the Thought of Death," *Angelaki* 23, no. 6 (2018): 102. Godley points out that death is not a restriction, so much as a satisfaction. Joan Copjec describes how the very satisfaction of the death drive is found through its inhibition. See, Joan Copjec, *Imagine There's No Woman* (Cambridge: The MIT Press), 30. John Raphael Staude notes that Lévi-Strauss and Freud (along with Carl Jung) are pessimistic because "the utilization of the theory of the unconscious itself creates a paradigm with strongly conservative and

anti-utopian implications" John Raphael Staude, "From Depth Psychology to Depth Sociology: Freud, Jung, and Lévi-Strauss," *Theory and Society* 3, no. 3 (1976): 331.

54. As Almeida writes, "time is irreversible because as time passes entropy increases. Conversely, machines that preserve some symmetry, reversible machines, require the arrest of the processes of entropy. Without this violation neither life nor culture would exist." Almeida, "Symmetry and Entropy," 375.

Chapter 5

Old Age and Entropic Decline

> For it is the exploitation of the workers, the pulverization of society, and the utter poverty of a culture confined to the privileged, educated few that leads to this kind of dehumanized old age. And it is this old age that makes it clear that everything has to be reconsidered, recast from the very beginning.
>
> Simone de Beauvoir, *La Vieillesse*[1]

> Our culture has lost its sense of death, so it can kill both mentally and physically, thinking all the time that it is establishing the most creative order possible.
>
> Robert Smithson, "A Sedimentation of the Mind"[2]

> People start aging from early, very early, on. Gradually it spreads over their entire body like a stain that cannot be wiped away.
>
> Haruki Murakami, *A Wild Sheep Chase*[3]

William Shakespeare's *King Lear* depicts the catastrophic decisions made by an old king. Lear, for reasons not altogether clear, divides his kingdom, distributing it among his three daughters. Following this calamitous pronouncement, he charges his newly empowered children to tend to him in his old age as he proceeds to "unburdened crawl toward death."[4] As he disowns his only loyal child, giving his future over to the other two daughters, he quickly realizes the tragic course upon which he has set his life. Unmistakably a poor decision by any measure, it speaks to one of the most pressing questions of the work: what would drive a person to make such an unreflective and disastrous choice about their future well-being?

Is Lear already mad at the beginning of the play? Is he simply old and desirous of being cared for by those he believes owe him this fulfillment of duty? Is his developing madness a result of his age or does he become prematurely old as he slips into lunacy? Whatever the answers to these questions may be, his story is a misfortune of senescence left to fend for itself when it is no longer useful. Giving away his power and assets, Lear has nothing left but the misplaced assumption that he will be cared for until death. But as his fool constantly reminds him: when he gave away his kingship, he gave away his identity, thereby becoming old before his time. Without power or purpose, those he trusted would care for him in perpetuity instead reject and abuse him.

Not only must Lear confront the disloyalty and cruelty of two of his daughters and his mistaken assessment of his only loyal child, he must also face his own total irrelevance. Without his crown, he becomes a useless and unwelcome figure, cast into the shadows of social and familial status. Regan's admonition stings to the core: "O, sir, you are old; Nature in you stands on the very verge of his confine. You should be ruled and led by some discretion that discerns your state better than you yourself."[5] Father become child, the two daughters charged with his care demand that he give up the illusion of patriarchal sovereignty and willingly submit to their rising tyrannical power.

The play reveals a stark and terrifying truth that Lear's irrelevance stems from his lack of having anything more to offer. As the Fool sings, "Fathers that wear rags do make their children blind, but fathers that bear bags shall see their children kind."[6] Without material wealth or political power, Lear becomes nothing more than a nuisance, ultimately thrust out of his daughters' homes, breaking under the recognition of his foolishness, and driven mad by the consequences of his actions. Shakespeare reminds us that there is no purpose for an ex-king.

Lear's tragedy centers around his own self-imposed worthlessness. Once he resigns as monarch, there is nothing left for him to do. This state of affairs cannot be mapped on identically to the modern age, even if it too largely disdains the elderly. Late-stage capitalism produces, exploits, and ultimately discards old people. Like Lear, those without purpose or wealth are often cast aside without social or material support. However, the modern capitalist machine operates to take as much as possible before this abandonment. Within this oppressive situation, the elderly take on a doubled alterity—both terrifying and repugnant (the ghosts from the future come to haunt the present) as well as self-effacing (marginalized to the point of being practically invisible).[7] There is nothing natural about this position at the crumbling margins of social identity. Rather, systems that seek to maximize output of goods, energy, and labor, with minimum input of those very same things actually produce social exclusions. Among the many groups that are harmed by these practices (including those sidelined by race, class, sex, geography, and ability), I focus on the aged, as their position in society is unique, insofar as age is the future that awaits us all. Unlike the ageless Hesiodic golden race, the facts of the present are far more dire. "Die early or grow old," Simone de Beauvoir writes, "there is no other alternative."[8]

The entropic metaphor allows for diagnosing some of the horrors lurking in the shadows (and often in the light of day) in advanced capitalism. I have argued throughout this book that entropy's potency lies in its versatility as an umbrella concept that is both generative (in that it expands our ability to think through central ideas in the history of Western thinking) and connective (in that it links seemingly diverse phenomena together). Whereas myriad avenues could be explored,[9] this chapter focuses on an acute manifestation of entropics that holds sway in particularly pernicious forms: the loss of energy and decline of the aging body, exploited and exacerbated by advanced capitalism's demand for constant increase of production and profit.

Capitalism necessitates maximum extraction of energy from labor with minimum input for rejuvenation and sustenance.[10] Neoliberalism demands that individuals take moral responsibility for their own upkeep while ignoring the systemic roadblocks prohibiting shared care and just allocation of resources. Responsibilization (making individuals responsible for the situation produced by economic structures) coupled with the refusal to acknowledge and address systemic obstacles to care intersect in the exploitation and erasure of the aged. The entropy metaphor provides a lens through which to understand how bodies are constituted as machines that age and fall apart, while also offering a language to speak to the phenomenological experiences of slackening and the anxiety of doing so in a society that views people as exploitable and disposable energy resources. While the historical treatments so far explored do not suggest a fixed line of causality to the experiences discussed in this chapter, they do provide tools with which to analyze the situation of the elderly in advanced capitalist society.

As the origin of entropy emerged as a law describing the increase in energy unavailable to do work, studying the aging body is particularly salient in showing some of the more destructive aspects of entropics emergent in the modern era. The lawfulness of entropy makes the desire to escape it delusional and dangerous—it is inexorable. All that can be done is to acknowledge how it operates and to work to mitigate its effects, forestalling the inevitable by carefully borrowing energy from systems such that human and ecological flourishing can be enjoyed for as long as possible. This requires a reorientation toward the *entrepic* that focuses on care and reverence of finite life rather than the callous hastening of harm for the temporary benefit of the few. As it currently stands, the overt denial of overly taxed systems and bodies continues an accelerationist mentality toward already dwindling energies, therefore not only confounding flourishing but overtly furthering total social and environmental collapse. The formulation of the human body as a machine, coupled with the maximization of output from bodies with dwindling abilities, produces an abused and misused group. Importantly, this population, unlike Lear, is not to blame for its social positioning because the chips have been stacked against it from the beginning.

Advanced capitalism attempts to cheat entropy by capturing all the energy it can, through whatever means, and forcing the inevitable waste onto those who gain the least benefit. In part, this chapter offers a pointed application of Freud's death drive and Lévi-Strauss' entropology by illustrating, in current social practices, the ways that societies in decline employ short-sighted methods that try to forestall the byproducts of entropy. The modern era of globalization and mass production functions in a direct denial of and war against entropic breakdown. The resulting social, cultural, and environmental fallout produces a temporary expansion of profit and production of material goods for a small minority, while creating rapidly growing numbers of depleted populations. In particular, advanced capitalism seeks to ward off entropy through the myth of eternal expansion, but in so doing actually accelerates entropy through the production of refuse, the commodification of individuals, and the mistreatment of the aged.

To explore the effects of entropic acceleration on the working aged, I read Karyn Ball's "Losing Steam After Marx and Freud: On Entropy as the Horizon of the Community to Come" with Beauvoir's analysis of old age in *La Vieillesse*. Together these works show how (1) the metaphor of the body as machine provides insight into the ways in which systemic breakdown is inevitable yet staunchly repudiated; (2) the configuration of the aged in contemporary society amplifies their abject status; and (3) developed societies extract maximum capital and work before ultimately discarding unusable bodies. Even as bodies fail to achieve maximum productivity—through ableist and ageist practices and/or inescapable bodily degeneration exacerbated by overwork and senescence—merciless efforts continue unchecked to wring every ounce of energy possible through compulsory capacitation until death.

MACHINE AND PROFIT

The forward movement of time's arrow necessarily involves aging, understood as inescapable biological and physiological breakdown. As Georgescu-Roegen observes:

> Every human being ages because of the entropic factors which begin to work at birth, nay, before it, and work slowly but cumulatively. . . . By the same token,

it is the degradation of man's dowry of low entropy as a result of his own ambitious activity that determines both what man can and cannot do.[11]

While it does not have to be something feared or despised, aging beyond prime years has come to be so for all but the very rich and privileged. Human beings, like all living organisms, require constant utilization of low entropy (understood as useful fuel and energy) for maintenance and survival. Yet, the dowry of energy and resources is not inexhaustible, and no amount of exploited labor will overpower this limit.

Karl Marx and Friedrich Engels laid bare the reduction of the worker to little more than a cog in the machine—one with only labor to sell, whose meager earnings maintain minimum health and bodily functioning until the worker can no longer effectively produce capital. At that point, they are discarded and replaced by another who will suffer the same fate in a process without end. The production of unusable labor produces bodies that no longer contribute to wealth accumulation for the material elite and therefore become a social drain. In an attempt to obviate such antagonisms to profit and material accumulation, capitalism works to reabsorb, whenever possible, its inevitable byproducts. One way to do this is to boost labor and consumption in aging bodies, which otherwise appear to capitalism as threats to be neutralized or rejected. However, as Luciana Parisi and Tiziana Terranova note, "There is only so much surplus value you can extract out of disciplined bodies within anti-entropic institutions" because "while you do that, entropy keeps increasing."[12] While resources dwindle, bodies age, and systems unravel, capitalism attempts to extricate as much as possible before it morbidly threatens itself with its own excesses.

The human being is particularly receptive to tactics of this nature because it both is and is not like a machine. Katherine Hayles observes that while the human body is "like a heat engine because it cycles energy into different forms and degrades it in the process," the contrary also holds so that "the body is not like a heat engine because it can use energy to repair itself and to reproduce."[13] Human bodies thus become a place where the battle against entropy is heightened, often yielding (largely unnecessary) devastating consequences. Bodies wear out, but given appropriate nourishment, rest, and care, they are capable of recovery and repair. Yet, the denial of entropics forces bodies to produce and consume far beyond what is necessary or ethical. Ball argues that the metaphor of entropy allows for discussing the limitations of human energy without necessarily falling into earlier forms of pessimisms regarding decline. She designates a "poetics of entropics" that centralizes an "affectivity of depletion" in order to provide a framework for the experiences of physical and affective exhaustion.[14] Harmonizing with the idea of entropy as a metaphor operative throughout this book, Ball uses "figurative language" as it aids in the "assessments of contemporary problems and the strategies we might pursue to resolve them."[15] Whether or not the human body is rightly framed as a kind of machine that eventually wears out, it certainly *feels* as if this is the case.[16] The lived experience of aging, losing abilities and capacities, fatigue, illness, and social vulnerability produce effects of depletion and fatigue. Neither infinitely resilient nor adaptable, nevertheless, the body has come to be conceived as a human motor, an ideal perpetual motion machine that will still ultimately falter.

The notion of the human being as a motor dates to the middle of the nineteenth century and results from changes in modes of production. With the industrial revolution in full swing, machines come to dominate the cultural imaginary of those developed societies in which they are most concentrated. At the same time, the second law of thermodynamics emerges, carrying with it a descriptive and normative allure as a law. Descriptively, the law allowed for a kind of analogy between rapid developments in technology and transformations in labor evolving in tandem. In addition, it created a novel language for the body understood as a machine. Normatively, it enabled a language morally condemning a laborer's lack of energy and subsequent fatigue, providing a scientifically supported criticism of the failure to maintain the proper functioning of the machine. The machine formulation, Ball explains, is an amalgamation "of scientific, social, and philosophical metaphors portraying the body as a thermodynamic economy, a psychophysical *energetics* with conservation as its condition and exhaustion (heat death) as its horizon."[17] Ball's interest lies in the ways in which entropy provides a poetics of the body, particularly adept at unfolding the affective body as it degrades with age and use. Conceiving of human beings as motors helps to describe the *feeling* of what happens when these motors metaphorically "lose steam." Entropics gives voice to experiences of slackening energy and degeneration in general, as well as of specific groups who suffer them most dramatically.

Since Marx and Engels were engaged in the emerging science of thermodynamics,[18] Ball analyzes Marx's understanding of wage laborers being worked like machines in order to maximize surplus value. Rather than progressing toward flourishing, living energy is expended in mere survival, an exercise that remains to this day. Ball points out that

> Marx and Freud acknowledge the tolls that physical and psychic work take on finite stores of energy, they imagine people who might *feel like bounded subjects* in becoming more self-protective as they desperately struggle to conserve energy and fend off entropy. Entropics is intended to convey the demoralizing experience of waning capacity over time in the conflict between a death-driving capitalism and an inertia-inclining psychophysical economy.[19]

Such practices require that workers be denied time outside work, sleep, meaningful and sustaining meals, leisure, and entertainment. All that is required of the wage laborer is utmost production with negligible sustenance.[20] The worker, while undergoing constant entropic loss, expends all of their energy simply to endure. In a parallel vein, Freud's psychoanalytics exposes how undischarged drives can manifest in anxiety that exhaust vital energy without producing anything socially or individually beneficial. As shown in the previous chapter's discussion of the death drive's thrust toward organic quiescence, Freud joins Marx in providing another important insight into the lived experiences of modern bodies subject to entropy. The constant anxiety generated by living in the frenetic capitalist landscape produces little in the way of happiness and satisfaction and instead exhausts subjects who are at its relentless mercy. Instead of working, creating, or living an engaged life, anxiety expends energy in a self-referential cycle of affective buildup. Certainly, precarious conditions are key producers of anxiety in contemporary labor practices. In neoliberal markets, workers are forced to act as if this is not the case in order to maintain their insecure positions. This produces "a *maniacal entropy machine* that makes gains in 'capacitation' by extracting relative and absolute value while compelling 'smooth' behavior as its components become more tense, fatigued, unhealthy, indebted and desperate."[21] In both the exploited Marxian laborer and the anxious Freudian subject, energy that could be diverted to human thriving is instead focused on mere survival or empty expenditure. This produces exhausted and broken bodies and increasing psychological harm from failure to convey social and organic resiliency.

Concentrating on the experience of what it means to work and decline as a laborer, Ball convincingly argues that much of the virtual and materialist turn in post-Marxist and Freudian affect studies are ill-equipped (if not outwardly hostile) to address considerations of concrete lived experiences of embodied depletion in the twenty-first century. Critics go too far in decentering the neoliberal "subject," almost to oblivion. In their desire to critique outdated and exclusionary vocabularies of subjectivity, Ball argues that the reality of suffering gets lost. For example, the Deleuzian move toward de-individuating the body (making it an open and porous system interacting with and being affected by numerous other systems) is indeed helpful in conceiving of organizations and flows of energy beyond the anthropocentric. Thinking from a de-subjectified perspective allows for considerations of forces, energies, life, and materialities that form dynamic interactive fields. This in turn helps to counter neoliberalism's heavy-handed accent on individual agency and responsibility (themes I take up in the following chapter). However, as Ball points out, such models fail to adequately address the suffering of sentient bodies that labor under oppressive systems. The physical and psychic experiences of depletion, and the fear dominating those most vulnerable and abused by these systems, cannot find adequate representation in a framework of pure becoming and potentiality. Theories that de-emphasize bodily borders and over-emphasize materiality and force undermine the value of affective life trying to exist in these conditions. Even if bodily borders and systems are porous, giving lie to any sense of inviolable sovereignty, the ability to talk about what it is like to feel "survival under siege" is of foremost significance if systemic, rather than individual, change is the goal.[22] A culture of forced labor requires thinking bodies as self-aware systems vulnerable to the predations of entropy and not merely as matter on a continuum.[23]

Ball continues by showing how shifting dramatically toward notions of immanence and becoming fails to provide a sense of agential personhood or to motivate against exploitation and abuse. This "virtually turned liberation scientism" combines scientific paradigms with metaphors of matter containing infinite potentiality, which is useful for deconstructing modern subjectivity, but it ultimately lacks concrete political power.[24] As compelling as the gestures toward liberation are in such theories, they end up recapitulating "capital's turgid powers of expansion through compulsory capacitation, which smooth over the affective economies that stratify the embodiment of different working conditions."[25] The move toward desubjectification thus defangs critical abilities to call out the effects of entropic patterns in our modern world: health decline, psychological disorders such as depression and anxiety, malaise, apathy, lowering levels of empathy, class alienation and exploitation, racial oppression, and the shaming of gender expression. Ball asserts that

> in promoting a morphology that traces lines of force, quantum indeterminacies, and super-empirical thresholds, cognitively laboring affect theorists do not "give us back" a body; instead, they molecularize and thereby elide the social distribution of survival anxiety, or write as though the experience of economic uncertainty can go without saying for the sake of emancipatory post-humanist thinking.[26]

While I acknowledge Ball's criticisms here, and I agree that the suffering body must maintain a place of privilege in the critiques of the terrifying entropy machine of late-stage capitalism, I return to the notion of matter and materiality largely rejected by Ball in the following chapter in order to investigate ways in which the affective experience of slackening does not require stable bodily boundaries. In fact, the entropic metaphor not only speaks about the feelings of depletion and anxiety as described by Ball but can widen the field to consider systems in which humans function and of which they are largely unaware. I suggest this not as a refutation of Ball's arguments, but rather as a supplement to the poetics of entropics and its focus on affective life.

The anxiety of being an aging, laboring body requires not only that we problematize what a body is but that we also speak to the lived experience of those positioned at the battle-front of the anti-entropic warfare promoted by capitalism. To this end, I turn to *La Vieillesse* (*The Coming of Age*) by Simone de Beauvoir, itself a monumental description of the forces that use and abuse elderly bodies. Beauvoir's inquiry testifies to the affective, existential dimension of the lived experience of aging in Western cultures. Her approach provides a necessary addition to Ball's poetics of entropics as well as a framework from which to analyze current treatments of the aged in the United States.

BEAUVOIR AND ENTROPIC DENIAL

La Vieillesse details the biological, cultural, mythological, and experiential phenomena of aging. Mirroring the basic framework of *The Second Sex*, Beauvoir studies the ways in which the aged are produced by culture so as to be its other—at once abject and yet wholly necessary to provide the borders of social and material identity. This work explores the various threads that lead to what she considers to be a near-universal attitude in both developing and technologically developed cultures, all of which share, in varying degrees, a revulsion, dread, and avoidance of decrepitude. Even more mistreated than the women of her study in *The Second Sex* decades earlier, Beauvoir writes that "society looks upon old age as a shameful secret that is unseemly to mention."[27] Positioning herself as the voice of the silenced and forgotten, she begins by describing the aged from the perspective of the various social forces that consistently deprive them of agency and support. Afterward, she presents a variety of lived experiences of the elderly struggling under these institutional pressures. Society produces and subsequently neglects the elderly, creating a group as the "other" in order to justify its systematic exploitation and abandonment of it. "As far as old people are concerned," she reminds us, "society is not only guilty but downright criminal. Sheltering behind the myths of expansion and affluence, it treats the old as outcasts ... condemned to poverty, decrepitude, wretchedness and despair."[28] Society generates the elderly as abject through maximal vital extraction and then turns away from them as soon as they become economic and social drains. I argue that the elderly reveal the extent to which modern capitalist society accelerates and denies the workings of entropics.

Beauvoir acknowledges that one cannot study age without a multiperspectival approach, nor can one understand aging without cross-cultural reference. This sort of project can never be completed but must necessarily remain open-ended because no single factor determines what it means to be aged in any given time or society. Beauvoir's ethics of ambiguity allows for soft universals in terms of what it means to be old. Since the experience of aging (or the possibility of aging to come) is shared by all human beings, it is possible to make certain connections across differences without reducing them to sameness. For example, all bodies require energy and maintenance; thus all people share the affective experience of entropic slackening and loss of available energy to do work even as these experiences are situationally dependent. In the most general terms,

> life is an unstable system in which balance is continually lost and continually recovered; it is inertia that is synonymous with death. Change is the law of life. And it is a particular kind of change that distinguishes aging—an irreversible, unfavourable change; a decline.[29]

This decline, she observes, distresses every aspect of the biological organism: eyesight and hearing fade, muscle and organ strength decrease, sexual interest and function wane, and a general increasing fragility of mind and body set in. Of course, not all of these physical diminutions occur in the same ways; individual vigor matters, as does (and perhaps more significantly) one's place in a situation that either fosters health or leaves one without care and support. "A man's ageing and his decline," Beauvoir notes, "always takes place inside some given society: it is intimately related to the character of that society and to the place that the individual in question occupies within it."[30] Thus, decline doesn't necessarily have to be a frightening bogeyman as it is so often cast, even if it is so in many societies.[31]

To counter the widespread fear of aging, cultures must do that which is available to fewer old people: provide a safe and secure retirement, relatively free from financial fears, with plenty of availability for social and creative activities. Such a goal would reposition decline as something akin to rest and leisure. Although this has never been universally available in any capitalist culture, it shouldn't be seen as impossible even as it becomes progressively unrealistic for the vast majority of people. For most, capitalism increasingly demands that working life extends well beyond what is physically possible or desirable. This is an extension of what Lauren Berlant would call "slow death"—the wearing down of the poorest, most vulnerable populations over time.[32] Berlant's notion of slow death explores the social ramifications of precarity in the modern age, particularly tracking it "in terms of the desperation and violence that has been released when the capitalist 'good life' fantasy no longer has anything to which to attach its promises of flourishing, coasting, and resting."[33] In a blatant display of capitalism's war against entropy, the aged, disabled, and economically disadvantaged have every last ounce of available energy worked out of them—oftentimes to the point of literal or psychic death, because, as Jasbir K. Puar pointedly observes, "debility—slow death—is profitable for capitalism" in terms of both the extraction of labor and the economic benefits in the treatment of resulting disability.[34] The withdrawal of energy and resources from vulnerable populations occurs over spans of time that are difficult to take in at a glance, thus making it tempting to accept such practices as inevitable, even necessary. But the profiting off the backs of workers of varying degrees of capacitation is not necessary for societal health, and, in fact, works directly against it. For those who remain unemployed or unemployable, their social erasure is even more extreme.[35]

Although written in 1970, much of Beauvoir's observations have borne out more than she may have expected. Calling the lot of old people in the twentieth century "scandalous," she writes that as

> a general rule society shuts its eyes to all abuses, scandals and tragedies, so long as these do not upset its balance; and it worries no more about the fate of the children in state orphanages, or of juvenile delinquents, or of the handicapped, than it does about that of the aged. In the last case, however, this indifference does on the face of it seem more astonishing, *since every single member of the community must know that his future is in question.*[36]

As contemporary disability theorists observe, disability is inevitable given enough time. What awaits all of us is what Robert McRuer calls the "disabled community to come."[37] Beauvoir underscores the particularly unusual repudiation at work in the mistreatment of the elderly by those who will one day find themselves in the same position. She attributes this denial to a kind of self-defense mechanism. The flat rejection of a shared human experience can be explained existentially by the fear that the other—that which limits yet defines us—inspires in patriarchal capitalist cultures. Like the feminine, old age appears as repugnant and loathsome in order for younger populations to claim a kind of subjective superiority. Yet, unlike the feminine, it crosses all borders of race, gender, and class. Because of its absolute abject status, it fills most "with more aversion than death itself."[38] The old person is a kind of living corpse, a zombie frightening and following younger generations through life until they finally succumb and join its ranks, terrifying others in turn.

Beauvoir did not fully visualize the way in which capitalism would morph to fight against entropy by demanding the extension of labor beyond standard retirement. The old, according to her, basically become useless mouths to feed. While this may remain true for certain segments of the aging population who are forced (directly and indirectly) into "early" retirement to avoid paying them higher salaries and benefits, many (including some from the aforementioned category) are forced into extended, exhausting, and underpaid work. Markets and corporations seek to make as much money as possible out of elderly labor and consumption, which may temporarily lead to a forestalling of entropy on a local scale, but catastrophically contributes to global social abuse and waste.[39]

The entropic metaphor sheds light on the plight of the aged, whether senescence brings with it retirement from the labor force or continuation of work until death. No matter how much one desires to stay on top of scientific, cultural, political, and technological changes, with age what one cannot do inevitably increases. This creates conditions for greater marginalization in addition to exploitation. As a result, age often brings with it a kind of "inertia" wherein those things that once gave pleasure, or at least were interesting or curiosity-arousing, lose their allure. Boredom, indifference, and apathy come to fill the space that was occupied by curiosity and ambition.

> The sadness of old people is not caused by any particular event or set of circumstances: it merges with their consuming boredom, with their bitter and humiliating sense of uselessness, and with their loneliness in the midst of a world that has nothing but indifference for them.[40]

This sadness may take the form of intense melancholia, feelings of worthlessness, and paralyzing ennui, perhaps even a kind of madness like Lear. Such emotional states only contribute to the abject positioning of the aged. Crucially, none of this is a natural part of growing old but instead directly results from social and political practices that force many elderly into an existential space of isolation.[41] These feelings are all-too-easily exploited by the market which eagerly encourages low or no-paying labor or material goods to fill the void left by social oblivion.

AGING AND WORKING IN THE UNITED STATES

In the opening lines of *La Vieillesse*, Beauvoir speaks of the Buddha—unique for embracing all aspects of the human condition, including aging and decrepitude. Immediately following this praise, she observes how all others evade old age, noting "the Americans have struck the word death out of their vocabulary."[42] Beauvoir's words set the stage for the current situation of the elderly in many countries. Yet the American situation provides a unique example to study with Ball's entropic theory and Beauvoir's understanding of the aged as other. The current shifts in American politics work to consolidate wealth into the hands of an aging and entitled class, while refusing acknowledgment of growing systemic collapse. The so-called Baby Boomers—much maligned by the younger and less materially secure generations—serve as a constant lightening rod in the face of a tumultuous political and environmental situation. Although true that this generation grew into adulthood during a time of national prosperity and relative social security, it never was a golden generation experiencing universal privilege. Whether through racial or class exclusion that barred access to this wealth, or through the loss of savings due to the chaotic and cynical machinations of a predatory market, or simply through the cruelties of medical and housing establishments extracting money, the Boomers are the canaries in the coal mine of a culture that refuses to acknowledge entropic decline. The overall callousness toward the most vulnerable members of American society—immigrants, the disabled, the sick, the young, the poor—is acutely visible in the treatment of the elderly. The United States is a paramount example of the political prioritization to harness and consolidate materials and energies through the utilization of the poor and underprivileged. Such practices generate a vulnerable aged population that is paradoxically slandered as a threat to resources, while relentlessly badgered into spending what diminishing resources it has.[43]

In recent developments, for example, Andrew Cockburn writes about the appalling negligence shown toward the elderly in American nursing homes. The COVID-19 pandemic momentarily cast light on shadowy practices that have been left to fester and grow over decades of government changes to Medicare and Medicaid, as well as unchecked, predatory private equity firms. Nursing homes have become ripe for exploitation because of the helplessness of the population: "helpless because so often confined in a state of neglect and squalor. But despite or perhaps because of their conditions, they were worth a lot of money. In effect, they were being harvested for profit."[44] While many exposed populations were affected by the pandemic in a mismanaged country such as the United States (prisoners, meatpackers, teachers, students, etc.),

> the treatment of the aged stands out. As Simone de Beauvoir once wrote: "By the way in which a society behaves toward its old people, it uncovers the naked and often carefully hidden truths about its real principles and aims." The virus, it could be said, has made these truths self-evident.[45]

The pandemic only exposed practices that have been siphoning off money and energy from the elderly for decades.

American labor practices push the old and infirm to work for as long as possible before they are drained of every last dime in nursing homes. Many will never even get to that point. One need only look at the extension of retirement into a future that never arrives, as well as the poor pay and working conditions in which the elderly often find themselves, to see rampant entropic accelerationist tendencies. Jessica Bruder's recent work has explored how contemporary labor practices have relied on the exploitation of older, poorer, sicker groups. Her 2017 book, *Nomadland*, traces many of the ignominies suffered by these marginalized populations who are constantly faced with material deprivations and impossible choices. She writes that "these indignities underscore a larger question: *When do impossible choices start to tear people—a society—apart?*"[46] Bruder's 2014 article, "The End of Retirement," earlier investigated the grueling and uncertain situation facing many American seniors who, after long lives of work, are unable to afford to retire—ever. Her analysis of the working aged—those who must continue to work until they die or are simply physically unable to endure—connects to many of Beauvoir's observations on the French aged and much of the developed world of the twentieth century. In an era of disappearing pensions, wage stagnation, and widespread foreclosures, Americans are working longer and leaning more heavily than ever on social security, a program designed to supplement (rather than fully fund) retirement. Due to shrinking or nonexistent retirement savings or pensions, insufficient unemployment benefits, or a lack of robust familial networks, many workers who once thought they would be able to retire find themselves in a devastating situation, leaving them susceptible to homelessness, untreated illnesses, and death. As a result of this horrific reality, those who should be cared for as they are no longer able to be fully able-bodied workers must often take on limited seasonal work and physically taxing and low-paying jobs for minimum (or less than the minimum) wages. As with other forms of compulsory able-bodiedness, forcing aging workers to extend their work-life "functions by covering over, with the appearance of choice, a system in which there actually is no choice."[47]

Shockingly, only 17 percent of Americans envision that they will not work at all during their retirement years,[48] leaving many to become a migrating workforce seeking out temporary seasonal work as varied as selling Christmas trees, picking raspberries, selling fireworks, or maintaining campgrounds. Many live in mobile homes as "workampers," chasing jobs such as beet harvesting or joining Amazon's "Camperforce" during high volume sales times like Christmas. Others find more stable work as greeters or food demonstrators at large warehouse stores like Walmart or Costco. Generally perceived by corporations to be dependable and hard-working, the conditions of hard labor and material uncertainty take grave tolls on already hard-hit and declining bodies. "Retirement" is indeed a relatively new development (not even 150 years old). However, people in the developed world are living longer and have less communal support than previous generations. This state of affairs necessitates some kind of social safety net for the growing aging population, or, as in the United States, forcing individuals to work during old age.[49]

The inevitable decline of the aging body, exacerbated by the demands of physically punishing forms of paid work, prompts Bruder to ask,

What happens to all these people when they're too old to scrub campsite toilets or walk ten hours a day in an Amazon warehouse or lift thirty-pound sacks of sugar beets in the cold? When they can't see well enough to drive cumbersome rigs on the highway? Some geriatric migrants I met already seem one injury or broken axle away from true homelessness. Vans and trailers don't last forever. Neither do bodies.[50]

All aging bodies become less capable of work regardless of their privileges or lack thereof. But it would be a rude error to assume that all bodies are equally affected by the passage of time as class, race, gender, education, and geography all factor heavily into these calculations.[51] The push to legally raise the retirement age in the United States, coupled with the fact that even aged Americans who are well past it must continue to work, places a disproportionate burden on those workers who exist in lower economic brackets and who have largely engaged in labor throughout their adult lives that was already physically taxing and punishing.

Whether through the maximization of work extracted from bodies long past the ability to be fully productive contributors to working-class capitalism, or the proliferation of companies, programs, and products solely devoted to anti-aging propaganda, entropic decline and loss of vitality are considered to be the enemies against which all forces must be deployed. We are witness to a round-the-clock demand for vital energy that abides nothing short of complete commitment, with no room for depletion, fatigue, sickness, or age. Moral condemnation falls on less-than maximally producing and self-reliant individuals. Anything shy of the mythic demand of total able-bodiedness, twenty-four hours a day, from youth to death is intolerable and explicitly punished or ejected from the system as waste. If one is not born able-bodied, then one is treated as a "drain" on the system—forced either into the abject shame of social scorn and dependency or into producing as much as possible in order to justify one's place in the social network. If one is viewed as a potentially maximally producing worker, then one's education is geared from the earliest years toward becoming fully activated in the labor force (something that is particularly painful for the younger generations who labor under long hours, engaging in less fulfilling, lower paid, and scarcer work).[52] If perceived to be an able-bodied worker, one is expected to continue on this path of maximum output until death—a notion wholly irrational and antithetical to the second law of thermodynamics. Bodies, like all systems, eventually run out of energy to maintain themselves at maximum energy levels.[53] In a deeply embodied sense then, modern labor expectations flaunt a direct denial of entropics, while at the same time hastening it by forcing declining bodies into compulsory capacitation and poorer economic brackets into maximal spending of limited wealth.

Western capitalism produces entropic results while fearing and hating the actual appearance of them, particularly in the form of old age. The distaste for aging and disease has been found by various thinkers thus far studied. We find it in Timaeus' discussions of organic faltering, Hegel's formulation of organisms dying from the inborn disease of death, and Freud's discussions of the death drive. Barbara Ehrenreich argues that it was in the twentieth century wherein "medical science began to think of aging as a kind of disease as opposed to a normal stage of the life cycle."[54] In liberalism, individuals, rather than the complex overlapping organizations which both sustain and define them, bear the burden of system failure. This is not only impossible but politically and morally bankrupt. By way of illustration, Ehrenreich describes the contemporary spectacle linking health and virtue. Judging aging people as either virtuous or vicious based on how they maintain health reinforces the mythology of total personal responsibility and autonomy.[55] Of course, the body as a system can only stave off decline and death for so long before it must succumb to inorganic chaos. Not only are most aging bodies expected to work longer, with less social and financial support, they are also required to maintain health by their own actions or be judged as disappointments by an entropy-denying culture. Barred from material support, the aged must spend dwindling resources to maintain the veneer of total health and fitness. Puar additionally observes that debility is profitable, "but so is the demand to 'recover' from or overcome it."[56] Yet, the push against entropy on the individual (not to mention social) level is a losing battle from the start given the nature of time and limited available energy and resources. Even if one manages to escape hard labor past retirement, to shore up enough financial security to be protected, to take on individual responsibility to care for one's own health and affairs without being a social or familial "burden," there are ever-growing predators waiting in the wings.[57]

What is needed in the face of these gross abuses to the aged is to recall what Beauvoir emphasizes and modern disability studies highlight, that is, everyone, given enough time, will be disabled. This is not an unusual or special class of people to be drained and discarded but it is *all of us*. Echoing Beauvoir's earlier observations, McRuer reminds us that "if we live long enough, disability is the one identity we will all inhabit."[58] Such an observation underscores the constantly shifting, yet shared, experience of human finitude. Those who refuse to recognize this all but ensure their own abject future. We are all "temporarily abled" as nobody that lives to adulthood has not experienced illness, physical trauma, and, if given enough time, age and decrepitude.[59] It is no longer acceptable—and indeed never was—that the privileged and powerful garner all possible securities, leaving the vast majority to varying degrees of social exclusion and suffering.

I want to interrupt and conclude this discussion as we have reached a glimpse into just some of the damage wrought by practices that simultaneously deny and accelerate entropy. The time has come to change direction, both in the text and in our way of reflecting and acting in the world. At this point, thinking must start to turn away from the fatalism of entropic philosophy in order to receive the *entrepic* call for reverence and care.

Returning to *Oedipus at Colonus*, Sophocles describes the final journey of long-suffering Oedipus as a homeless, blind, old man who is totally dependent on the care and love of his daughter, Antigone. Ball's poetics of entropics illustrates how the lived experiences of aging, losing capacities, and social vulnerability can be terrifying and difficult to endure. Oedipus serves as a pointed illustration of this state of affairs. Fear and vulnerability are captured in the near helplessness of old Oedipus who has nothing to offer but his broken body and, ultimately, the gift of his death. Because of his worthlessness as a ruler and the tragic fallout from his previous actions, he, like King Lear, is displaced from his homeland by his own family. As the father and daughter make it to Athens, they wait in the holy grove of the Eumenides to see if they will be welcomed or forced to continue their ongoing exile. Oedipus has hope that he will find hospitality, as a prophecy promises a boon to the city that receives him and allows him to die within it. While Oedipus waits to know what will become of his last days (and more importantly, his corpse), he learns that Creon is on his way, hatching a plan to bury Oedipus outside of Thebes as a form of insurance against the curse he carries with him as the fallen king.

Even as his sons reject him and Creon dooms him to shame, "banished, a beggar, to wander forever,"[60] Antigone cares and sustains him in his wanderings. When Theseus, king of Athens, shows up to discuss his fate, Oedipus extends him the offering of his own death. But before Theseus can decide on whether or not to accept this gift, Oedipus warns that his sons will fight Athens for the corpse. Perplexed, because there is no quarrel between Thebes and Athens, Theseus asks why this would be the case. In the ensuing discussion, Oedipus laments: "O dearest son of Aegeus: only the gods know neither age nor death; everything else all-mastering time confounds. The strength of the earth, the strength of the body, dies."[61] Ultimately, in an expression of *entrepic* protection and veneration, Theseus grants hospitality and citizenship to Oedipus because the old man has claimed the king's respect.

In watching the events of the familial battle unfold in their homeland, the chorus rages against the injustices of aging. After having weathered the great upheavals of life's trials, all that lies in the future is "old age at the last, most hated, without power, without comrades, and friends, when every ill, all ills, take up their dwelling with him."[62] This stark picture of abhorrent senescence is the one largely fostered by the contemporary acceleration of capitalist entropic destruction. Decline is part of aging, but it is detestable because very few have Antigone to help alleviate it. Even more to the point, no one should have to rely on a single blood relative to care for them but should be situated in a society in which care and reverence are woven into all aspects of life to the greatest extent possible. Oedipus' situation does not require gerontological loneliness, as the play itself bears out. Theseus turns a reverential face to the vulnerable stranger who has nothing to offer but his own death, and in so doing shows the kind of consideration that does not accelerate or deny decay and dissolution, but rather honors and attends to it. As a result, the secret of death that Oedipus contains becomes a source of blessings upon the land. Despised and cast out from Thebes he becomes an act of consecration for Athens and its people, transforming from a burden to his family into a guide into the unknown secrets of finitude. The care shown by Theseus for the fragility of age is returned by the blessing of Oedipus' body.

Oedipus' exile makes him feel useless, abject, and parasitic. This is the situation of the elderly illuminated by Beauvoir's analyses. As she observes, "it is an empiric and universal truth that after a certain number of years the human organism undergoes a decline. The process is inescapable,"[63] but it does not have to be tragic, at least not in preventable ways. True, time's arrow sails forward at the individual and systemic levels; sometimes mitigation of the inconveniences of aging is the best that can be hoped for since they cannot be reversed or cured. However, without adequate social welfare structures, financial security, and meaningful familial relationships and friendships, aging becomes remarkably sad and isolating. How could it be otherwise? If, however, the social systems are changed to show *entrepic* reverence, turning toward that which has been cast out and rejected, then care can form the basis for protecting both the individual and the community from the worst effects of entropic decline.

Entropy as a metaphor certainly points to the inexorable breakdown of systems and the ultimate heat death of the universe, but until that final point far into an unforeseeable future, systems constantly borrow energy from each other. Whereas capitalism relentlessly "borrows" from the slackening energies of the elderly by taking their labor and their property, another community is possible wherein what is borrowed from the elderly is far less exploitative and more dutiful. Society must recognize that all have paid into the various systems that should in turn support them comfortably until death. Even that small minority of people who are limited in contributing substantially through work should be given a place of care and support. A society far less terrified of entropic decay wouldn't be bothered if it must tend to specific groups without recompense.

As it stands now, Beauvoir remains correct that the treatment of the elderly is a crime carried out on a national level and begins well before one is forced into senescence. It starts in childhood, carries forward throughout adulthood, and lies in wait the moment one is declared "old." Society "prefabricates the maimed and wretched state that is theirs when they are old. It is the fault of society that the decline of old age begins too early, that it is rapid, physically painful and, because they enter in upon it with empty hand, morally atrocious."[64] Rather than individual islands, human beings are interconnected and interdependent. Collective life must be envisioned as a dynamic system facilitating the transfer of energy to where it is most needed in order to preserve the vitality of the whole. Sites of entropic breakdown should signal where to divert and reinvest energy rather than producing shadow sites to be abandoned and shunned.

We would do well to embrace Ball's formulation of entropics as a poetics "anchored in the materiality of the tired, aching, and aging body as the horizon of eventual wear and tear that binds us all, disabled and temporarily-abled alike."[65] Such a reorientation of priorities can work against the madness of the anti-entropic march of late capitalism, opening up new ways of creating out of ruin, embracing change out of collapse, and conceiving of possible futures that are not plagued by pessimisms focused on annihilation. These are some of the avenues of thinking explored in the final two chapters. If decay and breakdown can be approached as irruptions of possibility, then groups such as the elderly do not have to be forced to the margins of social oblivion. In the end, tinkering with one social service over here, another over there, will not fundamentally change the poor treatment of the elderly. Rather, the call is nothing less radical than to "change life itself,"[66] and in so doing, to find possibility in impossibility and new life in death. It is with this view toward the *entrepic* in mind that I now turn to thinkers and artists who tasked themselves with this very project.

NOTES

1. Simone de Beauvoir, *The Coming of Age (La vieillesse)*, trans. Patrick O'Brian (New York, W.W. Norton & Company, 1996), 7. The English edition of *La Vieillesse* is *The Coming of Age*. I use the French because *Old Age* is a more accurate translation.

2. Robert Smithson, "A Sedimentation of the Mind: Earth Projects, 1968," in *Robert Smithson: The Collected Writings*, ed. Jack Flam (Berkeley: University of California Press, 1996), 107.

3. Murakami, *Sheep Chase*, 115.

4. William Shakespeare, *King Lear* (New York: Bantam Books, 1988) 1.1.40

5. Ibid, 2.4.147.

6. Ibid, 2.4.47–50.

7. Much like Derrida's specter, the aged, both individually and as an undifferentiated mass, occupy a shadow region of a visible/invisible menace. "At bottom, the

specter is the future, it is always to come, it presents itself only as that which could come or come back." Jacques Derrida, *Spectres of Marx: The State of the Debt, the Work of Mourning and the New International.* ed. and trans. Peggy Kamuf (New York: Routledge Classics, 2006), 48.

8. Beauvoir, *La vieillesse*, 283. For more extensive treatments in age studies see, for example, Geoffrey Scarre, ed., *The Palgrave Handbook of the Philosophy of Aging* (London: Palgrave Macmillan, 2016), and, Marc Schweda, Michael Coors, and Claudia Bozzaro, eds., *Aging and Human Nature: Perspectives from Philosophical, Theological, and Historical Anthropology* (New York: Springer International Publishing, 2020).

9. For example, political borders and their porousness and dissolution. The great migrations of people across the globe are a direct result of the exhaustion of low entropy resources which forces peoples to look elsewhere for sustenance. In this theme, the following chapter explores waste and pollution as high-entropy byproducts of low-entropy mining, production, and consumption.

10. Terranova and Parisi, "Emergence and Control." https://journals.uvic.ca/index.php/ctheory/article/view/14604/5455; Lynn Margulis and Dorion Sagan, *What is Life?* (New York: Simon and Schuster, 1995).

11. Georgescu-Roegen, *Entropy Law*, 305.

12. Terranova and Parisi, "Emergence and Control."

13. Hayles, *Posthuman*, 101.

14. Ball, "Losing Steam," 56.

15. Ibid.

16. The claims made in this chapter cannot be simply universalized to all cultures, which is why I focus on the United States as a particular case study.

17. Ball, "Losing Steam," 55. Ball continues: "The human motor remains an *idée fixe* in our cultural imaginary long after the name Helmholtz has lost its aura as a sign of the times." Ibid.

18. *Capital* was published in 1867, along with Clausius' *Mechanical Theory of Heat*. Clausius had coined the term "entropy" two years earlier in 1865.

19. Ball, "Losing Steam," 60. The concern with the affective dimensions of entropic decline is a continuation of Ball's general preoccupation with recuperating the notion of an experiential subject following the post-modern deconstruction of subjectivity. See Karyn Ball, "The Entropics of Discourse: The 'Materiality' of Affect Between Marx and Derrida," in *Encountering Derrida: Legacies and Futures of Deconstruction*, eds. Allison Weiner and Simon Morgan Wortham (London: Continuum International Publishing Group, 2007).

20. Ball, "Losing Steam," 58. Ball notes that "Marxian metabolics provides entropics with the image of a laboring body as an economy of energies distended between conservation and entropy." Ibid.

21. Ibid, 67.

22. Ball writes that "from an entropical standpoint, affect theory becomes more politically substantive when it distances itself from open-system motifs to draw attention to the differentially deadening impact of survival under siege." Ibid, 69.

23. Ibid, 64.

24. Ibid, 70. These moves can be seen not only in Deleuze and Guattari but also in Patricia Clough, Brian Massumi, Michael Hardt, and Antonio Negri.

25. Ibid, 64.

26. Ibid.

27. Beauvoir, *La vieillesse*, 1.

28. Ibid, 2. This is even more true with the exploited classes who experience all of this worse than the wealthy and privileged. Ibid, 541.

29. Ibid, 11.

30. Ibid, 37.

31. Decline is only a negative term for teleological beings: "the word decline has no meaning except in relation to a given end—a movement towards or farther away from a goal." Ibid, 86. Disorder and decline are, in fact, highly relative in entropic functioning.

32. Slow death is described by Jasbir K. Puar as "the debilitating ongoingness of structural inequality and suffering." Jasbir K. Puar, "Coda: The Cost of Getting Better: Suicide, Sensation, Switchpoints," *GLQ: A Journal of Lesbian and Gay Studies* 18, no. 1 (2012): 149. For an original discussion of this topic, see Lauren Berlant, "Slow Death: Sovereignty, Obesity, Lateral Agency," *Critical Inquiry* 33 (2007): 754–780. Judith Butler describes slow death as resulting from ongoing, rather than episodic processes captured by the term "precaritization" which "allows us to think about the slow death that happens to targeted or neglected populations over time and space." Jasbir K. Puar, "Precarity Talk: A Virtual Roundtable with Lauren Berlant, Judith Butler, Bojana Cvejić, Isabell Lorey, Jasbir Puar, and Ana Vujanović," *The Drama Review* 56, no. 4 (2012): 169.

33. Puar, "Precarity Talk," 171.

34. Puar, "Coda," 153.

35. David T. Mitchell and Sharon L. Snyder explain that "non-productive bodies are those inhabitants of the planet who, largely by virtue of biological (in)capacity, aesthetic non-conformity, and/or non-normative labor patters, have gone invisible due to the inflexibility of traditional classifications of labor (both economic and political). They represent the non-laboring populations—not merely excluded from—but also resistant to standardized labor demands of human value." David T. Mitchell and Sharon L. Snyder, "Disability as Multitude: Re-Working Non-Productive Labor Power," *Journal of Literary and Cultural Disability Studies* 4, no. 2 (2010): 4, http://dx.doi.org/10.3828/jlcds/2010.14.

36. Beauvoir, *La vieillesse*, 216; italics my own. This is well before Robert McRuer's proclamation of the inevitability of disability. Robert McRuer, *Crip Theory: Cultural Signs of Queerness and Disability* (New York: New York University Press, 2006), 200.

37. Ibid, 198. McRuer is careful to note that while this is not factually true, it functions very well as a remarkably generative rhetorical point. Ibid, 200, 207. Also cited in Ball, "Losing Steam," 266.

38. Beauvoir, *La vieillesse*, 539.

39. Beauvoir was also somewhat aware of the direction the world was headed, noting that the elderly person is unable to rest as "he is often compelled . . . to take on unpleasant and ill-paid jobs." Ibid, 232.

40. Ibid, 464. This is why, as Sonia Kruks frames it, "powerlessness is thus their [the elderly] common hallmark." Sonia Kruks, "Simone de Beauvoir: Engaging Discrepant Materialisms," in *New Materialisms: Ontology, Agency, and Politics*, eds. Dianna Coole and Samantha Frost (Durham: Duke University Press, 2010), 273.

41. In its most extreme forms, it can perhaps be understood as an extension of Lisa Guenther's "social death." Lisa Guenther, *Solitary Confinement: Social Death and its Afterlives* (Minneapolis: University of Minnesota Press, 2013), xx–xxiv. Or, of Jill Stauffer's "ethical loneliness" imposed onto other populations. Jill Stauffer, *Ethical Loneliness: The Injustice of Not Being Heard* (New York: Columbia University Press, 2015). While clearly and significantly different from the violence done to slaves (in Guenther's work) and ignored victims of mass violence (in Stauffer's work) the elderly often experience the violence of total exclusion from society—prey to homelessness, sickness, and profound, long-standing isolation.

42. Beauvoir, *La vieillesse*, 1.

43. In this vein, Jessica Bruder discusses the stereotype of the "greedy geezer." Jessica Bruder, *Nomadland: Surviving America in the Twenty-First Century* (New York: W. W. Norton & Company, 2017), 67.

44. Andrew Cockburn, "Elder Abuse: Nursing Homes, the Coronavirus, and the Bottom Line," *Harper's Magazine*, September 2020, 43.

45. Ibid, 49; Beauvoir's quote can be found in *La vieillesse*, 87.

46. Bruder, *Nomadland*, 247.

47. McRuer, *Crip Theory*, 8.

48. Jessica Bruder, "The End of Retirement: When you Can't Afford to Stop Working," *Harper's Magazine*, August 2014, 29. This data comes from an AARP survey cited by Bruder.

49. In fact, it was only the Great Depression that ushered in the need for retirement to make what little work there was available to the younger people who were entering the labor force. Ibid, 34.

50. Ibid, 36.

51. Puar, "Coda," 153.

52. See Malcom Harris' critique of how Millennials' entire education program is one geared toward making them nothing more than human capital, which then shames them for exhibiting all of the traits capital does: narcissism, anxiety about value, and entitlement. Malcolm Harris, *Kids These Days: Human Capital and the Making of Millennials* (Little, Brown and Company, 2017). As Beauvoir observed fifty years earlier, "society cares about the individual only in so far as he is profitable. The young know this. Their anxiety as they enter in upon social life matches the anguish of the old as they are excluded from it." Beauvoir, *La vieillesse*, 543.

53. Given that in the United States, "the U.S. Census Bureau reports that nearly 40 percent of people age sixty-five and older suffer from at least one disability," this is an impossible ideal. Ehrenreich, *Natural Causes*, 167.

54. Ibid, 171.

55. Ehrenreich notes, that in "the health-conscious mind-set that has prevailed among the world's affluent people for about four decades now, health is indistinguishable from virtue." Ibid, 2.

56. Puar, "Coda," 154.

57. One of many possible examples can be found in Rachel Aviv's reports on the use of "legal guardianship." Currently, a million and a half adults in the United States have their property and assets seized by family members or professional service providers under the auspices that they are no longer able to take care of themselves. Rachel Aviv, "How the Elderly Lose Their Rights," *The New Yorker*, October 9, 2017, https://www.newyorker.com/magazine/2017/10/09/how-the-elderly-lose-their-rights?mbid=social_facebook_aud_dev_kw_paid-how-the-elderly-lose-their-rights&kwp_0=712051. One element of decline where I do not have the space to do justice is the association of age and dementia. Dementia is particularly antagonistic to capitalism's demand for constant output and labor. The aging body can still be squeezed for every last drop of its productive capacities, but not so the body whose mind no longer operates according to the rules of normalcy in a given society. As Sallie Tisdale observes, "Perhaps dementia has always been with us in one form or another, and perhaps it always will be—an entropic response." Sallie Tisdale, "Out of Time: The Un-becoming of Self," *Harper's Magazine*, March 2018, 65.

58. McRuer, *Crip Theory*, 200; quoted by, Ball, "Losing Steam," 70.

59. Ibid, 68.

60. Sophocles, *Oedipus Colonus*, 493.

61. Ibid, 695–699.

62. Ibid, 1420–1424.

63. Beauvoir, *La vieillesse*, 539.

64. Ibid, 542. Why can't we create a world where aging is not to be feared but is conceived as a time "accompanied by enrichment and liberation"? Ibid, 486.

65. Ball, "Losing Steam," 70.

66. Beauvoir, *La vieillesse*, 543.

Chapter 6

Entropic Excess

Reconfiguring Matter and Waste

> Even the run-down nature of the high-rise was a model of the world into which the future was carrying them, a landscape beyond technology where everything was either derelict or, more ambiguously, recombined in unexpected but more meaningful ways. Laing pondered this—sometimes he found it difficult not to believe that they were living in a future that had already taken place, and was now exhausted.
>
> J. G. Ballard, *High Rise*[1]

> Are we not all at fault, in basing our judgments on periods of time that are too short? We should make the geologists our pattern.
>
> Freud, *The Future of an Illusion*[2]

The American poet, Robinson Jeffers, looked upon the world that humanity had created and despaired at its self-centered destructiveness. Preferring instead the quiet hardness of stones, the coldness of the sea, and the lone hawk to the company of his fellow human beings, Jeffers' perspective is notably one of the outsider. Deliberately placing himself beyond the norms and expectations of society (even, in many ways, outside of human temporality), Jeffers writes poetry about and from within the perspective of the inhuman. Admittedly, his poetry can be starkly gloomy, as his criticisms of humanity and the unnecessary violence and destruction that it wreaks upon the world cuts through its loud proclamations of virtue and goodness. Yet, the standpoint of "inhumanism" also reveals a far richer world than the merely human—one that is a complex, interweaving web of human, animal, plant, stone, and natural forces producing a cosmic, tragic beauty.[3]

In his poem, "November Surf," Jeffers writes about a fortuitous event on a November day each year when the ocean cleans away tourist rubbish left on the granite rocks of the shoreline. The waves rise to remove trash accumulated from half a year of visitors to the beach:

> The orange-peel, eggshells, papers, pieces of clothing, the clots/ Of dung in corners of the rock, and used/ Sheaths that make light love safe in the evenings: all the droppings of the summer/ Idlers washed off in a winter ecstasy.[4]

Jeffers stands awestruck at the way in which the ocean washes away human refuse, leaving behind no trace of the havoc and thoughtlessness of those creatures he often refers to as apes. He speaks a dream of a biblical storm that may one day clear away more than the tourists' trash, but also the scourge of humanity itself, taking down cities, bringing back nonhuman animals and culling society, a time "when the two-footed/Mammal, being someways one of the nobler animals, regains/The dignity of room, the value of rareness."[5] While the emphasis on the inhuman is not unique to this poem (it infuses much of Jeffers' corpus), the focus on the bits of waste and rubbish is exceptional. He applauds the purifying ocean waves as they remove evidence of humanity's recklessness since it not only produces waste but abandons it to the very nature it had traveled to to marvel at. However, more so than simply praising water's ablution, the materiality of that which the ocean takes into itself—orange peels, eggshells, clothing, feces, condoms—momentarily arrests him. This awareness signals a kind of reverence for materiality and even trash, marking a turn toward *entrepic* thinking that I believe produces care and wonder, rather than bleak pessimism about the future.

As discussed in chapter 2, Plato's *Timaeus* posits a perfect organism, a universe that consumes its own waste, never succumbing to death, old age, and disease. While this cosmological creature presents a powerful anti-entropic image, in reality, the cosmos produces more unusable waste than can be reincorporated, leading toward material homogenization and universal heat death. In his 1952 paper, "On a Universal Tendency in Nature to the Dissipation of Mechanical Energy," William Thomson (later Lord Kelvin) investigates the leftovers produced by machines and the measurable movement from warmer to cooler bodies. This irrevocable loss not only pointed to entropy continuously increasing but also to the alarming fact that humans are in a precarious state. Martin Meisel observes that one of Kelvin's main conclusions drawn from his study of heat and energy was that "within a finite period of time past, the earth must have been, and within a finite period of time to come, the earth must again be unfit for the habitation of man as at present constituted."[6] Kelvin's study of the inevitable movement of warmth to coolness constructs a vision of the true fragility of the human condition and an awareness that no matter how fecund the world appears now, it was not always so, nor will it continue to be in the future.

The previous chapter investigated the anti-entropic practices of maximizing capital and minimizing care resulting in the creation of an ever-expanding population of aging, laboring bodies. There, I explored how the elderly become fuel for a distressed economic system. This chapter takes a wider angle on the question of matter and waste in general, in order to study the possibilities of entropic philosophy reconceiving the human relationship to energy and its byproducts. The present task takes a perspective on materiality that extends beyond human agency into the inhuman, so as to explore different forms of world order and disorder with the goal of disrupting sedimented, nihilistic thinking.

Much of this book has focused on the ways in which influential thinkers grapple with the inescapable truths of decline, breakdown, and death. While the actual entropy law was a latecomer in the temporal flow of thinkers discussed, the reality of forces that work against progress, motion, and wholeness has always been undeniable. Entropic forces manifest their presence in many ways: tendencies toward disorder, homogenization, chaos, and slackening. The entropy metaphor speaks to all of these phenomena, struggling to understand the various ways that energy degrades. Regardless of how it appears, entropy is absolutely unidirectional and necessarily produces more waste than serviceable fuel. Ignoring this necessary component of entropic loss by substituting a mythology of recycling and reconditioning actually furthers environmental damage resulting from unthinking human practices.

This is not to say, however, that humanity should forego serious projects of energy reclamation and stewardship. In fact, directly engaging with entropics yields *precisely* this moral imperative. Recalling the Homeric and Sophoclean emphasis on respect and regard (which forms the essence of what I have been throughout referring to as *entrepic* philosophy), humanity must denounce the fantastical desire for incessant progress and instead turn toward that which calls for care and reverence in order to mitigate harm. In reality, true universal heat death does not concern us. But the vulnerable state of our shared world certainly does. Maximizing both human and world flourishing and minimizing excessive, unnecessary garbage production should be the global goal. This would have the obvious benefit of upending the practices of energy extraction and profit-making that currently direct global economic and political practices. Jeffers' dream of a flood washing away the sins of humanity needs to be replaced by a conscious choice to work within the parameters of entropics.

Liberalism emphasizes individual autonomy and responsibility, which directly contributes to entropic devastation of ecosystems, social structures, and energy. Combating such social and existential harms involves strategizing in terms of collectivities over individuals. Human beings belong to groupings larger and more diverse than we consciously realize. Systems overlap, feed into, and borrow from each other, constantly challenging each other's integrity. Matter organizes and ruptures in a flux of organic and inorganic mingling at macro and micro levels. Bodies and forces continually form and break apart. Even waste is involved in the cycling of energies between systems. Entropic philosophy therefore needs to ruminate on a much larger and more heterogeneous scale than simply the human.

This chapter looks at the intersecting issues of collectivities and waste, using Jane Bennett's vital materialism, as a starting point to explore the ways in which the "human" is porous, composed by multiple intersecting materialities, existing far beyond the boundaries of the body and even the organic as such. I also borrow from Barbara Ehrenreich's book *Natural Causes* to further these considerations. These thinkers destabilize the borders of the person by amplifying non-(or not only) human forces, materialities, systems, and energies. Finally, I employ the thought of Robert Smithson, who exemplifies the inhuman using artworks that directly engage, rather than circumvent, entropy. Accentuating the inevitable waste that comes from all systemic organizations does not automatically lead to despair but rather builds ways to see matter and refuse as ineluctable components of life that require attention and consideration.

MATTER AND WASTE

In one of his most important essays, "The Question Concerning Technology," Martin Heidegger describes a particularly dangerous way in which technologically advanced (but in many ways philosophically retrograde) societies share a warped experience of the world. Rather than nature disclosing itself in its vast, wide, marvelousness, "progressive" societies view it as nothing more than arrangements of stored energy to be exploited for financial gain and world domination. This disclosure challenges nature with "the unreasonable demand that it supply energy that can be extracted and stored as such."[7] In direct defiance of the entropy law, the modern era approaches nature as a kind of warehouse of energy without concern for the devastation energy extraction and utilization wreaks upon the world, or the irrecuperable waste that it leaves in its wake. Refusing to acknowledge the finitude of the reserves it extricates, modern practice "expedites in that it unlocks and exposes. Yet that expediting is always itself directed from the beginning toward furthering something else, i.e., toward driving on to the maximum yield at the minimum expense."[8] With the sole purpose of taking, using, and profiting before the collapse of the targeted systems, capitalist production and consumerism fly directly in the face of the inevitability of the entropy law. Of utmost importance for Heidegger is to heed attitudes that reveal the world to us in ways that do not frame nature as simply a repository of exploitable resources.

Approaching modernity's treatment of nature from an economic framework, Georgescu-Roegen's work, *The Entropy Law and the Economic Process*, understands how human economies are necessarily tied to thermodynamics. This orientation makes entropy a uniquely *human* experience of energy loss. The concepts of "bound" (high entropy) and "free" (low entropy) energy make sense from a goal-oriented, human perspective. Without the notion of purpose, there are only constantly shifting energy fields. Energy loss matters only for beings that set ordered plans and projects that require vigor to maintain or that would otherwise collapse.[9] From the human perspective, entropy breaks down order and structure, producing waste in the form of dissipated and unusable energy. Quite often this waste is not only unable to be reabsorbed but actually works counter to goals posited by the organization or organism. However, this entropic truth is only true for a very specific set of existents. Beyond that, definitive claims about the nature of matter and refuse are only speculations.

In his application of the law of entropy to economics, Georgescu-Roegen emphasizes the *irrevocability* of entropic processes, because "if the entropic process were not irrevocable, i.e., if the energy of a piece of coal or of uranium could be used over and over again ad infinitum, scarcity would hardly exist in a man's life."[10] Since free energy is clearly and observably limited, to behave as if it is not produces some of the most egregious world catastrophes. According to Georgescu-Roegen, the failure to recognize limitations "in relation to space, to time, and to matter and energy" leads to "the idea that we may defeat the Entropy Law by bootlegging low entropy with the aid of some ingenious device."[11] This magical technology would be a self-perpetuating, inexhaustible, and waste-less form of energy. Such a goal, while laudable insofar as it encourages developments in renewable energy and energy recapture through recycling, is ultimately a fantasy that does not recognize limited resources. There is no conceivable way to stop entropy's unidirectionality toward useless matter, but there are most certainly ways to work within these parameters to maximize thriving.

One of liberalism's central tenets maintains that economic development necessarily benefits not only developed societies but the rest of the world that interacts with them through trade, tourism, and politics. Certainly, as developed in chapter 4, Lévi-Strauss showed that this is patently false as unchecked development obliterates world diversity. Instead of bringing less-developed nations into a higher quality of life, capitalist expansionism extinguishes difference, crushes cultures and environments, and produces homogeneity and garbage in its wake. Modern forms of agriculture and industry exponentially accelerate this movement. Recycling promises a solution to the massive production of globalization's waste.

While such efforts make sense, they falsely promote the idea that the effects of human production and consumption can be alleviated, perhaps entirely so. But no amount of recycling can ever stop, let alone reverse, the movement from low entropy fuel to high-entropy waste. Even the most efficient mechanisms that sort and recycle waste themselves require energy to run. Copper can be recycled, for example, but the energy used to initially mine and process it into something useful produces an increase in entropy that cannot be neutralized through recycling. Whatever energy is used, by whatever mechanism employed, at whatever level to sort or mine, always increases entropic degradation. Georgescu-Roegen muses,

> to sort out the scrap molecules scattered all over the land and at the bottom of the seas, would require such a long time that the entire low entropy of our environment would not suffice to keep alive the numberless generations of Maxwell's demons needed for the complete project.[12]

Although true that matter and energy can be neither created nor destroyed, the critical point lies in the difference between energy available to do work and energy that is not. Economically speaking, there is no motivation to slow entropic increase because capitalism's focus is on short-term surplus, rather than long-term preservation.[13]

Organisms and systems can be threatened by their own refuse to varying degrees. Waste can grow to such proportions that it becomes toxic, effectively destroying its creator. Many succumb to the delusional fantasy that someone, somewhere, somehow, will invent a solution to save humanity from the consequences of its foolishness and fix what has hitherto been only an exponentially growing catastrophe. Such fantasies only produce inaction.[14] Heat death in itself is not the problem (as this is so distant as to be irrelevant) rather capitalism is insofar as it configures its production of waste and loss as necessary evils to be pushed onto vulnerable peoples and lands (as explored in the previous chapter). In an additional movement of denial, modernity configures a very law of nature—the inevitable dissipation of energy and heat—as a foe to be conquered, or a ghost unheeded, rather than as a vital element in the service of the creation of the new. No matter how extreme forced capacitation and labor become, or how many recycling centers are constructed, this monster cannot be defeated and ignorance of entropics only heightens the danger. The goal should instead be one in which societies reorganize around a model of "low-input/low-output" as Robert Biel observes, "not just to avoid *importing* into the social system finite stocks, but more profoundly to avoid the *export* of waste (another representation of entropy)."[15] I would add that thinking *entrepically* by turning toward the precariousness and vulnerability of life in the face of death is the further step that must be taken.

A narrow focus on anthropocentric progress inhibits thought and action. Our very bodies comprise amorphous and uninterested colonies that operate below conscious awareness. Expanding entropics beyond the human compels thinking into broader forms. Jane Bennett is one such thinker to do this well. Bennett proclaims a philosophy of "vital materialism" and "thing-power," describing the different kinds of collectivities that evoke wonder. Building on the notion of assemblages from the work of Spinoza, Deleuze, and Guattari, Bennett explores these collectivities that make up the shared world. Assemblages challenge bodily inviolability and stability insofar as they are composed of multiple living and non-living participants sharing porous and dynamic borders.[16] Much of her work focuses on the formations of matter that intersects (though not intentionally) with the human, providing a way to work through entropics unbeholden (or at least not entirely so) to human purpose and action. Thus, Bennett's vital materialism offers not only an imaginative ontology of naive realism but also an ecological and ethical dimension that takes seriously the nonhuman webs of matter and energy that compose the world.[17]

Like Jeffers, Bennett asks that we open ourselves up to being struck by the world in its various material dimensions. Doing so brings to light how we are shaped and formed by energies and flows that far exceed the boundaries of human bodies and communities. Vital materialism emphasizes the

> recognition of human participation in a shared, vital materiality. We *are* vital materiality and we are surrounded by it, though we do not always see it that way. The ethical task at hand here is to cultivate the ability to discern nonhuman vitality, to become perceptually open to it.[18]

In response to this task, Bennett urges lingering on those experiences when objects become strange and fascinating (like the trash strewn on Jeffers' November beach). Doing so exposes us to connections across ontological boundaries: things, plants, elements, animals, minerals, forces, etc. As human life is undeniably affected by these material dimensions at every moment, such attunement awakens a powerful exposure to the world's continual emergence.

Bennett explores the implications of thing-power in order to illuminate the blurring of seemingly stable borders and boundaries in things. Foregrounding nonhuman materialities, she focuses on integrated and interweaving material systems.[19] Significantly, she highlights how thing-power manifests in trash stuck in a storm drain: a dead rat, a bottle cap, a plastic glove, and a piece of wood. Rather than being inert "things" revealed by a perceiving "subject," they oscillate between garbage and unique matter:

> each thing is individuated, but also located within an assemblage—each is shown to be in a relationship with the others, and also with the sunlight and the

street, and not simply with me, my vision, or my cultural frame. Here thing-power rises to the surface. In this assemblage, *objects* appear more vividly as *things*, that is, as entities not entirely reducible to the contexts in which (human) subjects set them.[20]

Vital materialism's focus on thing-power brings to light the volatile boundaries of things by destabilizing the borders between human subjects and material objects. Through this practice, it creates conditions wherein different kinds of systems and energy flows become perceptible.

I submit that openness to the fascination evoked in entropics creates a dynamic and ultimately creative relationship to phenomena that appear to humans as decay and slackening. Rather than concentrating on individual agential or community decline, both can be experienced as part of the energy exchanges constantly at work in interweaving organic and inorganic levels. Lingering in those moments of decay and dissolution (instead of denying them) shows the new bursting forth from the old, bringing to the foreground the fundamental truth of *change*. The world is of a web of materialities actively working and being worked upon. Agency is distributed across multiple entities and forces. Through this lens, what may appear as thriving in one system is actually diminishment in another and vice versa. Regardless, wonder can be found in the interconnectedness of energies and systems and through attunement to the various material assemblages that make up the world. Once done, the emphasis becomes less about human praise for achievement and blame for failure, and more about how to work within, rather than against the inevitable dissipation of limited resources.

For example, the energy disaster that affected the state of Texas in February of 2021 brought to light the multiple human and nonhuman forces at work in daily life. As temperatures plummeted due to a winter storm, the electrical grid crashed. Blame for the power collapse ranged from the state's failure to invest in winterizing pipelines and wind turbines, to the over-reliance on fossil fuels, to the fact that the power grid in Texas is not shared with neighboring states that could provide energy during times of emergency.[21] While not all of the hypotheses were equally reasonable, the event brought to light the various interlocking and interweaving systems that compose the amorphous entity, the "energy grid." Blame can certainly be attributed to individual agents who failed to look after the well-being of Texans, but it is also clear that the problem is far larger than can easily be attributed to individuals since weather, electricity, politics, and matter dynamically bleed into each other.

Bennett takes up a similar incident, with the 2003 Northeast power blackout that affected fifty million people, to show how one might think an event on multiple registers according to distributive agency. Similar to the 2021 Texas power failure, the 2003 blackout spanned across human and nonhuman registers, revealing complex, unpredictable, and unstable assemblages. For Bennett, bodies as assemblages means

> ad hoc groupings of diverse elements, of vibrant materials of all sorts. Assemblages are living, throbbing confederations that are able to function despite the persistent presence of energies that confound them from within. They have uneven topographies, because some of the points at which the various affects and bodies cross paths are more heavily trafficked than others, and so power is not distributed equally across its surface.[22]

Bennett hypothesizes that assemblages allow us to conceive materiality as a connection of heterogeneous yet interactive components. In the case of the 2003 blackout, she describes the electrical power grid as in some senses bounded but in other ways not. While technically created by human beings for the purposes of human power usage (and thus involving political, economic, and environmental factors directly produced by people), the grid comprises numerous nonhuman elements: electrons, trees, wind, and so on. The vital materialist considers the electrical grid as "a volatile mix of coal, sweat, electromagnetic fields, computer programs, electron streams, profit motives, heat, lifestyles, nuclear fuel, plastic, fantasies of mastery, static, legislation, water, economic theory, wire, and wood," among many other actants.[23] The North American blackout can be seen through all of these overlapping registers. True, there was a clear systemic breakdown—the electrical grid as a power-generating system succumbed to the inevitability of entropic decline. From Bennett's position, this event should not be understood as solely the result of human failure. To interpret this breakdown as simply the result of greed and mismanagement misses the untold nonhuman agents that participated in the collapse:

> There is not so much a doer (an agent) behind the deed (the blackout) as a doing and an effecting by a human-nonhuman assemblage. This federation of actants is a creature that the concept of moral responsibility fits only loosely.[24]

Displacing agency and responsibility away from human decision-making exposes the ebbing and flowing of matter and energy within a heterogeneous landscape. It can, therefore, allow for a much more creative way to think through energy collection, use, lessening, and waste. Additionally, decentering agency minimizes devastation insofar as it encourages a multiperspectival approach to investigating energy transformation instead of a dangerously reductive one. For a thing-power materialist like Bennett, the place in which we live "is a dynamic flow of matter-energy that tends to settle into various bodies, bodies that often join forces, make connections, form alliances."[25] The ecological hope lies in divesting humanity from shortsightedness by opening it up to the *"energetic forces* that course through humans and cultures without being exhausted by them."[26] As a result, her work focuses on the *increase* of power between the human and nonhuman, rather than a curtailment of them.

Similarly, entropic systems are not to be conceived as simply exhausting themselves in a downward death spiral, but rather as diverse arrangements borrowing energies from each other in their circuitous, spiraling transformations. Borders are constantly under negotiation in such formulations. Like Bennett, Barbara Ehrenreich also encourages us to think in a specifically inhuman manner. In *Natural Causes: An Epidemic of Wellness, the Certainty of Dying, and Killing Ourselves to Live Longer*, Ehrenreich talks about how the natural world has been stripped of agency since the mid-seventeenth century. The elevation of efficient causality and the diminution (and ultimate extinction) of final causality has removed a significant, essential component of what any given thing *is*. Just as Bennett's materialism criticizes anthropocentric prejudice, so Ehrenreich lambastes the hyper-prioritization of human agency over everything else. The resulting conception of nature "as a passive, ultimately inert mechanism was a mistake, and perhaps the biggest one humans ever made."[27] Ehrenreich's characterization of the tragic error of conceiving of nature as passive matter recalls the way Hegel earlier formulated matter in nature as having its center outside of itself. As seen in chapter 3, such a rendering leads directly to the notion that the only way to salvage exhausted nature is to demand its sacrifice to divine and human spirituality, which is not so decentered. Reducing the natural world to passive stuff promotes agency as something reserved for the select spiritual few and results in devastating world depletion. "Agency," in other words, becomes synonymous with self-conscious, rational decision-making, and "world," as Heidegger earlier suggests, becomes a repository of resources to be used and exploited.

However, agency spans far beyond self-conscious human beings. By way of example, Ehrenreich denies that cells, viruses, or particles have sentience, yet maintains that "what they possess is *agency*, or the ability to initiate an action."[28] Certain cells, such as macrophages, are not acting according to the telos of human life, but rather following their own goals, even as their activity is in direct contact with animal bodies. In this model, agency does not require self-consciousness or even organic structure. Akin to Bennett's vital materialism, agency simply becomes the intrinsic ability to act in the world; it "is not concentrated in humans or their gods or favorite animals. It is dispersed throughout the universe, right down to the smallest imaginable scale."[29] Viruses, atoms, and electrons act without consciousness, following their own paths and effecting the world directly and impactfully. Thus, to conceive of oneself as a being in the world means taking into account the ways that *all* life and matter are busy going about doing their own things, intersecting with human goals, but rarely, if at all, actually concerned with them. The *entrepic* entreats us to still show care and reverence even for these nonhuman entities because our worlds constantly overlap and intermingle. Our world is in fact multiple worlds. The onus is upon us to care about them because they traverse our own at every minute. Reverence must be extended not only to humanity but to manifold registers of material existence because that *is* human reality.

Bennett and Ehrenreich are more interested in expanding, or better, challenging dominant conceptions of moral agency by considering the vast and nebulous beings that form and break apart and have motivations of their own. These entities don't necessarily align with humanity, and in fact are often directly antagonistic to it. For both Bennett and Ehrenreich, the human is much smaller and much larger than the strict borders of the body, family, home, or society. The constant dances of energy and activity extending from voracious black holes to blinking quarks paint a picture of a universe that defies boundaries as much as it creates them. In this context, entropy's unidirectionality points to energies that are not infinitely self-sustaining, but only temporarily borrowing from each other. Yet, it also illuminates how breakdown and decay show the new bursting forth from the old. On the way toward cosmic heat death, birth and beauty continually emerge and dynamically shape worlds. What often appears to us as loss is most certainly the birth of countless material excesses.

While these observations do not directly give rise to an ethics or ecology, they inform the quest to confront the modern condition on the human scale. Ehrenreich writes, "the natural world is not dead, but swarming with activity, sometimes perhaps even agency and intentionality."[30] Vitality is omnipresent. Because the universe "is restless, quivering, and juddering, from its vast vacant patches to its tiniest crevices,"[31] humanity must disabuse itself of the bloated sense of self-importance and challenge customary notions of autonomy and responsibility. I now move to explore in more detail how assemblages bring to light various intersections of power and matter that yield sites of creation and novelty. Turning to Smithson, for whom entropy as creation maintains a primary focus, furthers these considerations.

ROBERT SMITHSON'S MATERIALITY

Bennett's vital materialism highlights the ways that matter is just as active (or vastly more so) in shaping the world as is human agency. Some agents know better than others that human activity does not simply form passive matter. Bennett notes that "artisans (and mechanics, cooks, builders, cleaners, and anyone else intimate with things) encounter a creative materiality with incipient tendencies and propensities, which are variably enacted depending on other forces, affects, or bodies with which they come into close contact."[32] Among other people who work with the various emergent properties of things, artists are closely familiar with the kind of creative materiality that dissolves borders in thinking and production. Jeffers, for example, was not only a poet but a stonemason who often venerates the magic of the inhumanity of rock.

Another poet of matter, Smithson, embodies the notion of creative materiality. Much of Smithson's art uses assemblages of glass, rock, and metal in various states of transition to foreground rather than mask entropy. His writings and art never shy away from the most insidious and lethal products of human achievement. In fact, many of his most important works can only be understood as a direct engagement with matter and waste. He creates experiences that intentionally evoke the kind of naive realism described by Bennett. Manipulating and displacing rocks, sand, glass, metal, water, and dirt reveals what is usually hidden in artistic production: the effects of time and decay on all matter. His fascination with what Bennett calls assemblages (such as abandoned mines, commercial wastelands, and the polluted and forgotten dumping grounds of technological accomplishment) brings Smithson to artistic places not usually seen as fertile, let alone aesthetically valuable.[33]

In his incredibly prolific, but brief writing career, Smithson wrote a number of articles about his approaches to and understanding of artistic creation. In his first published piece, "Entropy and the New Monuments," he demarcates a group of artists, who he clearly identifies as workers of a "new kind of monumentality," as they are those who celebrate

> what the physicist calls "entropy" or "energy-drain." They bring to mind the Ice Age rather than the Golden Age, and would most likely confirm Vladimir Nabokov's observation that, "The future is but the obsolete in reverse." In a rather round-about way, many of the artists have provided a *visible analog for the Second Law of Thermodynamics*, which extrapolates the range of entropy by telling us that energy is more easily lost than obtained, and that in the ultimate future the whole universe will burn out and be transformed into an all-encompassing sameness.[34]

While bringing the entropy law into visibility may not be an obvious choice for aesthetic celebration, Smithson scraps the idea that only timeless and ideal presentations of the natural world are worthy of artistic treatment. In fact, art that conceals the machinations of time and decay is in some senses *less* interesting and even *more* dangerous than art that makes these forces visible. The everyday experiences of false idealism conceal the vibrant transformations of entropic change:

Only commodities can afford such illusionistic values; for instance, soap is 99 $^{44/100}$% pure, beer has more spirit in it, and dog food is ideal; all and all this means such values are worthless. As the cloying effect of such "values" wears off, one perceives the "facts" of the outer edge, the flat surface, the banal, the empty, the cool blank after blank; in other words, that infinitesimal condition known as entropy.[35]

Rather than eliding the banality and dullness of modern architecture and commercial products composed of high-entropy materials, the artists whose media are plastic, fluorescent bulbs, sheet aluminum, and Formica embrace the desolation and nullification of modernity because it affords the real possibility of stripping away the veil of idealism: a veil that necessarily perverts relationships to time by refuting the persistent workings of entropy.

Many entropic artworks appear as if somehow produced by (perhaps even as the discarded byproducts of) anonymous workings of technology and industry. Instead of the future tending toward "progress," the new monumentalists show the future as tedious repetitions of the same: labor, consumption, and interpersonal relationships, which all become interchangeable and identical. This sameness emerges in the repetitious shapes (lines, blocks, holes, cones) and materials (plastic, metal, rocks, dirt) used in much of the art. This artist collective brings to light the tendency toward entropic homogenization and ties it to the destruction of consumer capitalism. Manifesting the machinations of the entropy law as leading to heat death helps to foreground uniquely human destructive social and cultural practices. This approach provides a way to contemplate how human beings are actively producing an inhospitable future. Yet, the artworks of the new monumentalists embrace the entropic movement toward homogenization with a sense of irony rather than despair.[36]

Smithson offers the Union Carbide building as an example of "architectural entropy." "If ever there was an example of action in entropy," he writes, "this is it. The action is frozen into an array of plastic and neon, and enhanced by the sound of Muzak playing in the background."[37] Such architecture, abounding in the contemporary landscape of mass-produced repetitions of cheap, uninspiring dwellings, works in a bizarre framework of aesthetic idealization. Cookie-cutter architecture is not a perfection of a form, but rather the entropic tendency toward homogeneity writ large. Much of the mono-architecture of the past (and current) century enacts material repetition. These dwellings, "or slurbs, urban sprawl, and the infinite number of housing developments of the postwar boom have contributed to the architecture of entropy."[38] Smithson is far less interested in the existential toll such spaces have on the collective psyche than he is in the way that artists of his loose collective take these banalities and turn them into artworks. Yet, the very sites of decay, breakdown, pollution, and waste (while clearly problematic for ethical, political, and biological concerns) also express what Bennett calls "an emergent causality."[39] While not directly worried about ethical or ecological matters (often, in fact, rejecting those concerns), Smithson's art gives form to the emergent causality of the nonhuman world which, in turn, provides the opportunity to ask ethical and ecological questions in different ways.

Matter does what it does regardless of human designs for mastery and control. The aforementioned power failures illustrate the intersecting and overlapping world of human and nonhuman actants. Smithson also explores the phenomenon of an electrical blackout but from a different orientation. He speaks of a kind of "cosmic joy" that erupted following a massive blackout in the Northeast in 1965, which, "far from creating a mood of dread [. . .] created a mood of euphoria."[40] It might be tempting to interpret this euphoria as only the ecstasy of our own demise: the perverse pleasure of seeing the end and welcoming it. And certainly, entropism in art allows us to experience the joy in destruction, even if that destruction is our own. Smithson talks about the coupling of waste and enjoyment and acknowledges that "there's a certain kind of pleasure principle that comes out of a preoccupation with waste," insofar as the more luxuries we have, the more waste we produce.[41] Pleasure comes not only from the possession of and enjoyment in goods that use low entropy fuel in their production but also in the high-entropy waste that their fabrication and consumption create. We have to admit the unique kind of (certainly manufactured) pleasure that comes from producing waste if we are to be honest about how to confront its accelerating, irrecuperable accumulation. This pleasure is necessarily tied up in disrespect and disdain rather than grounded in an *entrepic* turning toward and reverence for the fragility of the world.

Smithson's art foregrounds waste because he believes entropy discloses the inevitable movement toward a wasteland, which simply presents a realistic state of affairs.[42] He finds that the languages of environmentalism, recycling, and energy conservation are too often disingenuous. Although every bit as true today, he points to the fact that these movements often miss an underlying truth: entropy. Smithson's tour of the Passaic in the 1960s, with its vast badlands of technological and environmental waste, causes him to muse as to whether the degraded areas of twentieth-century New Jersey have replaced Rome as the "Eternal City."[43] Sites filled with urban blight perform material irreversibility. No matter how much energy pours into restoring an earlier state of affairs, this goal remains forever unattainable. To illustrate, Smithson offers a simple entropic thought experiment:

> Picture in your mind's eye the sand box divided in half with black sand on one side and white sand on the other. We take a child and have him run hundreds

of times clockwise in the box until the sand gets mixed and begins to turn grey; after that we have him run anti-clockwise, but the result will not be a restoration of the original division but a greater degree of greyness and an increase of entropy.[44]

Smithson's thought experiment illustrates entropy's movement. Once things become mixed up, they cannot be put back into their original order without the input of additional energy from without. In this case, the sandbox would require a perfect machine, akin to Maxwell's Demon, to sort out the millions of grains of white and black sand. Order, particularly from the human perspective, always tends toward disorder, and any environmentalism that omits this fact will exacerbate, rather than alleviate, the dire problems it seeks to address.

More importantly, Smithson emphasizes the movement of entropy toward homogenization as both an artistic and a political point. Lévi-Strauss' anthropological observations of cultures moving toward a great flattening is not unlike the industrial wastelands Smithson chooses to highlight. Only, whereas Lévi-Strauss expresses the profound existential sadness produced by modern technology and its leveling tendencies, Smithson works this into an artistic entropics at once discomforting and revelatory of human and inhuman exchanges. He acknowledges the profundity of Lévi-Strauss' insight, as well as gesturing beyond the enticement of hopelessness:

> Lévi-Strauss suggested that they change the word anthropology to entropology, meaning highly developed structures in a state of disintegration. I think that's part of the attraction of people going to visit obsolete civilizations. They get a gratification from the collapse of these things.[45]

What draws us to ruins is in part historical interest (or perhaps obligatory tourism) but also the fascination of seeing what was once great and self-confident in its supposed permanence, reduced to rubble and dust. The distinct pleasure associated with the destruction can smack of cruelty but can also acknowledge that destruction is necessary for life. This is why Smithson advocates an artistic collaboration with entropy:

> Unlike Buckminster Fuller, *I'm interested in collaborating with entropy*. Some day I would like to compile all the different entropies. All the classifications would lose their grids. Lévi-Strauss had a good insight; he suggested we change the study of anthropology into "entropology." It would be a study that devotes itself to the process of disintegration in highly developed structures. *After all, wreckage is often more interesting than structure.* . . . Utopian saviors we can do without.[46]

Directly rejecting utopian aesthetics, Smithson's decision to use technologically blighted locations forms the ground of Non-Sites, those works that emphasize physicality and the disruption of matter.[47] The artworks transport materials (rocks, sand, dirt, concrete) from industrial locations into museum spaces (bounding them with mirrors, boxes, or crates, or depositing them in piles on the museum floor) simultaneously drawing the amorphous landscape into a relationship with the restricted space around a piece. His choice of a site (such as a quarry or abandoned mine, usually indicated by a map in the museum adjacent to the piles) foregrounds otherwise unproblematized industrial waste and degraded landscapes. Non-Sites emerge out of the ruined physical world, highlighting the materiality (rather than ideality) of art and emphasizing the fact that the work will necessarily return to the rubble out of which it came.

Most human beings in the Western tradition have a delusional commitment to the notion of progress, so much so that contrary evidence is summarily abandoned, ignored, or denied. The museum often contributes to this artificial narrative of human progress winning the war against time. Smithson's Non-Sites challenge this progress-based narrative by fixing the materials in the space of the museum, causing a simultaneous disruption of both the sharp enclosure of the gallery and the unrestrained site location. Thus disoriented, the spectator is carried back and forth between the categories of inside/outside, progress/regress, and bounded/unbounded, provoking experiences of constant flux:

> The bins of containers of my *Non-Sites* gather in the fragments that are experienced in the physical abyss of raw matter. The tools of technology become a part of the Earth's geology as they sink back into their original state. Machines like dinosaurs must return to dust or rust. One might say a "de-architecturing" takes place before the artist sets his limits outside the studio or the room.[48]

The emergent material vitality becomes the central focus of bins of rocks, sand, and glass. No longer inert, they vibrate in connection with the museum, the spectators, and the photos and written descriptions. Possibility, rather than pessimism, emerges in this space specifically honed to the forces of materiality, waste, and entropy.

As Smithson's sand mixing example above illustrates entropics on an intellectual level, Non-Sites do so on an aesthetic level. He explains that the latter produces a confused orientation by rejecting clearly demarcated boundaries:

> The points of pick-up, or the points of collection tend to be scattered throughout the site, yet there's no possible way of defining those points. So if you go to the sites, there's no evidence other than the site, you're sort of thrown off

the nonsite. This is the coming together of those particular points. And those points tend to cover the landmasses so that, in a sense, all this terrain will be homogenized.[49]

Just as the industrial wastelands of discarded concrete, sand, runoff, and broken machinery have leveled the environments that preceded their creation, so Non-Sites disrupt rigid notions of "art" and "technology." Additionally, Non-Sites unsettle system boundaries. As the center of the piece resides neither in the museum piece, the map of the location from which the materials came, nor the actual site in which the materials were originally scattered, the system is inherently unbounded and amorphous, and thus not really closed. Smithson clarifies: "That's why it's entropic. . . . The information tends to obliterate itself so that there is obviously information there, but the information is so overwhelming in terms of its physicality that it tends to lose itself."[50] Importantly, Smithson takes himself as an artist out of the picture, denying that he is doing the scattering. Rather, the scattering has already occurred, and he simply unveils it. This face of entropy is the force that he calls the "one dominant theme that runs through everything," functioning not so much to induce social awareness, but spotlighting the inevitable natural occurrences ensnaring animate and inanimate matter.[51] Centering these forces in the work of art elevates them as something central to creation, rather than as its Mephistophelean threat.

Prioritizing geological over existential time, Smithson does not form the work as a self-conscious agent but rather inserts himself into an ongoing and largely uncontrollable rippling material event. He adheres to a kind of modified evolutionary entropism of geological movement wearing down and wearing out, ultimately rejecting teleology because there is nothing to indicate, and no reason even to desire, the overcoming of time or an idealized future.[52] The entropic sense of time that permeates Smithson's works and writings reorients perspective away from the fleetingness of human beings and toward the material, capturing grand scales of the geologic and crystalline. Jennifer L. Roberts explains that,

> Smithson's crystalline model of time disregards linear, progressive, or triumphalist models by imagining time as an opaque encrustation around a fault or fracture. Here time has no connection to an animate origin or center; it begins with a "dislocation" and merely accumulates from without. Time does not "pass" or "fly," it builds up as a material sediment that remains on hand indefinitely.[53]

Existential time passes, stretching and compacting according to specific projects of the lives in question. But this is not the only way that time *happens*. Geological and crystalline time shows human temporality as only an inconsequential ripple in a stream without end or beginning, which can be seen as any or no time at all.[54]

Displaying an uneasy balance between these two radically different temporalities (existential and geological), one of the first scenes of his eponymous *Spiral Jetty* film, shows torn bits of maps fluttering down the side of a hill. Joining the purposeful and human with the material and geological, the falling bits of maps speak to an inevitable decline. Ultimately, nothing is safe from the predations of the second law, but this does not produce a univocal meaning.[55] Printed matter comprises various concretions of human experience. The fixity of the printed page, the map, the diagram, and so on grant an illusory sense of solidity and realness. The map grounds space, the newspaper society, and the diagram rationality. But the sheer act of tearing them into pieces and watching them tumble down a hill, pulled by the forces of gravity and reduced to unusable information, reveals the deception at work in rational attempts at unifying meaning. All attempts at grounding will be entropically ungrounded.

The illusion of fixity is even more obvious in digital media which obfuscate materiality even further. While digital and digitized truths may more readily expose ceaseless transformation, the very real materiality that allows them to function at all is eclipsed. And yet, the slow server, the dropped signal, and the malfunctioning SIM card all produce an anxiety deeply wedded to entropics. At those moments, we catch glimpses of how much energy is required to maintain the fantasy of reliability and progress, the delusion that it can be interminably maintained, and the cost indefinitely deferred. Focusing on the *entrepic* turning, these finite and precious resources should be attended to rather than carelessly obliterated. Otherwise, it's merely a race to total and irreversible depletion.

In one of the final scenes in the *Spiral Jetty* film, the spectator moves through a red-filtered view of the Hall of Late Dinosaurs in the American Museum of Natural History. Ominous sounds appear to echo from the room filled with dinosaur remains but completely absent human life. One of the more remarkable disjunctions produced by this particular scene is the way the glass cases and wall illustrations attempt to capture the "facts" about the dinosaurs. Human constructs look puny compared to the dead husks of the great lizards and the obvious truths they reveal: no life is permanent, no system can withstand change, destruction is inevitable. "These fragments of a timeless geology laugh without mirth at the time-filled hopes of ecology."[56] As the camera pans over the dinosaur remains Smithson's voice, reading from Samuel Beckett's, *The Unnamable*, emerges:

> Nothing has ever changed since I have been here. But I dare not infer from this that nothing ever will change. Let us try and see where these considerations

lead. I have been here, ever since I began to be, my appearances elsewhere having been put in by other parties. All has proceeded, all this time, in the utmost calm, in the most perfect order apart from one or two manifestations the meaning of which escapes me. No, it is not just that their meaning escapes me, my own escapes me just as much. Here all things, no, I shall not say it, being unable to. I owe my existence to no one: these faint fires are not of those that illuminate or burn. Going nowhere, coming from nowhere.[57]

Beginning in entropy and ending in entropy. The journey through the Hall of Dinosaurs shows death as absolute rest. The skeletal remains appear to be a timeless and stable eye of a fluctuating hurricane. However, Beckett's words portray the so-called order as unnamable, inaccessible, and wholly inhuman. Ultimately, all is matter and flux, and the human is merely a wasteful byproduct, just like the oil of the once-thriving dinosaurs roaming the earth now captured in bones behind museum glass.

The shift away from the human, toward the Pleistocene, and ultimately toward the inorganic impacts not only temporality but also morality. Waste is a necessary byproduct of entropic decay. While garbage can never be fully recycled, it is madness to exponentially hasten its production. What is needed is a new *entrepic* perspective. Entropic art refuses to lament the workings of change and decay in the material world and instead celebrates these as vital, cosmic forces. I see this as a starting point for turning toward the *entrepic* because this kind of art makes visible and beautiful what is otherwise hidden and scorned. When waste and matter become perceptually dominant, we are called upon to notice and care about them. Bennett's vital materialism and Smithson's entropic art alters the locus of morality in such a way that human thinkers and spectators are thrown into a productive disturbance of boundaries and borders, of matter and subjectivity. Bennett and Ehrenreich ask us to heed the multiple intersecting and vibrating materialities that make purely human responsibility impossible. Smithson shifts away from existential time to the material temporality of geology and crystals, the time of astral formations and planetary death. While they trouble human subjectivity, these thinkers do not encourage avoidance of responsibility for environmental and social decay. Rather, they show the lie behind the wildly fantastic idea that any single person, group, or government, can solve it. The release from humanity's grand self-importance toward a humbler orientation is not meant to produce passivity or disassociation but rather to expose new engagements with the material world. With this prospect, I turn to the final chapter in order to explore the life and existence-affirming occasions created through *entropic* philosophy and the celebration of flux, transformation, and life.

NOTES

1. J. D. Ballard, *High Rise* (New York: W. W. Norton & Company, 2012), 176.
2. Freud, *Pleasure Principle*, 70.
3. Erik Reece explains that for Jeffers, inhumanism means "simply to develop an ethos that reached beyond man as the measure of all things. Inhumanism entailed 'the rejection of human solipsism and recognition of the transhuman magnificence.'" Erik Reece, "Bright Power, Dark Peace," *Harper's Magazine*, September 2020, 55.
4. Robinson Jeffers, "November Surf" in *The Norton Anthology of Poetry*, ed. Arthur M. Eastman (New York: W. W. Norton & Company, 1970), 991.
5. Ibid.
6. Meisel, *Chaos Imagined*, 385.
7. Martin Heidegger, *The Question Concerning Technology and Other Essays*, trans. William Lovitt (New York, Harper & Row, 1977), 6.
8. Ibid, 7.
9. Georgescu-Roegen, *Entropy Law*, 277.
10. Ibid, 6.
11. Ibid.
12. Ibid, 280.
13. To see how the production of garbage is linked to global debt, see Nathan Gorelick, "The Real (of) Debt: Notes Toward and Ethics of Trash," *Continental Thought and Theory: A Journal of Intellectual Freedom* 1, no. 2 (2017): 490–517.
14. Inaction is in part caused by what Terranova and Parisi observe: "Entropy is energy which cannot be reabsorbed back into the industrial social machine; it is energy which becomes a threat to the disciplinary order once it is pushed outside its walls. Heat-death was not just the end of the universe in a far, far future; it was the necessary tendency of industrial capitalism." Terranova and Parisi, "Emergence and Control." This is ultimately why they criticize the thermodynamic model since it encourages social orders built upon such principles to exhaust themselves. Although this is accurate, it is too facile to simply reject it and instead advocate for a Deluezian-Spinozistic one built upon affect and turbulence because bodies deteriorate according to entropy, no matter how porous and deterritorialized their boundaries may be.
15. Robert Biel, *The Entropy of Capitalism* (Chicago: Haymarket Books, 2012), 22.
16. Giles Deleuze and Félix Guattari explain that "an assemblage is precisely this increase in the dimensions of a multiplicity that necessarily changes in nature as it expands its connections. There are no points or positions in a rhizome, such as those found in a structure, tree, or root. There are only lines." Gilles Deluze and Félix Guattari, *A Thousand Plateaus: Capitalism and Schizophrenia,* trans. Brian Massumi (Minneapolis: Minnesota University Press, 1987), 8.
17. Matter and materialism have a far broader history to which any one chapter can do justice. There are many contemporary theorists of speculative realism and object-oriented ontology that orbit this discussion but are not addressed directly. One helpful source for thinking of matter as other than thought can be found in Richard A.

Lee Jr., *The Thought of Matter: Materialism, Conceptuality, and the Transcendence of Immanence* (London: Rowman & Littlefield International, 2016).

18. Jane Bennett, *Vibrant Matter: A Political Ecology of Things* (Durham: Duke University Press, 2010), 14. Bennett's theory is related to Theodor Adorno's philosophy of nonidentity, insofar as both frameworks emphasize attentiveness to what is outside the human but in which the human is intertwined. Bennett's work on vital materialism is also related to Deleuze and Guattari's idea of nomadism in *A Thousand Plateaus*.

Elsewhere, Bennett explores the notion Henri Bergson's *élan vital* and the notion of *entelechy* in Hans Driesch to elaborate her conception of vital materialism. "A Vitalist Stopover on the Way to New Materialism," in *New Materialisms: Ontology, Agency, and Politics*, eds. Diana Coole and Samantha Frost (Durham: Duke University Press, 2010).

19. Bennett explains that "thing-power materialism is a speculative onto-story, a rather presumptuous attempt to depict the nonhumanity that flows around but also through humans." Jane Bennett, "The Force of Things: Steps toward an Ecology of Matter," *Political Theory* 32, no. 3 (2004): 349. Bennett belongs to the new materialists who emphasize how "materiality is always something more than 'mere' matter: an excess, force, vitality, relationality, or difference that renders matter active, self-creative, productive, unpredictable." Diana Coole and Samantha Frost, "Introducing New Materialisms" in *New Materialisms: Ontology, Agency, and Politics*, eds. Diana Coole and Samantha Frost (Durham: Duke University Press, 2010), 9.

20. Bennett, "Force of Things," 351.

21. See, Dionne Searcey, "No, Wind Farms Aren't the Main Cause of the Texas Blackouts." *The New York Times*, February 2, 2021, https://www.nytimes.com/2021/02/17/climate/texas-blackouts-disinformation.html. Also see, Reuters Staff, *Reuters*, "Fact Check: the causes for Texas' Blackout go Well Beyond Wind Turbines." February, 19 2021, https://www.reuters.com/article/uk-factcheck-texas-wind-turbines-explain/fact-check-the-causes-for-texas-blackout-go-well-beyond-wind-turbines-idUSKBN2AJ2EI.

22. Bennett, "Vitalist Stopover," 24.

23. Ibid, 25.

24. Ibid, 28.

25. Bennett, "Force of Things," 365.

26. Ibid, 367. Diana Coole uses Maurice Merleau-Ponty to explore a similar notion of matter. Dianna Coole, "The Inertia of Matter and the Generativity of Flesh," in *New Materialisms: Ontology, Agency, and Politics*, eds. Dianna Coole and Samantha Frost (Durham: Duke University Press, 2010), 92.

27. Ehrenreich, *Natural Causes*, 160. See also, Coole and Frost, "New Materialisms," 10–11.

28. Ehrenreich, *Natural Causes*, 158.

29. Ibid, 160.

30. Ibid, 202.

31. Ibid, 203.

32. Bennett, "Vitalist Stopover," 56. These incipient properties of matter indicate the incredible movement and dynamism within every bit of matter. Bennett emphasizes, in line with Deleuze and Guattari, that the "aim is here to rattle the adamantine chain that has bound materiality to inert substance and that has placed the organic across a chasm from the inorganic. The aim is to articulate the elusive idea of a materiality that is *itself* heterogeneous, itself a differential of intensities, itself *a* life. In this strange *vital* materialism, there is no point of pure stillness, no indivisible atom that is not itself aquiver with virtual force." Ibid, 57.

33. Northern New Jersey made a strong impression on Smithson. As Jack Flam explains, "the very shoddiness of the New Jersey suburbs seemed to be a tangible embodiment of the entropic condition, constantly falling apart at the same time that it was in the process of being rebuilt." Jack Flam, "Introduction: Reading Robert Smithson," in *Robert Smithson: The Collected Writings* (Berkeley: University of California Press, 1996), xxi.

34. Robert Smithson, "Entropy and the New Monuments, 1966," in *Robert Smithson: The Collected Writings*, ed. Jack Flam (Berkeley: University of California Press, 1996), 11. The twentieth-century artists such as Smithson, Sol Le Witt, Dan Flavin, Donald Judd, and other entropically minded creators made visible manifestations of the movement toward homogenization, sameness, and loss.

35. Ibid, 13. Artists continue to use the entropic as inspiration for work. See, for example, Iván Navarro's *Molotov Cocktail Nostalgia* (2001), Simon Starling's *Tabernas Desert Run* (2004), Alora & Calzadilla's *Puerto Rican Light* (2003), Daniel Roth's *Cabrini Green Forest* (2004). Francesco Manacorda, "Entropology: Monuments to Closed Systems." *Flash Art* (2005): 76–79.

36. For more on how irony functions in Smithson's art, see Shannon M. Mussett, "Irony and the Work of Art: Hegelian Legacies in Robert Smithson," *Evental Aesthetics* 1, no. 1 (2012): 45–73.

37. Smithson, "New Monuments," 12.

38. Ibid, 13. Peter Lloyd Jones clarifies that for Smithson, "the terminal state of maximum entropy in a closed system has been taken as a metaphor for the boredom and enervation of affluent American life." Peter Lloyd Jones, "Some Thoughts on Rudolf Arnheim's Book 'Entropy and Art,'" *Leonardo* 6 (1973): 33.

39. Bennett, "Vitalist Stopover," 59.

40. Smithson, "New Monuments," 11.

41. Robert Smithson, interview by Alison Sky, "Entropy Made Visible (1973)," in *Robert Smithson: The Collected Writings*, ed. Jack Flam (Berkeley: University of California Press, 1996), 303.

42. Robert Smithson, "Four Conversations Between Dennis Wheeler and Robert Smithson (1969–1970)," ed. Eva Schmidt, in *Robert Smithson: The Collected Writings*, ed. Jack Flam (Berkeley: University of California Press, 1996), 230. Smithson mentions Marcel Duchamp, Buckminster Fuller, and Norbert Weiner as visionaries of entropy. Smithson, "Made Visible," 301.

43. Robert Smithson, "A Tour of the Monuments of Passaic, New Jersey, 1967," in *Robert Smithson: The Collected Writings*, ed. Jack Flam (Berkeley: University of California Press, 1996), 74.

44. Ibid.

45. Robert Smithson, interview by Gianna Pettena, "Conversation in Salt Lake City (January 1972)," in *Robert Smithson: The Collected Writings*, ed. Jack Flam (Berkeley: University of California Press, 1996), 299.

46. Robert Smithson, interview by Gregoire Müller, "The Earth, Subject to Cataclysms, is a Cruel Master' (1971)," in *Robert Smithson: The Collected Writings*, ed. Jack Flam (Berkeley: University of California Press, 1996), 256–257 (italics my own). This leads Francesco Manacorda to argue that of all the artistic positions that engage destruction, "the most extreme position remains the one that is attracted to entropy, verging on an appeal for decay, which has its main apologist in Robert Smithson." Manacorda, "Entropology," 77.

47. The site is "the physical, raw reality—the earth or the ground that we are really not aware of when we are in an interior room or studio" and the indoor Non-Site "is an abstract container." Robert Smithson, "Frederick Law Olmsted and the Dialectical Landscape, 1973," in *Robert Smithson: The Collected Writings*, ed. Jack Flam (Berkeley: University of California Press, 1996), 178. The Non-Site "contains the disruption of the site. The container is in a sense a fragment of itself, something that could be called a three-dimensional map. Without appeal to 'gestalts' or 'anti-form,' it actually exists as a fragment of a greater fragmentation." Smithson, "Sedimentation of Mind," 111.

48. Ibid, 104.

49. Smithson, "Four Conversations," 218.

50. Ibid, 219. See also, Smithson, "New Monuments," 17–18. His choice of sites, these "low profile landscapes, the quarry or the mining area which we call an entropic landscape, a kind of backwater or fringe area," has everything to do with the movement toward dedifferentiation and breakdown. Robert Smithson, interview by Paul Cummings, "Interview with Robert Smithson for the Archives of American Art, 1972," in *Robert Smithson: The Collected Writings*, ed. Jack Flam (Berkeley: University of California Press, 1996), 293.

51. Smithson, "Archives," Ibid.

52. Smithson explains that "if we consider the earth in terms of geologic time we end up with what we call fluvial entropy. Geology has its entropy too where everything is gradually wearing down." Smithson, "Made Visible," 303.

53. Jennifer L. Roberts, "The Taste of Time: Salt and Spiral Jetty," in *Robert Smithson*, eds. Eugenie Tsai with Cornelia Butler (Berkeley: University of California Press, 2004), 98.

54. This hearkens to Heraclitus' time, where from a universal temporal perspective, "changing it rests." Heraclitus, *Presocratics Reader*, Fr. B84a.

55. Smithson explains that these scenes show how "'printed matter' plays an entropic role. Maps, charts, advertisements, art books, science books, money, architectural plans, math books, graphs, diagrams, newspapers, comics, booklets and pamphlets from industrial companies are all treated the same." Smithson, "New Monuments," 18.

56. Robert Smithson, "The Spiral Jetty, 1972," in *Robert Smithson: The Collected Writings*, ed. Jack Flam (Berkeley: University of California Press, 1996), 152.

57. Robert Smithson, *Spiral Jetty*, directed by Robert Smithson (New York: VAGA at ARS, 1970), 16-mm film on video.

Chapter 7

Destruction and the Joy of Creation

> Disintegration and decay are, he knew, predicates of physical things indicating simply that they have taken off one form and put on another, as when water turns to air, or air to water, or when plants become soil or ashes, or soil becomes a plant. This is the meaning of breakdown.
>
> Ibn Tufayl, *Hayy Ibn Yaqzan*[1]

> This is the sadness clinging to all finite life, and if in God, too, there is a condition which is at least relatively independent, then within him there is a well of sadness, which, however, never comes to actuality, but serves only for the eternal joy of overcoming.
>
> J. F. W. Schelling, "On the Essence of Human Freedom"[2]

Goethe's *Faust* paints a singular picture of evil. The main antagonist, Mephistopheles, has a rather lackadaisical approach to being a devil. When Faust asks his name, Mephistopheles is evasive. He does, however, reveal that he is a "part of that force which would do evil evermore, and yet creates the good,"[3] clarifying that he is the "spirit that negates."[4] The devil introduces himself as negative but necessary to the good. He is a share of darkness that creates light and thus is, as Faust names him, "a peculiar son of chaos."[5] While Mephistopheles is only an agent of evil, a servant of darkness, he is clearly the most visible and active one.

Despite the tragic undoing of Faust by his own hands, his despoiled soul is saved in the end. While this matters significantly in his redemption arc, Faust's salvation pales in comparison to Mephistopheles's celebration of corruption. The uniqueness of Goethe's devil lies in the fact that he is unnervingly charming. He initially appears on the stage like a dog (a poodle nonetheless) and transforms into something as nonthreatening and almost disappointing as a traveling scholar. These disguises disarm Mephistopheles' malevolent threat. Dressed as a dandy, speaking glibly, and making light of the seriousness of the soul-sacrificing arrangement into which he enters with Faust, his allure is still undeniable and irresistible. He plays with an earnest student by mocking philosophy and logic, encouraging instead the pursuit of sex. He toys with the drunken patrons of a Leipzig pub, and ruthlessly mocks the witches and animals that serve him. Mephistopheles thus presents sin and corruption (and the ruin they threaten) by simultaneously undermining their menace, transforming them into a playful spectacle. Darkness produces laughter and not only despair. The play captivates in part with the depiction of evil through humor, and in so doing, Goethe transmutes corruption into sublime comedy, providing a glimpse of affirmative ways to work within entropic thinking. What corrupts is not only necessary for goodness but, more importantly, for creation as such.

Eric Zencey observes that one of the noteworthy features of entropy as a modern root metaphor is that it is pessimistic, meaning that it "is a convenient shorthand for articulating a sense that things are running downhill, falling apart, getting worse."[6] While this book has so far explored many of the ways that this darker aspect of the entropic metaphor manifests, this chapter devotes itself to challenging this particularly enticing but ultimately cynical feature in a move away from the entropic and toward the *entrepic*. Recall that the Introduction to this book traced out the notion of the *entrepic*—the other, quieter sister of entropics found in Homer and Sophocles. *Entrepic* thinking conveys a turning toward the fragility of life in the face of death. The overwhelming evidence of decline demands a reorientation toward the world that involves respect for dwindling energy that keeps multiple human and nonhuman systems thriving. The entropy metaphor must shift away from pessimism and instead name more life-affirming possibilities. The task of thought and action needs nothing short of a total transformation away from resignation and the acceptance of the status quo.

Friedrich Nietzsche and Robert Smithson encourage precisely this kind of alternative worldview. Both respond to entropics by emphasizing creation out of destruction. Nietzsche's vision of the cosmos and his theory of the eternal return posit existence as non-teleological and entirely self-sustaining. Every moment is the beginning of creation and therefore pure potentiality. As explored in the previous chapter, Smithson's works highlight the processes of entropy, decentering subjectivity and ushering in new conceptions of time. His temporality celebrates the geologic and crystalline, thereby largely circumventing the anxiety of human time and instead highlighting aesthetic transformation. While coming at the riddle of entropics from different orientations, both Nietzsche and Smithson ultimately imagine powerful philosophies of time from within the movement of becoming. These unique formulations provide a glimpse into how entropics can yield novelty and, most importantly, life and existence-affirming joy.

NIETZSCHEAN ENTROPICS

I return one final time to Sophocles' *Oedipus at Colonus*, where the chorus offers an insight that will come to play a critical role in Nietzsche's *The Birth of Tragedy* (and ultimately, his philosophy as a whole). Noting that death is the final consummation of life, awaiting all who come into existence, the chorus in the tragedy proclaims: "Not to be born is best of all; when life is there, the second best to go hence where you came, with the best speed you may."[7] The lightness of youth inevitably gives way to the agonies of aging, so tragic wisdom encourages us to leave this life as quickly as possible since we cannot avoid having been born. As Goethe transforms evil into laughter, so Nietzsche translates this tragic insight into praise of the ancient Greeks. In the face of such potentially nihilistic wisdom, the Greeks affirm finite life with gods who intensify, rather than disdain it:

> Thus do the gods justify the life of man: they themselves live it—the only satisfactory theodicy! Existence under the bright sunshine of such gods is regarded as desirable in itself, and the real pain of Homeric men is caused by parting from it, especially by early parting: so that now, reversing the wisdom of Silenus, we might say of the Greeks that "to die soon is worst of all for them, the next worst—to die at all."[8]

Nietzsche explores how Greek religion in the tragic age reverses the negativistic kernel of entropic decline by showing how the gods live like magnified humans. The Olympians conquer the wisdom of Silenus insofar as they are divine beings praising and loving existence. This joy becomes a transformative mirror reflecting the need to respect, care for, and enjoy finite life. The Olympian gods represent an attitude of overcoming suffering through a celebration of it. Similarly for Nietzsche, Sophoclean tragedy, through an *entrepic* turn, praises the beauty of life despite suffering. I have suggested throughout this book that such care and joy can be achieved by turning attention to and respecting that which needs consideration, that which is vulnerable, that which comes into and passes out of existence. The *entrepic* transformation requires attentiveness and reverence for all life which fans out through a wide register of human and nonhuman manifestations. While it does not require attending to *everything* that lives (an impossible goal) it demands awareness that all systems are interconnected, and what one does affects more than just oneself.

In this spirit, Nietzsche's writings confront the irrefutable evidence of human stupidity and the tragic wisdom of mortality by affirming life and joy. There is no "solution" to the trials of living, but there is a way in which they can be sanctified by a kind of holy atheism. Rejecting the domination of the past and the stifling vice of monotheism in all of its forms, Nietzsche praises existence as an unstable flux, hailing destruction just as much as construction: "*My first solution: Dionysian wisdom.* Joy in the destruction of the most noble and at the sight of its progressive ruin: in reality joy in what is coming and lies in the future."[9] Nietzsche elevates destruction to the most profound delight. To welcome this, one must first of all jettison any notion of an absolute fixed and knowable origin or purpose of the world. Embracing radical historicism, Nietzsche believes in a vast and varying explosion of different tables of values in space and time. Fundamentally, whether in nature or culture, all creation involves destruction. "Whoever must be a creator always annihilates."[10] To ignore this cycle leads to a joyless, ahistorical, and monolithic vision of reality.

In "Nietzsche, Genealogy, History," Foucault provides an elegant exploration into Nietzsche's deployment of the critique of origin-hunting in morality. Origins—those elusive, fabricated, yet successful deployments of power—prove to be irresistible treasures sought by philosophers, theologians, and theorists of all stripes. Foucault discusses how Nietzsche's genealogical method shows the ways in which history, time, and power work to turn accidents and errors into concretions of incontestable truth. The genealogist, Foucault explains, pushes against the pursuit of origins as they erroneously purport to uphold a timeless essence of entities. In other words, the essence of things is to have no essence, to have no secret to be discovered. There are, however, moments of the new, what Foucault names "emergences" (*die Entstehungen*). These emergences are not origins in the sense of complete ideas or things that inevitably descend from being into becoming but are rather "non-places," born from the interstices of conflictual accounts. No one is responsible for emergences; rather, they are eruptions of power bursting chaotically from within the apertures of conflict. From this perspective, struggle and breakdown between artificially bounded ideas, objects, and systems create the very conditions for unpredictability and revolution. Those institutions, cultures, and people that seek to prevent or "cure" this fluidity are regressive and, ultimately, nihilistic. Taking the *entrepic* turn redirects urgency away from the pursuit of origins and instead focuses on limited resources and energies so that they can be attended to more carefully.

Nietzsche's diagnoses of the state of Europe in the nineteenth-century frequently crystallize into a study of nihilism as an illness. Contracted through millennia, forged in the fires of religious and scientific ideologies guided by the will to truth, nihilism emerges as a symptom of physiological, biological, and cultural degeneration. *On the Genealogy of Morals* notoriously provides many different origin stories to explain the causes of current decline in "this decaying, self-doubting present."[11] While not meant to provide definitive answers (only better fictions), these stories offer provocations for reopening and reinterpreting accepted philosophical, religious, and scientific truths. Exploding the morality that has risen to a monolithic, ahistorical dogma, Nietzsche's utilization of entropic thinking can be found in the unforgiving critique of cultural degeneration on the one hand and the praise of destruction necessary for life and creation on the other.

Regarding the critique of degeneration, Nietzsche asks whether or not there is a symptom of regression inherent in what we mean by the "good" (person, society, leader, ideology, etc.). Insofar as "good" is synonymous with unsullied, this produces "a danger, a seduction, a poison, a narcotic, through which the present was possibly living *at the expense of the future.*"[12] The unquestioning acceptance of this notion of the "good" has had devastating social, psychological, and even environmental consequences. The ascetic impulse, which can sometimes sharpen philosophy and art, is mostly a practice of self-denial and abuse. It advocates for a kind of cruel purification meant to cure but that only hurries and heightens degeneration. Dedicated to practicing pain and misery against oneself, allowing the death drive to do its destructive work in the creation of a soul, what is "good" is actually the perfection of a morality based in world rejection. Calling the Earth a distinctively ascetic planet, Nietzsche bemoans the "offensive creatures filled with a profound disgust at themselves, at the earth, at all life, who inflict as much pain on themselves as they possibly can out of pleasure in inflicting pain—which is probably their only pleasure."[13] Asceticism looks suspiciously at the pleasures of beauty and joy because it is a "discord that *wants* to be discordant, that *enjoys* itself in this suffering and even grows more self-confident and triumphant the more its own presupposition, its physiological capacity for life, *decreases.*"[14] Nietzsche's penetrating observation of a tendency manifest in life to work *against itself* is of central importance to understanding the fundamentally retrograde character operating in tandem with the movement of life to expand and overcome. The interplay between creation and entropy follows a similar kind of tug-of-war between cessation and vitality.

While the contradictory appearance of a drive that directly works against itself may not initially appear to be entropy-related, it is in rather striking ways. Nietzsche's ascetic ideal describes a force directed toward the preservation of the human organism in order to torment it, which is a curious expenditure of finite energy sources. Rather than harnessing the expansive aspects of life, the ascetic ideal works specifically to try to correct, even halt, the aggressive and exploitative drive of life to grow. Asceticism works specifically to curtail the extensive and energy-devouring movement of life in a misguided drive to remedy it. Herein lies its danger: it is harmful insofar as it internalizes outwardly expressive instincts. Yet, Nietzsche acknowledges that without the repression of these instincts, humanity would never have transformed beyond the purely animal. Thus, his philosophy brings awareness to the ways in which the repressive movement is necessary for the creation of human art, culture, philosophy, and even religion. Regression and destruction, however, do not manifest in identical ways. Accordingly, vigilance is necessary to be ever-mindful toward what works to enhance life through redirection and innovative deployments of power and what suffocates it through eradication.

The connections between Freud's death drive and Nietzsche's ascetic ideal are remarkable. Both find unconscious, instinctual life to be the bulk of human experience. Consciousness is a mere modification of the unconscious drives of the organism seeking expression.[15] Both theorists locate the paradox of an instinct driven toward the attainment of quiescence that is yet somehow completely necessary for prolonging and sustaining life. This enigmatic drive displays entropic slackening along a twofold path: one toward decline and death, and one toward preservation and advancement:

> *The ascetic ideal springs from the protective instinct of a degenerating life* which tries by all means to sustain itself and to fight for its existence; it indicates a partial physiological obstruction and exhaustion against which the deepest instincts of life, which have remained intact, continually struggle with new expedients and devices. The ascetic ideal is such an expedient; the case is therefore the opposite of what those who reverence this ideal believe: life wrestles in it and through it with death and *against* death; the ascetic ideal is an artifice for the *preservation* of life.[16]

The ascetic ideal is thus a response to the harshness of existence, one that tarries constantly with obstruction and exhaustion. Life bursts forth in nearly infinite configurations for Nietzsche, and asceticism is one way that it manifests—pointedly, as life confronts extinction. Even though it runs counter to life, this ideal is paradoxically still an effective and likely indispensable expression of it. Put in terms of entropic philosophy, that which produces physiological exhaustion and organic degeneration also unexpectedly and necessarily preserves and proliferates different forms of it. Just as the elements and planets are created through the death of stars, so the ascetic ideal engenders conditions that create and preserve certain forms of life. The problem (as it is in Freud) is therefore *not* that such drives exist, but that they are overtly denied, perversely quickened, or come to be dominant. These excessive tendencies ultimately work against the care and reverence needed for the flourishing of vital diversity and joyful existence. Here lies a critical distinction between Freudian and Nietzschean entropics.

As explicitly addressed in chapter 4, Freud's treatment of the death drive is largely pessimistic (it may be puzzlingly necessary for existence, but still threatens to swallow humanity in total destruction). Nietzsche walks a fine line between acknowledging the retrograde tendency toward self-preservation as being necessary while ultimately siding with life's ability to overcome itself. In *Beyond Good and Evil*, he writes:

> Physiologists should think before putting down the instinct of self-preservation as the cardinal instinct of an organic being. A living thing seeks above all to *discharge* its strength—life itself is *will to power*; self-preservation is only one of the indirect and most frequent *results*.[17]

Expansion into different forms captures the principal expression of life, making self-preservation merely epiphenomenal. While most certainly true that the ascetic ideal's dominance produces a profound world-sickness, it can also be seen as critical in making new forms.[18] Existence, in its expansive desire for dominance, exploits and appropriates energy from various systems.

The relentless pull of torpor is constant, blooming in the institutions and practices that seek to deny death by promising a perfect future. But this anti-entropic faith in the eradication of death and decline only produces the more devastating and corrupting effects of them. Not only recognizing, but embracing, even actively willing demise, Nietzsche writes that "even a partial *diminution of utility*, an atrophying and degeneration, a loss of meaning and purposiveness—in short, death—is among the conditions of an actual *progressus*."[19] Death is not only necessary but should be *willed* in the service of creation and novelty. While this can be read in more or less ominous ways (as found in Nietzsche's example of the overman which often promotes a sacrifice of the present for a stronger future), the overarching point is sound: no development, no growth, no innovation is possible without death and sacrifice of what is no longer (or never was) vital and life-promoting. "If a temple is to be erected *a temple must be destroyed*: that is the law—let anyone who can show me a case in which it is not fulfilled."[20]

Nietzsche consistently reiterates that the attraction of life-denying asceticism poses the greatest seduction and danger for humanity. The cold stillness of heat death and the allure of stability proves a powerful soporific for an exhausted human condition. While he happily provides the diagnosis of the sickness, he is reluctant to give a clear roadmap for how to cure it. This is not, to his mind, his problem to solve. Rather, Nietzsche champions a new way of thinking about eternity and the moment. In a wildly speculative, and yet captivating, move, he posits the theory of the eternal return as a challenge to entropic stasis. Abandoning the tranquilizing effects of a heavenly hereafter, one must focus on the moment as the only thing that exists: not the moment as a singular event that arises and passes away, but the moment that repeats eternally. For Nietzsche, the hardest and yet most liberating thought is that what has happened has happened in the past and will happen in the future in an infinitely repeating cycle. Moving away from heat death, he exclaims that the way out of pessimism and nihilism involves thinking through the eternal return of the same. The moment in which we exist is one that must be *willed* through all eternity because it has existed before and will exist again in a tight knot of unbreakable causality.[21] This is, for Nietzsche, both a psychological and cosmological principle. His universe (perhaps like the self-contained organism postulated by Plato's *Timaeus* or Fechner's universal organism) is one that cycles perfectly through itself with no irrecuperable waste.[22] Rejecting all teleological interpretations, Nietzsche maintains that *if* there was a goal to existence, it would have already been reached. As a result, all becoming and change would have come to a standstill, thus showing that the absurdity is in positing any universal purpose or goal.[23]

While the first law of thermodynamics asserts that matter and energy are neither created nor destroyed, the second law shows how they are necessarily reorganized such that stasis and homogeneity are the ultimate universal terminus. Nietzsche's formulation takes a different approach to these laws. The world as force is *not*, in fact, unlimited in his physics. Infinite force is impossible. Mechanistic theory would require that the world had already reached its finished state, thereby making it an imperfect and provisional theory. Nietzsche's own hypothesis on the eternal return embraces the following:

> If the world may be thought of as a certain definite quantity of force—and every other representation remains indefinite and therefore useless—it follows that, in the great dice game of existence, it must pass through a calculable number of combinations. In infinite time, every possible combination would at some time or another be realized; more: it would be realized an infinite number of times. And since between every combination and its next recurrence all other possible combinations would have to take place, and each of these combinations conditions the entire sequence of combinations in the same series, a circular movement of absolutely identical series is thus demonstrated: the world as a circular movement that has already repeated itself infinitely often and plays its game *in infinitum*.[24]

This unending process, with a definite quantity of available force, contains all the energy needed to sustain it as a perfectly recycling universe. Much like the perpetual motion machines haunting the entropy-averse human imagination,

Nietzsche's universe would be both cause and effect of itself without wear, without death: "This world, a monster of energy, without beginning, without end; a firm, iron magnitude of force that does not grow bigger or smaller, *that does not expend itself but only transforms itself*; as a whole, of unalterable size, a household without expenses or losses, but likewise without increase or income."[25] The movements from complexity to simplicity, hot to cold, rigid to fluid, are not unidirectional but rather infinite in their back and forth flow. Nietzsche's cosmos never runs out of free energy—never requires outside sustenance in order to maintain itself. It is, rather, a perfectly self-contained organism, joyfully creating and destroying itself for all eternity. Entropics denies expansion that does not take into account the ultimately finite nature of any system in which life appears.[26] Nietzsche's conception of the world as will to power necessarily overcomes the unidirectionality of entropic dissipation into equilibrium, replacing it instead with an eternally self-renewing and excessive creation.

The only liberating choice in the face of this awesome eternally recurring universe is to will it, rather than passively resign to it. Such willing is the source of joy. In *Thus Spoke Zarathustra*, Nietzsche's eponymous protagonist exclaims: "to redeem all 'it was' into a 'thus I willed it'—that alone should I call redemption.... Willing liberates."[27] The creative will says, "thus I willed it ... thus I will it; thus shall I will it" in the ultimate move to liberate every moment of existence.[28] This choice brings with it the highest affirmation of joy in the chance game of existence.

Nietzsche's advocacy of the eternal return over linear time shields him from the entropic thought of ultimate universal heat death insofar as all that has been will be again in an unending cosmic cycle. Ultimate stasis is impossible. This thought brings a kind of jubilant welcoming of this moment, here and now, as the true meaning of eternity. While not overtly engaging it, Nietzsche advances a powerful revaluation of the entropy law itself. Destruction and deterioration are necessary for life and creation, but time is not a one-way movement to universal homogenization. The infinite play of forces combines and dissolves in an eternal repetition of all possible combinations.

Many artists are creators who inhabit this joyful yes-saying to existence, refusing to capitulate to the conservative and ultimately nihilistic ascetic drive. Philosophers contribute esteemed analyses of their times, but artists model true self-overcoming. True artists, for Nietzsche, move within a milieu of action, unconcerned with conscious, rational choice; they break apart form and boundary in order to give birth to manifold new shapes and subjectivities. This process of creation rejects fixed essentiality and abjures a robust sense of sovereign agency. In the process of creation, artists "no longer do anything 'voluntarily' but do everything of necessity, their feeling of freedom, subtlety, full power, of creative placing, disposing, and forming reaches its peak."[29] The portrait of the artist as a subject self-consciously creating an art object is replaced by the idea of the artist expressing the process of creation itself, playing the role of facilitator of power rather than rational agent of production.

In order to explore the possibilities of art for reimagining and reconfiguring the more pessimistic and nihilistic tendencies of entropics, I return to Smithson. The previous chapter took up his ability to heighten awareness of materiality and degradation rather than mask them, only briefly touching upon his unique use of entropic temporality. In order to develop this sense of time more fully, I now show Smithson to be an artist in the Nietzschean mold, one who thoroughly commends entropic creation out of destruction.

SMITHSONIAN ENTROPICS

Contemplating entropy from the human perspective, and more to the point, from lived experience, often evokes a kind of dread at the relentless march of time's arrow. Human beings have a visceral understanding of the amount of energy required to keep the systems of our bodies, our homes, our labor, and our communities intact. And we also "know" (whether consciously or not) that it is a losing battle. Eventually, all the structures that provide human shelter—from the clean house, the organized city, up to the universe itself—will fall apart. This insight can induce a kind of existential despair, engendering profound anxiety about slackening, breakdown, and death. However, focusing on the prehistoric past of the great lizards or the inhuman future of the inorganic and crystalline produces a different kind of truth, one that circumvents dread, instead generating a kind of wonder. This approach is critical to twentieth-century land art in general, and specifically to Smithson's creations. Gary Shapiro highlights the ways in which earthwork artists embrace temporal decay rather than timelessness or progress. An artist in Smithson's vein

> is deeply suspicious of progress and conscious of industrial devastation, decay, waste, and the general tendency toward entropy. Rather than attempting to catch up with "progress," he regressively allows the waste and the ground to emerge in its wake; the very contrast will suggest that history and "progress" are limited by entropy, the ineluctable undertow of all human and natural processes.[30]

Instead of bemoaning finitude, the entropic artist foregrounds and ultimately discards aspirations toward timeless perfection. Not only is the latter a well-traveled, uninteresting artistic path, but it is inevitably pessimistic insofar as it prioritizes an unrealistic, idealized, and ultimately unattainable vision of static truth.

While celebrating the Nietzschean joy in destruction, Smithson takes a different approach to entropy than one advocating eternal cosmic repetition. He regards unidirectional entropy precisely as the place of emergence and creation. The lack that gnaws at the edges of formal perfection, the appearances of decay and ruin, the experiences of time's relentless forward movement don't evoke anxiety, even if they reveal the inhuman and elemental. Through works that heighten awareness of the second law—commending it rather than deprecating it—Smithson produces an understanding of entropy as one of a galactic explosion and dispersion, churning out creation every moment. From the orientation of human subjectivity, this can be a terrifying and dark thought. As Asimov's Lupov and Adell realized in their moment of self-congratulation in "The Last Question," heat death inevitably evokes unease, no matter how far into the future it may be. From the orientation of the inorganic and crystalline, however, this thought produces awe and wonder. Centering geology and materiality and down-playing human progress allows for new modes of valuation.[31] While Nietzsche's eternal return challenges the despair over a universe hemorrhaging energy, and Smithson's art celebrates the power of dispersal and collapse, both agree that moving beyond the exhaustion of human morality is necessary to conceive of new relationships to the Earth. His artistic character underscores the idea that the entropic need not be merely frightening but also engaging and perhaps almost welcoming. The transformation of energy from one state to another counterbalances the movement toward homogenization and ultimate heat death. His art embodies the many possibilities that exist between the two poles of maximum entropy.[32]

Smithson advocates for the development of an artistic "entropy of technique" in which the artist regresses from rationality into the primordial condition of undifferentiation, thereby avoiding stifling boundaries and limitations. "This entropy of technique leaves one with an empty limit, or no limit at all. All differentiated technology becomes meaningless."[33] He speaks of the way in which artists abandon themselves into an oceanic dispersal such that boundaries and containment melt away and rationality itself appears as only a second-order production. Such a process is exemplified in Smithson's *Spiral Jetty*, where the geologic decomposition of the massive spiral of stones in the Great Salt Lake dissolves human perspective and elicits a kind of calm within the entropic—the tranquility of the water, stones, sand, salt, and spiral that are at once totally inhospitable, and yet, strangely familiar.[34]

Disavowing an aesthetics that rescues the material from such temporal destruction, Smithson's works instead "set aside European culture by sweeping away history itself and by addressing instead the metahistorical extremes of time—the remote past and the remote future."[35] Time, on the micro, macro, and human levels, is always at play in Smithson's creations insofar as he puts in motion a non-progressive dialectic vacillating between pre-, post-, and current history. Dialectical thinking can avoid pessimism, but unlike that found within Hegelian or Marxist frameworks, Smithson's dialectic does not go anywhere specific. Shifting between the past and the future, mind and matter, and form and formlessness, this non-teleological dialectic inhibits the overwhelming sense that everything is going downhill. "You have to have this dialectic, otherwise you have the tragic view where everything is sort of fatalistic, but with this [dialectic] you can somehow go back and forth."[36] Moving between the prehistoric past and the inhuman future places humanity as part of the temporal flow and not its destination. In so doing, it loosens time's unidirectionality, much like the Heraclitean proclamation that "the road up and the road down are one and the same."[37]

What would it look like to embrace a kind of aesthetic acceptance of the grinding, ceaseless machinations of entropy? For one thing, it clearly means welcoming all that entropy elicits: disorder, chaos, disruption, even death. Turning to Heraclitus to give voice to this cosmic celebration, Smithson writes that the "*disruption* of the earth's crust is at times very compelling, and seems to confirm Heraclitus' *Fragment 124*, 'The most beautiful world is like a heap of rubble tossed down in confusion.'"[38] The most beautiful world is a random heap, scattered by chance, given over to the workings of time. Heraclitus illuminates the constant forces of motion that simultaneously heap things together in creation and scatter them apart in destruction. The two processes are the same, which is why Smithson adopts it as a description of his aesthetics. Through Heraclitus, Smithson points to beauty in (or as) rubble and confusion. Stated differently, beauty actually *is* the rubble and confusion resulting from the disordering *and* formative workings of entropy.

Smithson is well aware of the environmental effects of entropy, as well as the human desire to completely ignore it through half-hearted (or no-hearted) attempts to recuperate waste.[39] Economies largely disregard systemic breakdown because they "seem to be isolated and self-contained and conceived of as cycles, so as to exclude the whole entropic process," when in fact they are interrelated and porous systems constantly borrowing from each other.[40] Art brings to light systemic breakdown in such a way that it causes appreciation and contemplation, rather than the far more prevalent economic and governmental denial. This artistic ideal is captured in most of Smithson's work, but perhaps in no greater way than in the *Spiral Jetty*.

Outside of Corinne Utah, the *Spiral Jetty* endures a constant flux of environmental and human decay. Jutting out from the northeastern shore of the ancient remnants of Lake Bonneville, the *Jetty* is one of the most important artworks of the twentieth century. The massive spiral, composed of basalt rocks, hauled in by bulldozer over the course of a week, was conceived by

Smithson to be a substantial performance of the workings of entropy. The rocks that compose the spiral are subjected to the brutal conditions of the Utah landscape, ranging from submersion for years under the saline lake, emersion into the harsh rays of the desert sun, and the chilling conditions of winter. In addition, thousands of people walk on and around it each year, rapidly contributing to the decomposition of the porous rocks and the spiral's form. These extreme conditions affect the *Jetty* in such a way that it never appears to be the same work of art. In fact, one of the most remarkable things about the *Jetty* is the way in which it so clearly and dynamically reacts to and with the environment. Its Protean nature captures the visceral experience of temporality. Rather than creating work for preservation in a museum, Smithson deliberately highlights time and decay in the piece, underscoring the inevitability of entropic transformation on all objects and systems. Instead of producing a foreboding pessimism about systemic breakdown, however, it leads to the revelation that dissolution and destruction are necessary for all creation. The breakdown *is* the art.

The Utah setting chosen for the piece helps to connect to a sense of prehistory, or what the poet Robinson Jeffers would name the "inhuman." Evidence of a past (and therefore future) absent of humans becomes obvious throughout the deep geological stratifications and layerings of the land. This "fluvial entropy"[41] will outlive the brief foray of humanity on the planet as it stretches back for billions of years before our arrival and will continue for billions of years after we are gone. The slow-motion breakdown of the earth's surface shows that much has happened and will happen that is utterly indifferent to human struggle and accomplishment.[42] As a result, human centrality diminishes. Like the *Jetty*, humanity is but a spur in the proliferation of organic and inorganic assemblies. Just as dinosaurs lived for millions of years and vanished, Smithson's work reminds us that "it may be that human beings are just different from dinosaurs rather than better."[43] By extension, life itself, is in the end, just different from other forms of matter, rather than categorically better.

For all of these reasons, Smithson's choice of the Salt Lake is significant for the creation of the *Spiral Jetty*. "My own experience is that the best sites for 'earth art,'" he explains, "are sites that have been disrupted by industry, reckless urbanization, or nature's own devastation. For instance, the *Spiral Jetty* is built in a dead sea."[44] The Salt Lake's twofold deadness results from its feature as a land-locked terminal body of water and from the years of industrial waste pumped into its waters. The lake has no constant source of water (such as a river or spring), nor does it have an outlet (such as a conduit to the ocean) allowing water to regularly flow out. Its smell and texture evoke mortality (due to the high salinity as well as the industrial pollution). Yet, the Salt Lake is filled with life ranging from the scores of brine shrimp, brine flies, and the algae upon which they feed (often giving the lake its "tomato soup" color that so fascinated Smithson). Further, the lake shelters dozens of species of migrating birds that rest and feed in the surrounding marshes. While small waves lap at the ever-changing shoreline, the lake often displays a kind of glasslike placidity, mirroring the landscape and sky around it in a kind of upside-down Carrollian juxtaposition. The sun, when visible, can be blinding (a theme played upon in the *Spiral Jetty* film) or hidden behind atmospheric alterations. Rather than using the Platonic notion of the sun as metaphysical symbol of unity and generation (ideas that Smithson bluntly calls "crap") he instead calls the sun a "portent of entropy" insofar as it is itself "a kind of groaning circle of hot marmalade" that behaves as a harbinger of death and madness.[45] The mirroring effect of the lake fails to elicit calm serenity for Smithson, but rather provides a glimpse into the dissolution of all: "the reflective aspect of the lake and the lake itself, especially the Salt Lake, is a kind of ocean of entropy, because it's a shrunken vestige of the great ocean that once existed there."[46] Thus, the lake brings together earth, water, sky, and sun into a self-contesting unity that defies easy categorization into a more classical art form.[47]

Smithson speaks of his "great pleasure" with the Rozel Point as a site because it is a jumble of natural and human-made structures in various forms of decay. "This site gave evidence of a succession of man-made systems mired in abandoned hopes," which fills Smithson's mind with possibility.[48] A somewhat unspectacular landscape at first glance, Rozel Point rests between abandoned oil rigs and natural tar pools. Provocative on many levels, the location is largely free of overdetermined scenic meaning (the hills are unspectacular compared to the austere beauty of much of the rest of the Utah landscape) the vast lake itself appears boundless (but lacks the drama of large waves or an abundance of diverse marine life) and it exists in a kind of wasteland.[49] Rozel Point thus avoids overly romanticizing nature as pristine or untouched by the human. In addition, Smithson sidesteps glorifying the human: the dilapidated and abandoned mining operation is not an achievement, but rather a discarded and obtrusive remnant of technology. He observes that

> the mere sight of the trapped fragments of junk and waste transported one into a world of modern prehistory. The products of a Devonian industry, the remains of a Silurian technology, all the machines of the Upper Carboniferous Period were lost in those expansive deposits of sand and mud.[50]

Finally, the specific location between the ATK missile facility and the Golden Spike Museum (commemorating the meeting of the Union and Pacific Railroads) plays human and monumental time against geological time.[51] The *Jetty* therefore emerges as an anchor of dialectical exchanges between (imperfect) nature and (imperfect) technology, highlighting the entropic movement of both. In short, he found a quintessential "entropic landscape" in which to create a quintessentially entropic work of art.[52]

Smithson rejoices at the ways in which sites of extraction and pollution rebuff attempts at artistic purification. The sky and the earth, nature and industry, art, and technology, all become confused in the place of the *Jetty*. "Ambiguities are admitted rather than rejected, contradictions are increased rather than decreased—the *alogos* undermines the *logos*. Purity is put in jeopardy."[53] The quest for purity—whether rational, artistic, or scientific—has always worked in the service of entropy (in the tendency toward homogenization) and against it (in denial of the real waste byproducts).[54] This is why the *Jetty* continues to captivate: it wears down and wears out right before our eyes. Rather than eliciting feelings of despondency at its inevitable disappearance, the breakdown of the *Jetty is* the aesthetic performance. In this manner, it points toward a future where entropy functions as an openly respected creative force. The *Jetty* shows that the path toward universal heat is a long one, but there are incalculably diverse formations possible along the way.

Smithson's artworks give voice to the beautiful possibilities emergent from entropic decline, working from within the heart of destruction and rejecting a kind of utopian approach to nature. In a somewhat surprising twist toward what I have named the *entrepic*, he advocates the partnering of industry and art. Their separation hinders both—making art irrelevant and industry rapacious in advanced capitalist society. "Modern day ecologists with a metaphysical turn of mind still see the operations of industry as Satan's work. The image of the lost paradise garden leaves one without a solid dialectic and causes one to suffer an ecological despair."[55] The false ideal of a lost garden necessarily creates the feeling of decline, failure, and consequently a pronounced desire to overcome or ignore entropy. Ultimately, the *entrepic* denies such a false paradise by not only embracing the necessity of entropy but in so doing, creating an attitude of stewardship for the finite, vulnerable, and declining. While this is not the ultimate direction of Smithson's thinking, using his philosophy sets us on the path to an *entrepic* orientation to nature and technology. Art is capable of acting as a mediator between the devastating consequences of industry and the impossible utopia of environmentalism:

> A dialectic between mining and land reclamation must be developed. Such devastated places as strip mines could be recycled in terms of earth art. The artist and the miner must become conscious of themselves as natural agents. When the miner loses consciousness of what he is doing through the abstractions of technology he cannot cope with his own inherent nature or external nature. Art can become a physical resource that mediates between the ecologist and the industrialist.[56]

Humans cannot "fix" entropy because it is inextricably part of our essence, just as it is for every other bit of matter. Since the return to an impossible past or the creation of a utopian future is neither desirable nor possible, the world must exist in the nexus of endless devastation and creation. For Smithson, the artist is well primed to serve as an intermediary between industry and environment.

Something like a working or abandoned industrial site actually brings humanity's destructive tendencies to light in all of their power *and* ugliness. Smithson's art makes present the possibilities generated by entropic decay— even in the obscenest excesses of capitalism.[57] Recalling chapter 6's discussion of materiality, catastrophes, waste, and pollution can appear as sites of action if human bias is decentered. In one of his most ambitious proposals for earth art from within environmental devastation, Smithson imagined placing a massive revolving disk at the bottom of the mile-deep Bingham Copper Mine (now the Kennecott Copper Mine) in Utah. Such a project, suggested, ignored, and minimally preserved in his writings and sketches, would force the viewer to confront the yawning void caused by one of the world's largest open-pit mines, while also drawing attention to how human technology functions in the larger workings of entropy. Rejecting the idea of refilling the massive hole once the mining was complete (an impossible return to pristine nature) Smithson decries the naiveté of both environmentalism and industry. This "humpty dumpty" approach attempts "to recover a frontier or a wilderness that no longer exists. Here we have to accept the entropic situation and more or less learn how to reincorporate these things that seem ugly."[58] He refuses the stalemate between the miner and the environmentalist—each rejecting the validity of the other—instead encouraging a "dialectics of entropic change." Both sides have to "recognize this entropic condition rather than try to reverse it."[59] The environmentalist should give up any idea of "return" as time does not run backward. Paradise not only remains lost but never was. The industrialist must abandon all notions of "progress" and admit that destruction and waste are irrevocably linked in extraction and production. Ultimately, Smithson's unrealized earthwork would have revealed the utter futility of human technology to master nature and environmentalism's failure to restore it by instead extolling the entropic forces widespread throughout both technology and nature.

Whether viewed from the perspective of profit or environmental devastation, the confrontation with our own monstrous power makes us uneasy. Smithson's artworks bring to surface the mechanisms of Freud's death drive, showing humans as agents of destruction, but also as fragile beings slated for psychic and organic dissolution. Encountering this ruin (without repressing or idealizing it) encourages a turn that is neither anti-technological nor anti-environmental, but *artistic*. Without attempting to ameliorate the destructive forces of entropy, Smithson shows their inherent possibilities. Art thus provides temporary relief from the realities of death and decay and in this way evokes the sense of *entrepics* promoted throughout this book. Although the crystalline and geological senses of time strip away rational privilege, they also provide a space in which to confront finitude and vulnerability. Eschewing an Edenic past or a utopian future through a novel understanding of time works to minimize the dangers that threaten the world right now.

Smithson proposes an alternative to the despair that many feel in the face of real or perceived entropic decline. It requires, first and foremost, forsaking the attachments to the notion of time as progressive and the prioritization of the human perspective. Taking instead the position of geological time, everything slows down and expands, allowing for the exploration of entropy as productive and creative. This is one point of possible departure into the notion of the *entrepic*, which goes further than detached, inhuman observation, and instead encourages thoughtfulness, care, and reverence for the shared world. As one system dies, so its energy, like a dying star, feeds other systems. What may appear as the march into decline and death is from another perspective the bubbling, vibrating, interactive universe of which we are but a small part. Here is where our attention must turn.

Goethe's seductive and frustrating Mephistopheles enacts the transformative power of philosophy and art. The devil cuts a figure of mockery and levity. The spirit that negates is ultimately transformed through laughter in the face of the crushing realities of existence. For his part, Nietzsche rejects god and devil, heaven and hell, in order to free humanity from the nihilism that he believes necessarily follows from them. In order to be rid of the pessimism resulting from a world crushed by submission to eternal truths grounded in nonexistent ideals, values must be the project of individuals and whole peoples. It is time to create new values that work within the bounds of the entropic and that foster *entrepic* care so as to reject the spirit of gravity that breeds despair.

Nietzsche rejects the weight of hopelessness in *Thus Spoke Zarathustra*. There he describes a vision of a shepherd choking on the snake that seeks his ruin. Once he bites off the snake's head, the shepherd rises from the experience transformed:

> No longer shepherd, no longer human—one changed, radiant, *laughing!* Never on earth has a human being laughed as he laughed! O my brothers, I heard a laughter that was no human laughter; and now a thirst gnaws at me, a longing that never grows still. My longing for this laughter gnaws at me; oh, how do I bear to go on living! And how could I bear to die now.[60]

A godlike, divine laughter challenges mortals, forcing us to ask how can we live, and how can we die, once we have heard such laughter in the face of the entropic forces of the universe? Nietzsche's answer lies in the affirmation of the moment and revaluation of values that disdain and abuse the Earth.

Smithson too believes in laughter. He recounts that R. Buckminster Fuller was told that the fourth dimension was laughter. "Laughter is in a sense a kind of entropic 'verbalization.' How could artists translate this verbal entropy, that is 'ha-ha,' into 'solid-models'?"[61] Proceeding from this account with the utmost "seriousness," Smithson categorizes laughter ranging from the giggle to the snicker, and the titter to the guffaw, in terms of six main crystal systems. It is possible, he believes, to apply these crystal concepts to artists who make certain forms of art entwined with materiality. This "solid-state hilarity allows us not to think of Laughter as a laughing matter, but rather as the 'matter-of-laughs.'"[62] The crystalline structure is rigid and heavy, and yet, Smithson uses it to crack open aesthetic laughter. This laughter reconfigures the boundaries of meaning and value and allows for new arrangements to appear in their dissolution. Harnessing the potential for joy in destruction makes destruction itself a site of jubilant creation, thus permitting the entropic to manifest primarily as a generative, rather than simply devastating force. Laughter sets humanity on a course freed from the heaviness of fear about devastation and annihilation, instead engendering possibilities of creation, affirmation, and reverence for the world.

NOTES

1. Portions of this chapter on Robert Smithson were previously published in Shannon M. Mussett "Irrationality, Entropy, and Nature: The Aesthetic Collision of Hegel and Smithson" in *Rendezvous with the Sensuous: Readings on Aesthetics*, eds. Linda Ardito and John Murungi (Newcastle upon Tyne: Cambridge Scholars Publishing, 2014) and "Robert Smithson, Entropic Art, and the West." In *Philosophy in the American West: A Geography of Thought*, eds. Gerard Kuperus, Brian Treanor, and Josh Hayes (New York: Routledge, 2020).

Ibn Tufayl, *Hayy ibn yaqzan*, trans. Lenn Evan Goodman (Chicago: University of Chicago Press, 2009), 136.

2. Schelling, "Philosophical Investigations," 271.
3. Goethe, *Faust*, 159.
4. Ibid, 161.
5. Ibid, 163.
6. Zencey, "Brief Speculations," 9.
7. Sophocles, *Oedipus at Colonus*, 1410–1413. These words recall the wisdom of Silenus. Nietzsche, Birth of Tragedy, 42, which is also echoed by Goethe's Mephistopheles who, as the negating spirit, claims that his role is called for "since

all that comes to be/ Deserves to perish wretchedly; 'Twere better nothing would begin.'" Goethe, *Faust*, 161.

8. Nietzsche, *Birth of Tragedy*, 43. Albert Camus describes Sisyphus as a mythological hero who lived and died by this motto. Albert Camus, *The Myth of Sisyphus and Other Essays*, trans. James O'Brien (New York: Vintage International, 1991), 119–123.

9. Friedrich Nietzsche, *The Will to Power*, trans. Walter Kaufmann and R. J. Hollingdale, ed. Walter Kaufmann (New York: Vintage Books, 1968), 224.

10. Friedrich Nietzsche, *Thus Spoke Zarathustra*, trans. Walter Kaufmann (New York: Penguin Books, 1978), 59.

11. Friedrich Nietzsche, *On the Genealogy of Morals and Ecce Homo*, ed. and trans.Walter Kaufmann (New York: Vintage Books, 1989), 96.

12. Ibid, 20. The present living at the expense of the future is *exactly* what a culture that hastens entropic decline promotes.

13. Ibid, 117. The ascetic ideal's fundamentally conservative expression seeks pleasure in "ill-constitutedness, decay, pain, mischance, ugliness, voluntary deprivation, self-mortification, self-flagellation, [and] self-sacrifice." Ibid, 118.

14. Ibid.

15. In *Beyond Good and Evil*, Nietzsche writes, "by far the greater part of conscious thinking must still be included among instinctive activities, and that goes even for philosophical thinking." Friedrich Nietzsche, *Beyond Good and Evil*, trans. Walter Kaufmann (New York: Vintage Books, 1989), 11.

16. Nietzsche, *Genealogy of Morals*, 120.

17. Nietzsche, *Good and Evil*, 21. See also, Ibid, 203.

18. Nietzsche, *Genealogy of Morals*, 88.

19. Ibid, 78.

20. Ibid, 95. Apple Zefelius Igrek's work on entropic affirmation is in line with Nietzsche's link between creation and destruction. Igrek notes that change is infinite and absolute: "change *qua* infinite and *qua* absolute is real. It will never be stopped or contained by the human constructs of eternal truth, discrete elements, or the immortal soul." Igrek, *Entropic Affirmation*, 42.

21. Nietzsche hypothesizes: "supposing the world had a certain quantum of force at its disposal, then it is obvious that every displacement of power at any point would affect the whole system—thus together with sequential causality there would be a contiguous and concurrent dependence." Nietzsche, *Will to Power*, 340.

22. Nietzsche imagines that "the world exists; it is not something that becomes, not something that passes away. Or rather: it becomes, it passes away, but it has never begun to become and never ceased from passing away—it maintains itself in both.— It lives on itself: its excrements are its food." Nietzsche, *Will to Power*, 548.

23. Ibid, 546.

24. Ibid, 549.

25. Ibid, 550.

26. This is why Babette Babich argues that, in a direct rejection of chaos as stasis, Nietzsche returns to a Hesiodic vision of chaos as generative. Babette E. Babich, "Nietzsche's Chaos Sive Natura: Evening Gold and the Dancing Star," *Revista*

Portuguesa de Filosofia 57 (2001): 230. Babich also makes a case for reading chaos in Nietzsche as the site of wild excess, rather than the homogenous, undifferentiated coldness of heat death. Ibid, 234.

27. Nietzsche, *Thus Spoke Zarathustra*, 139.
28. Ibid, 141. See also, Nietzsche, *Good and Evil*, 136.
29. Ibid, 140.
30. Gary Shapiro, *Earthwards: Robert Smithson And Art After Babel* (Berkeley: University of California Press, 1997), 36.
31. While disagreeing on the fundamentals of entropics, Smithson exemplifies a Nietzschean artist exclaiming: "Good and bad are moral values. What we need are aesthetic values." Robert Smithson, "What is a Museum? A Dialogue between Allan Kaprow and Robert Smithson, 1967," in *Robert Smithson: The Collected Writings*, ed. Jack Flam (Berkeley: University of California Press, 1996), 50. Even his philosophical lens embraces a kind of Nietzschean multiperspectivalism: "I think the more points the better, you know, just an endless amount of points of view." Ibid, 51.
32. Even though there was stability in the beginning and will be again at the end of the universe, there exists a vast, nearly infinite proliferation of forms in between because, even from the perspective of physics, the "gap between actual and maximum possible entropy represents possibility." Hester, *Entropy Redux*, 66.
33. Smithson, *Sedimentation of Mind*, 102.
34. As an artist, Smithson is most known for his land art (including *Broken Circle* [1971], *Partially Buried Woodshed* [1970], and *Amarillo Ramp* [1973]) and his Non-Sites (discussed in chapter 6).
35. Flam, "Introduction," xxi. For Smithson's views on imperfection and finitude in contrast to Hegel's aesthetics' emphasis on perfection and eternity, see Shannon M. Mussett, "Irrationality, Entropy."
36. Smithson, "Four Conversations," 211.
37. Heraclitus, *Presocratics Reader*, Fr. B60.
38. Smithson, *Sedimentation of Mind*, 102. This is actually Fragment 46, which Daniel Graham translates as "the fairest order is a random heap of sweepings." Heraclitus, *Presocratics Reader*, Fr. B60. Κεχυμένων (heap) means both "heaping together" and "scattering apart." Lidell and Scott, *Greek-English Lexicon*, 1989. Gary Shapiro also notes that Smithson echoes Heraclitus when he claims that is it "death to the artist's soul to become moist." Gary Shapiro,"Entropy and Dialectic: The Signatures of Robert Smithson," *Arts Magazine*, Summer 1988, 104.
39. Smithson observes that "one might even say that the whole energy crisis is a form of entropy. The earth being the closed system, there's only a certain amount of resources and of course there's an attempt to reverse entropy through the recycling of garbage." Smithson, "Made Visible," 302.
40. Ibid, 309. This entropic denial is why, Smithson believes, there is little to no consideration of the landscape after the extraction of low entropy resources.
41. Ibid, 303.
42. This is why the location is so important for the *Jetty*; the work "appears to be a prehistoric or even natural formation that has become increasingly at home in its surrounding site." Ann Reynolds, "At the Jetty," in *Robert Smithson Spiral Jetty: True*

Fictions, False Realities, eds. Lynne Cooke, and Karen Kelly with Bettina Funcke and Barbara Schröder (Berkeley: University of California Press, 2005), 74.

43. Smithson, "Made Visible," 303.

44. Smithson, "Dialectical Landscape," 165.

45. Kenneth Baker, "Talking with Robert Smithson," in *Robert Smithson Spiral Jetty: True Fictions, False Realities*, eds. Lynne Cooke and Karen Kelly with Bettina Funcke and Barbara Schröder (Berkeley: University of California Press, 2005), 160.

46. Ibid.

47. This insight becomes all the clearer as Smithson considers the *Spiral Jetty* to be not only the physical work but a triad including the earth work, the film, and the essay all of which share the same name.

48. Smithson, "Spiral Jetty," 146. Lytle Shaw provides a fascinating account of the ways in which the choice of site and Smithson's writing about it in the "The Spiral Jetty" essay shows his lifelong interest in apocalyptic science fiction (such as found in the work of J. G. Ballard and Eric Temple Bell). Lytle Shaw, "Smithson, Writer," in *Robert Smithson Spiral Jetty: True Fictions, False Realities*, eds. Lynne Cooke and Karen Kelly with Bettina Funcke and Barbara Schröder (Berkeley: University of California Press, 2005), 160.

49. He likes how "the piece is right near a disused oil drilling operation and the whole northern part of the lake is completely useless." Smithson, "Conversation in Salt Lake," 297.

50. Smithson, "Spiral Jetty," 145–156.

51. For more on the various ways Smithson uses time in this piece, see Roberts, "Taste of Time."

52. Robert Smithson, "Interview with Robert Smithson, 1970," eds. Paul Toner and Robert Smithson, in *Robert Smithson: The Collected Writings*, ed. Jack Flam (Berkeley: University of California Press, 1996), 239. Smithson also refers to the *Spiral Jetty* movie as an example of entropic film. Baker, "Talking With Smithson," 160.

53. Smithson, "Spiral Jetty," 147.

54. As Smithson clarifies, sites that magnify ambiguity and contradiction "are kind of entropic situations that hold themselves together. It's like the *Spiral Jetty* is physical enough to be able to withstand all these climate changes, yet it's intimately involved with those climate changes and natural disturbances." Smithson, "Conversation in Salt Lake," 298.

55. Smithson, "Dialectical Landscape," 161.

56. Robert Smithson, "Untitled, 1972," in *Robert Smithson: The Collected Writings*, ed. Jack Flam (Berkeley: University of California Press, 1996), 379.

57. Smithson, "Made Visible," 305.

58. Ibid, 307.

59. Ibid.

60. Nietzsche, *Zarathustra*, 160.

61. Smithson, "New Monuments," 21.

62. Ibid.

Conclusion

For man will be blotted out, the blithe earth die, the
brave sun
Die blind and blacken to the heart:
Yet stones have stood for a thousand years, and pained
thoughts found
The honey of peace in old poems.

                        Robinson Jeffers, "To the Stone-Cutters"[1]

But the woman with her hands removed the great lid of the jar
and scattered its contents, bringing grief and cares to men.
Only Hope stayed under the rim of the jar
and did not fly away from her secure stronghold.

                                    Hesiod, *Works and Days*[2]

In the 1973 essay, "Poetry is Not a Luxury," Audre Lorde speaks about poetry emerging from a "nameless and formless" space of feeling within women.[3] Rejecting the European emphasis on ideas as the site of freedom, Lorde celebrates dreams and feelings as necessary for radical, liberatory action. Her proclamation that poetry is not a luxury but a necessity challenges "living structures defined by profit, by linear power, by institutional dehumanization" where feelings are "not meant to survive."[4] In a direct challenge to the linearity of capitalism's dehumanization, she acclaims poetry's promise, showing reverence for the core and fountain of her power. Rejecting the construction of the feminine as scourge of man since Eve and Pandora, Lorde's poetry embraces the Black poetess as a deep source of creation.

In the college address, "Difference and Survival," Lorde denies safety and sameness and praises the courage to hail difference in oneself and in others. What makes people different can either be affirmed or it can be used against them by a capitalist "profit economy which needs groups of outsiders as surplus people."[5] Social structures that exacerbate harm, violence, and oppression through the manipulation of diversity inevitably *produce* racism, ageism, and heterosexism. Noting the urgency of these matters that must be immediately addressed before the future is irreparably truncated, Lorde couples the individual existential onus to define oneself and one's unique contributions to the world with the necessity to care about others. Her admonition is clear: the eradication of difference, or the mistaken move to make difference sameness, forecloses any hope for change and real advancement. To push toward homogenization is a form of spiritual and, ultimately, *actual* death. But the future is not determined. Warning that this is "not a theoretical discussion," she claims that:

> our differences are polarities between which can spark possibilities for a future we cannot even now imagine, when we acknowledge that we share a unifying vision, no matter how differently expressed; a vision which supposes a future where we may all flourish, as well as a living earth upon which to support our choices.[6]

Despite the forces that work to level variations, or that seek them as fodder for appropriation, or that foster exclusion and hatred, Lorde sees our fight as one in which diversity must be respected, tended to, and fought for.

There is no reason to hope for a future where all is reconciled, where the struggles, the wars, the losses, and the waste will somehow be recuperated in a grand historical payout. This kind of thinking falls into the trap of sacrificing the present in the name of a future that never comes. The maniacal push to outwit death only ushers it in at a dizzying pace. The greater the struggle for immortality, the more destruction is wrought upon the earth. In the face of these dilemmas, the thinkers and works addressed in this book confront the mighty forces of breakdown and decay by employing various strategies of denial, control, exacerbation, and respect. Some offer philosophies that claim to master these forces through metaphysical and theological powers, some give in to a fatalism that views waste and loss of diversity as inevitable, and some try to think beyond anthropocentrism to foster new orientations toward entropic phenomena without pessimism.

What has become clear is that we must reject fatalisms that proclaim our path as fixed, inevitably marching us to annihilation. Avoiding this sense of impending doom requires that we think in and through the fissures of systemic interruption. The great machines of progress, capitalism, and colonialism continue to purport that there is only one way to live, which is little more than an acceleration of homogenization and death. Yet, as Mark Fisher writes:

> The long, dark night of the end of history has to be grasped as an enormous opportunity. The very oppressive pervasiveness of capitalist realism means that even glimmers of alternative political and economic possibilities can have a disproportionately great effect. The tiniest event can tear a hole in the grey curtain of reaction which has marked the horizons of possibility under capitalist realism. From a situation in which nothing can happen, suddenly anything is possible again.[7]

Thinking the absolute limits of entropic philosophy reveals that eventually every structure decays. Yet, as explored throughout this book, there are different ways to face this reality: denial, control, hastening, and care. The time has come to embrace care.

While the modern condition feels like destructive human activity is unstoppable, it is imperative that total heat death and energy dissipation not be seen as the only destination. There is no way to defeat entropy and the desire to do so must be abandoned because overcoming it would impede all change and transformation. Entropic philosophy acknowledges that death and decay are essential to existence. No bound system can sustain itself indefinitely and to even desire this is misguided. Entropic breakdown allows for new permutations and forms to come into being through transformation and combination. Death in one system is potentially life for another. The withering of one form often contributes to the prospering of another. Degeneration in one arrangement can become a stimulant to another. Chaos and destruction are also nurseries of creation.[8]

This book has largely followed the entropic metaphor through its development as a concept naming those forces that work against life and threaten order, even as they are necessary for them. There are two prominent, noisy responses to this inescapable lawfulness: upholding an anti-entropic idealism through various divine mechanisms such as Plato, Aristotle, Kant, and Hegel attempt to do, or giving in to the inevitability of it, as found in the writings of Freud, Lévi-Strauss, and modernity's treatment of humans as, what Lorde above calls, "surplus" to be used and discarded. But there are other ways in which to engage the entropic, such as focusing on materiality beyond the human, or in the philosophical and artistic celebration of change and transformation located in Nietzsche and Smithson. Then there is the quieter but perhaps more vital vein of *entrepic* thinking unearthed in Homer and Sophocles: the turning toward and care for all creation caught up in the waves and spirals of entropic forces. The *entrepic* is more closely aligned to Lorde's configuration of poetry and feeling, drawing us not only to the artistic force of creation, in the Nietzschean and Smithsonian sense, but to community, love, and protection.[9]

Chapters 1-5 surveyed moments in the development of Western thought where attempts to name, control, and succumb to entropic phenomena appear in stark illumination. First, gods are imagined to harness and form the unpredictable and disorderly chaos of matter until privation is brought under the domination of form. The supersensible substratum of nature makes rational life feel as if the world is made for its purpose and place (even if it is not) and the irrationality of natural life sacrifices itself to keep the threat of disorder and death under Spirit's dominion. Once the law is named, its workings are seen in the destruction of the death drive and civilization's razing of diversity. This process steamrolls into contemporary harms done to aging, laboring bodies. Chapters 6 and 7 think from materiality and inhuman temporality so as to destabilize the pessimism and fatalism manifest in much entropic philosophy. This shift moves humanity toward aesthetic joy and world flourishing, and, ultimately, to the *entrepic*.

The *entrepic* turn reveals fragile structures as often what must be protected and nourished. Beauvoir reminds us in *The Ethics of Ambiguity* that it is *because* we are finite that we can envision new and better futures:

> From that formless night we can draw no justification of our acts, it condemns them with the same indifference; wiping out today's errors and defeats, it will also wipe out its triumphs; it can be chaos or death as well as paradise: perhaps men will one day return to barbarism, perhaps one day the earth will no longer be anything but an icy planet. In this perspective all moments are lost in the indistinctness of nothingness and being. Man ought not entrust the care of his salvation to this uncertain and foreign future: it is up to him to assure it within his own existence; this existence is conceivable, as we have said, only as an affirmation of the future, but of a human future, a finite future.[10]

Humanity must actively seek out ways to promote flourishing amid finite resources. This can be done by developing social and cultural organizations that are beautiful precisely because they work within entropic limitations through respect and care for all that is destined to end. This redirection promotes different attitudes about life than those that deny and accelerate production and waste, advocating instead for new ideas about the structure and purpose of civilization. Delight in destruction as seen in Nietzsche and Smithson is a starting point, but it is not enough. The *entrepic* motions toward a goal of world prospering that emphasizes stewardship of systems that constantly borrow from each other. Such attentiveness seeks out sites of breakdown that are sometimes inevitable, but that also signal what may require responsiveness and healing. The *entrepic* thus brings us into the orbit of an ethics of care.

Conclusion

This project began with a twofold concern: first, studying the various ways humanity has taken up entropic phenomena, and second, finding strategies to work within the limitations of entropics with a mind toward the guardianship of finitude. While I can only gesture to it here, this latter purpose is one I see contributing to care ethics and the concerns many care ethicists have with vulnerability, dependency, and precariousness, all of which the *entrepic* turn involves. In *Precarious Life*, Judith Butler describes the shared condition of human vulnerability as an ontological fact, "one that emerges with life itself," the source of which cannot be recovered, insofar as "it precedes the formation of 'I.'"[11] Vulnerability is directly associated with finitude and contingency, both of which are constitutive of the human condition insofar as human beings are fundamentally interdependent, incomplete, and exist in an existential state of original precariousness. Vulnerability, understood as fundamental openness, is one core aspect of being in a world that demands attention and respect. Born into a world that must tend to us before any possible reciprocation, each of us is constitutively incomplete and dependent on others. No human is an island, and sovereign subjectivity, built as it is upon the foundation of autonomy, inviolability, and independence is splintered through recognition of our deeply exposed and fragmentary condition. Ontological vulnerability forms the ground of our ability to be either recognized or dehumanized, thus raising concerns about how precarity is unequally distributed onto different groups either trapped by or benefiting from systemic forms of oppression. To be open to others and the world can bring harm, but it can also bring connection and love. This is a central insight into the ethics of care and one to which *entrepic* philosophy connects.

In a virtual roundtable involving several prominent thinkers, Jasbir Puar pushes back against Butler's emphasis on the human in the discussion of precariousness and precarity. Puar argues that if Butler is serious about not rehabilitating the more dangerous ideas of humanism's emphasis on sovereign subjectivity, then the discussion needs to move beyond human vulnerability to engage "other animals, plant life, and ecologies of matter."[12] I believe *entrepics* offers a contribution to these larger concerns of care ethics because it promotes a form of thought and action that rejects nihilism by awakening concern for the many aspects of material finitude. This invites humanity to care not just for itself but to turn toward the many organisms, organizations, and structures that form the manifold worlds of which we are composed and in which we participate.

The benefit of care ethics is that "it addresses aspects of the human condition that other moral theories tend to overlook or underplay—our vulnerability to injury, our inevitable dependencies, and the ubiquity of our needs."[13] As the turn toward care and reverence for finitude in the face of death is at the heart of *entrepic* thought, what Sarah Clark Miller calls "the four faces of finitude" (need, vulnerability, dependence, and precariousness) are always in play.[14] The emphasis on finitude is directly in line with the goals of *entrepic* philosophy, which invokes consideration and reverence *precisely* at those moments when humans face mortality. These are universally shared experiences by all of us insofar as we are human, even as these are not by any means shared in the same ways.[15] Additionally, entropic philosophy shows this interdependence to be something that expands beyond the human and is part of the warp and weft of the cosmos itself.

There exists no one solution to the vast problems facing the planet right now. Rather, humanity must prioritize and collectively safeguard energy stewardship and material diversity. We must turn to the preciousness and fleetingness at the core of finitude and find ways to maximize flourishing. The urgency of world preservation eclipses individual preferences and benefits. The demand is certain: energy is finite and so we must put ourselves to the task of honoring and allocating it with forethought as it moves throughout the interrelated systems that compose the world. Entropic philosophy provides tools for diagnosing and evaluating human attitudes toward energy use and loss. The cluster of concerns that include decay, dissolution, and death evoke many different kinds of responses. Whether these produce denial and exacerbation of these very phenomena, or respect for finitude remains an open question. For our future, I hope that this book encourages the turn toward reverence and care.

NOTES

1. Robinson Jeffers, "To the Stone-Cutters," in *Robinson Jeffers: Selected Poems* (New York: Vintage Books, 1965), 3.
2. Hesiod, *Works and Days*, 95–100.
3. Lorde, *Selected Works*, 3.
4. Ibid, 6.
5. Ibid, 174.
6. Ibid, 177.
7. Mark Fisher, *Capitalist Realism: Is There No Alternative?* (Winchester: Zer0 Books, 2009), 80–81.
8. Many thinkers of entropy know this. Georgescu-Roegen says that entropy allows for "*the emergence of novelty by combination.*" Georgescu-Roegen, *Entropy Law*, 13. Greene notes that entropy "clarifies how beauty and order can be produced against a backdrop of degradation and decay." Greene, *End of Time*, 18. Hefner acknowledges that "chaos provides the possibilities without which there can be no actuality; it is the womb of creativity and actuality." Hefner, "God and Chaos," 483.
9. In *All About Love*, bell hooks advocates for expanding the notion of love, tapping into the notion of what I have named *entrepic care*. We will have evolved "when we see love as the will to nurture one's own or another's spiritual growth, revealed

through acts of care, respect, knowing, and assuming responsibility." bell hooks, *All About Love* (New York: Harper Perennial, 2000), 136.

10. Simone de Beauvoir, *The Ethics of Ambiguity*, trans. Bernard Frechtman (Seacaucus, NJ: Citadel Press, 1997), 120.

11. Judith Butler, *Precarious Life: The Powers of Mourning and Violence* (London: Verso, 2004), 31. Human beings are completely ontologically interdependent, so primary focus must be on acknowledging that becoming and thriving are wholly contingent upon others. See also Judith Butler, *Notes Toward a Performative Theory of Assembly* (Cambridge: Harvard University Press, 2015), 120.

12. Puar, "Precarity Talk," 171. Butler acknowledges that this is an important point insofar as any discussion of the human necessarily involves the nonhuman, yet she does not develop in detail what this means. Joshua Trey Barnett argues that even though Butler does not often speak in ecological terms, care ethics can take into consideration the multiple systems in which one is exposed, "which include not only other people, but also other kinds of animals, plants, chemicals, artifacts, places, buildings, objects, and other forces. Ecologies are teeming with others, which is why ecology and the social are never far apart." Joshua Trey Barnett, "Thinking Ecologically with Judith Butler," *Culture, Theory and Critique* 59, no. 1 (2018): 20–39. Daniel Ross, who studies many of the same thinkers I do, concludes that we must find "a way of caring not just for our biospheric negentropic fate, but also for our psychospheric and noospheric neganthropic fate." Daniel Ross, "The End of Metaphysics of Being and the Beginning of the Metacosmics of Entropy," *Phainomena* 29 (June 2020): 98. The logic of precariousness and precarity has other critics. Ritu Vij, for example, challenges Butler's universalizing discourse. Ritu Vij, "The Global Subject of Precarity," *Globalizations* (Routledge) 16, no. 4 (2019): 506–524. Rij argues that the move to say that all humans are precarious "ends up reinforcing the image of the Third World as a zone of abjection, now available to previously sovereign Western liberal subjects." Ibid, 514. See also, Puar, "Precarity Talk."

13. Sarah Clark Miller, "From Vulnerability to Precariousness: Examining the Moral Foundations of Care Ethics," *International Journal of Philosophical Studies* 28, no. 5 (2020): 644.

14. Miller clarifies that need names an absence, vulnerability expresses an openness to reception, dependence is leaning on another, and precariousness is a kind of teetering from a place where one could fall. Miller, *Vulnerability to Precariousness*, 646. Miller focuses primarily on precariousness as it highlights the instability and uncertainty in all lives.

15. I urge readers to read the many powerful essays in Hasana Sharp and Chloë Taylor's, *Feminist Philosophies of Life*, many of which critique a Butlerian emphasis on the human and instead celebrate "matter as a (self)-organizing, structuring, transforming force." Ladelle McWhorter, "Foreword," in *Feminist Philosophies of Life*, eds. Hasana Sharp and Chloë Taylor (Montreal & Kingston: McGill-Queens University Press, 2016), xii.

Bibliography

Aristotle. *The Nicomachean Ethics.* Edited and translated by Martin Ostwald. Upper Saddle River, NJ: Prentice Hall, 1962.

———. *The Complete Works of Aristotle.* vol. 1. Edited by Jonathan Barnes. Princeton: Princeton University Press, 1984.

———. *The Complete Works of Aristotle.* vol. 2. Edited by Jonathan Barnes. Princeton: Princeton University Press, 1984.

Arnheim, Rudolf. *Entropy and Art: An Essay on Disorder and Order.* Berkeley: University of California Press, 1971.

Asimov, Isaac. "The Last Question." *Science Fiction Quarterly* (November 1956). Accessed May 3, 2021. http://www.gdctangmarg.com/Photos/04_02_2001_35_54Sem%20II_Asimov.pdf.

Aviv, Rachel. "How the Elderly Lose Their Rights." *The New Yorker.* October 9, 2017. https://www.newyorker.com/magazine/2017/10/09/how-the-elderly-lose-their-rights?mbid=social_facebook_aud_dev_kw_paid-how-the-elderly-lose-their-rights&kwp_0=712051.

Babich, Babette E. "Nietzsche's Chaos Sive Natura: Evening Gold and the Dancing Star." *Revista Portuguesa de Filosofia* 57 (2001): 225–45.

Ball, Karyn. "The Entropics of Discourse: The 'Materiality' of Affect Between Marx and Derrida." In *Encountering Derrida: Legacies and Futures of Deconstruction*, edited by Allison Weiner and Simon Morgan Wortham. London: Continuum International Publishing Group, 2007.

———. "Losing Steam After Marx and Freud." *Angelaki* 20, no. 3 (2015): 55–78.

Ballard, J. D. *High Rise.* New York: W. W. Norton & Company, 2012.

Barbosa de Almeida, Mauro W. "Symmetry and Entropy: Mathematical Metaphors in the Work of Lévi-Strauss." *Current Anthropology* 31, no. 4 (1990): 367–85.

Barnett, Joshua Trey. "Thinking Ecologically with Judith Butler." *Culture, Theory and Critique* 59, no. 1 (2018): 20–39.

Beauvoir, Simone de. *America Day by Day.* Translated by Carol Cosman. Berkeley: University of California Press, 1990.

———. *The Coming of Age (La vieillesse)*. Translated by Patrick O'Brian. New York: W.W. Norton & Company, 1996
———. *The Ethics of Ambiguity*. Translated by Bernard Frechtman. Seacaucus, NJ: Citadel Press, 1997.
———. *The Second Sex*. Translated by Constance Borde and Sheila Malovany-Chevallier. New York: Alfred A. Knopf, 2010.
Benjamin, Walter. "Theses on the Philosophy of History." In *Illuminations*, translated by Harry Zohn. New York: Schocken, 1969.
Bennett, Charles H. "Demons, Engines and the Second Law." *Scientific American* 275, no. 5 (November 1987): 108–16.
Bennett, Jane. "The Force of Things: Steps toward an Ecology of Matter." *Political Theory* 32, no. 3 (2004): 347–72.
———. "A Vitalist Stopover on the Way to New Materialism." In *New Materialisms: Ontology, Agency, and Politics*, edited by Diana Coole and Samantha Frost. Durham: Duke University Press, 2010.
———. *Vibrant Matter: A Political Ecology of Things*. Durham: Duke University Press, 2010.
Berlant, Lauren. "Slow Death (Sovereignty, Obesity, Lateral Agency)." *Critical Inquiry* 33 (2007): 754–80.
Betz, Eric. "The Big Crunch Vs. the Big Freeze." *Astronomy*, January 2021, 50–52.
Bianchi, Emanuela. *The Feminine Symptom: Aleatory Matter in the Aristotelian Cosmos*. New York: Fordham University Press, 2014.
Biel, Robert. *The Entropy of Capitalism*. Chicago: Haymarket Books, 2012.
BigThink. "Hey Bill Nye, 'Does Science Have All the Answers or Should We Do Philosophy Too?" *YouTube*. February 23, 2016. https://www.youtube.com/watch?v=ROe28Ma_tYM.
Borges, Jorge Luis. *Labyrinths: Selected Stories and Other Writings*. New Directions Publishing Corp, 1964.
Briegas, Marta Torres. "Artificial Intelligence has Made its Way to Literature." *BBVA*. November 6, 2018. https://www.bbva.com/en/artificial-intelligence-made-way-literature/.
Brill, Sara. *Plato on the Limits of Human Life*. Bloomington: Indiana University Press, 2013.
Bruder, Jessica. "The End of Retirement: When you Can't Afford to Stop Working." *Harper's Magazine*, August 2014, 28–36.
———. *Nomadland: Surviving America in the Twenty-First Century*. New York: W. W. Norton & Company, 2017.
Buchdahl, Gerd. "Hegel on the Interaction Between Science and Philosophy." In *Hegel and Newtonianism*, edited by M. J. Petry. Dordrecht: Kluwer Academic Publishers, 1993.
Butler, Judith. *Precarious Life: The Powers of Mourning and Violence*. London: Verso, 2004.
———. *Notes Toward a Performative Theory of Assembly*. Cambridge: Harvard University Press, 2015.

Campbell, Jeremy. "Observer and Object, Reader and Text: Some Parallel Themes in Modern Science and Literature." In *Beyond the Two Cultures: Essays on Science, Technology, and Literature*, edited by Joseph W. Slade and Judith Yaross Lee. Ames: Iowa State University Press, 1990.

Camus, Albert. *The Myth of Sisyphus and Other Essays*. Translated by James O'Brien. New York: Vintage International, 1991.

Clough, Patricia T. "The Affective Turn: Political Economy, Biomedia and Bodies." *Theory, Culture & Society* 25, no. 1 (2008): 1–22.

Cockburn, Andrew. "Elder Abuse: Nursing Homes, the Coronavirus, and the Bottom Line." *Harper's Magazine*, September 2020, 43–49.

Cooke, Lynne and Karen Kelly with Bettina Funcke and Barbara Schröder, eds. *Robert Smithson Spiral Jetty: True Fictions, False Realities*. Berkeley: University of California Press, 2005.

Coole, Diana and Samantha Frost, eds. *New Materialisms: Ontology, Agency, and Politics*. Durham: Duke University Press, 2010.

Copjec, Joan. *Imagine There's No Woman*. Cambridge: The MIT Press, 2003.

Curd, Patricia, ed. *A Presocratics Reader: Selected Fragments and Testimonia*. Translated by Richard D. Mckirihan and Patricia Curd. Indianapolis: Hackett Publishing Company, 2011.

Delueze, Gilles and Félix Guattari, *A Thousand Plateaus: Capitalism and Schizophrenia*. Translated by Brian Massumi. Minneapolis: Minnesota University Press, 1987.

Derrida, Jacques. *Spectres of Marx: The State of the Debt, the Work of Mourning and the New International*. Edited and translated by Peggy Kamuf. New York: Routledge Classics, 2006.

Dick, Philip K. *Martian Time Slip*. New York: Vintage Books, 1995.

Dvorsky, George. "Neil deGrasse Tyson Slammed for Dismissing Philosophy as "Useless"." *Gizmodo*, May 12, 2014. https://gizmodo.com/neil-degrasse-tyson-slammed-for-dismissing-philosophy-a-1575178224.

Eddington, Arthur. *The Nature of the Physical World*. New York: Macmillian, 1948.

Ehrenreich, Barbara. *Natural Causes: An Epidemic of Wellness, the Certainty of Dying, and Killing Ourselves to Live Longer*. New York: Twelve, 2018.

Fanon, Frantz. *The Wretched of the Earth*. Translated by Richard Philcox. New York: Grove Press, 2004.

———. *Black Skin, White Masks*. Translated by Richard Philcox. New York: Grove Press, 2008.

Fechner, Gustav. *Einige ideen zur chöpfungs und entwicklungsgeschichte der organismen*. Leipzig: Breitkopf und Härtel, 1873. https://www.projekt-gutenberg.org/fechner/schoepfg/schoepfg.html.

Fisher, Mark. *Captitalist Realism: Is There no Alternative?* Winchester: Zer0 Books, 2009.

Foucault, Michel. *Language, Counter-Memory, Practice: Selected Essays and Interviews by Michel Foucault*. Edited by Donald F. Bouchard. Translated by Donald F. Bouchard and Sherry Simon. Ithaca: Cornell University Press, 1977.

Franklin, Allan and Paul M. Leavitt. "Borges and Entropy." *Review: Latin American Literature and Arts* (1975): 54–56.

Freud, Sigmund. *Totem and Taboo*. Edited and translated by James Strachey. New York: W. W. Norton & Company, 1950.

———. *The Ego and the Id*. Edited and translated by James Strachey. New York: W. W. Norton and Company, 1960.

———. *Beyond the Pleasure Principle*. Edited and translated by James Strachey. New York: W. W. Norton & Sons, 1961.

———. *Civilization and Its Discontents*. Edited and translated by James Strachey. New York: W. W Norton & Company, 1961.

———. *The Standard Edition of the Complete Psychological Works of Sigmund Freud*. Edited and translated by James Strachey. London: The Hogarth Press, 1999.

Fultot, Martin Flament. "Ethics of Entropy." *APA Newsletter Philosophy and Computers* 15, no. 2 (Spring 2016): 4–9.

Furlotte, Wes. *The Problem of Nature in Hegel's Final System*. Edinburgh: Edinburgh University Press, 2018.

Georgescu-Roegen, Nicholas. *The Entropy Law and the Economic Process*. Cambridge: Harvard University Press, 1971.

Godley, James A. "Infinite Grief: Freud, Hegel, and Lacan on the Thought of Death." *Angelaki* 23, no. 6 (2018): 93–110.

Goethe, Johann Wolfgang von. *Goethe's Faust*. Translated by Walter Kaufmann. New York: Random House, 1990.

Goldhill, Olivia. "Bill Nye, the Science Guy, Says I Convinced Him that Philosophy is Not Just a Load of Self-Indulgent Crap." *Quartz*. April 15, 2017. https://qz.com/960303/bill-nye-on-philosophy-the-science-guy-says-he-has-changed-his-mind/.

Gorelick, Nathan. "The Real (of) Debt: Notes Toward and Ethics of Trash." *Continental Thought and Theory: A Journal of Intellectual Freedom* 1, no. 2 (2017): 490–517.

———. "Psychoanalysis at the End of the World." In *Lacan and the Environment*, edited by Clint Burnham and Paul Kingsbury. London: Palgrave Macmillan, 2021.

GPT-3. "A robot wrote this entire article. Are you scared yet, human?" *The Guardian*. September 8, 2020. https://www.theguardian.com/commentisfree/2020/sep/08/robot-wrote-this-article-gpt-3.

Graham, Daniel W., ed. *The Texts of Early Greek Philosophy*. Cambridge: Cambridge University Press, 2010.

Greene, Brian. *Until the End of Time: Mind, Matter, and Our Search for Meaning in an Evolving Universe*. New York: Vintage Books, 2021.

Gregory, Andrew. *Ancient Greek Cosmogony*. London: Bristol Classical Press, 2007.

Grosz, Elizabeth. *Volatile Bodies: Toward a Corporeal Feminism*. Bloomington: Indiana University Press, 1994.

———. *Space, Time, and Perversion: Essays on the Politics of Bodies*. New York: Routledge, 1995.

———. "Darwin and Feminism: Preliminary Investigations for a Possible Alliance." In *Material Feminisms*, edited by Stacy Alaimo and Susan Hekman. Bloomington: Indiana University Press, 2008.

Guenther, Lisa. *Solitary Confinement: Social Death and its Afterlives*. Minneapolis: University of Minnesota Press, 2013.

Hardt, Michael and Antonio Negri. *Multitude: War and the Democracy in the Age of Empire*. New York: Penguin, 2004.

Harris, Malcolm. *Kids These Days: Human Capital and the Making of Millennials*. Little, Brown and Company, 2017.

Hayles, N. Katherine. *How We Became Posthuman: Virtual Bodies in Cybernetics, Literature and Informatics*. Chicago: University of Chicago Press, 1999.

Hefner, Philip. "God and Chaos: The Demiurge Versus the Ungrund." *Zygon* 19, no. 4 (1984): 469–85.

Hegel, G. W. F. *Philosophy of Nature: Being Part Two of the Encyclopaedia of the Philosophical Sciences*. Translated by A. V. Miller. Oxford: Clarendon Press, 1970.

———. *The Philosophy of History*. Translated by J. Sibree. Amherst, NY: Prometheus Books, 1991.

———. *Hauptwerke in sechs bänden*. vol. 6. Hamburg: Felix Meiner Verlag, 1992.

Heidegger, Martin. *The Question Concerning Technology and Other Essays*. Translated by William Lovitt. New York: Harper & Row, 1977.

Hesiod. *Theogony, Works and Days, Shield*. Translated by Apostolos N. Athanassakis. 1st ed. Baltimore: Johns Hopkins University Press, 1983.

Hester, Jeff. "Entropy's Rainbow." *Astronomy* (October 2017): 16.

———. "Entropy Redux." *Astronomy* (November 2017): 66.

Homer. *The Iliad*. Translated by Robert Fagles. New York: Penguin Books, 1991.

———. *The Odyssey*. Edited and translated by Robert Fagles. New York: Penguin Books, 1999.

hooks, bell. *All About Love*. New York: Harper Perennial, 2000.

———. *Feminism is for Everybody: Passionate Politics*. Cambridge: South End Press, 2000.

———. *Writing Beyond Race: Living Theory and Practice*. New York: Routledge, 2013.

Horn, Christoph. "Why Two Epochs of Human History? On the Myth of The Statesman." In *Plato and Myth: Studies on the Use and Status of Platonic Myths*, edited by Pierre Destrée, Francisco J. Gonzalez, and Catherine Collobert. Leiden: Brill, 2012.

Houlgate, Stephen, ed. *Hegel and the Philosophy of* Nature. Albany: SUNY Press, 1998.

Igrek, Apple Zefalius. *Entropic Affirmation: On the Origins of Conflict in Change, Death, and Otherness*. Lanham: Lexington Books, 2018.

Jeffers, Robinson. "To the Stone-Cutters." In *Robinson Jeffers: Selected Poems*. New York: Vintage Books, 1965.

———. "November Surf." In *The Norton Anthology of Poetry*, edited by Arthur M. Eastman. New York: W. W. Norton & Company, 1970.

Johnston, Adrian. "The Voiding of Weak Nature." *Graduate Faculty Philosophy Journal* 33, no. 1 (2012): 103–57.
Jones, Peter Lloyd. "Some Thoughts on Rudolf Arnheim's Book 'Entropy and Art.'" *Leonardo* 6 (1973): 29–35.
Lee, Richard A., Jr. *The Thought of Matter: Materialism, Conceptuality, and the Transcendence of Immanence.* London: Rowman & Littlefield International, 2016.
Kant, Immanuel. *Perpetual Peace and Other Essays.* Translated by Ted Humphrey. Indianapolis: Hackett Publishing Company, 1983.
———. *The Critique of Judgment.* Translated by Werner S. Pluhar. Indianapolis: Hackett Publishing Company, 1987.
Kierkegaard, Søren. *Fear and Trembling and Repetition.* Edited and translated by Howard V. Hong and Edna H. Hong. Princeton: Princeton University Press, 1983.
Kunzru, Hari. "Easy Chair: Complexity." *Harper's Magazine,* January 2021, 7.
Lacan, Jacques. *Science and Truth.* Edited and translated by Bruce Fink. New York: W. W. Norton & Coompany, 2006.
Layzer, David. "The Arrow of Time." *Scientific American* (1975): 56–69.
Le Guin, Ursula K. *The Lathe of Heaven.* New York: Avon Books, 1971.
Lévi-Strauss, Claude. *Structural Anthropology.* Translated by Clair Jacobson and Brooke Grundfest Schoepf. New York: Basic Books, 1963.
———. *The Elementary Structures of Kinship.* Edited and translated by James Harle Bell and Richard von Sturmer. Boston: Beacon Press, 1969.
———. *Tristes tropiques.* Translated by John Weightman and Doreen Weightman. New York: Penguin Press, 2012.
Lidell, Henry George and Robert Scott. *A Greek-English Lexicon.* 9th ed. Oxford: Clarendon Press, 1940.
Lorde, Audre. *The Selected Works of Audre Lorde.* Edited by Roxane Gay. New York: W. W. Norton & Company, 2020.
Malabou, Catherine. "Plasticity and Elasticiy in Freud's 'Beyond the Pleasure Principle.'" *Parallax* 15, no. 2 (2009): 41–52.
Manacorda, Francesco. "Entropology: Monuments to Closed Systems." *Flash Art* (2005): 76–79.
Margulis, Lynn and Dorion Sagan. *What is Life?* New York: Simon and Schuster, 1995.
McKibben, Bill. *The End of Nature.* New York: Bloomsbury Publishing PLC, 2003.
McRuer, Robert. *Crip Theory: Cultural Signs of Queerness and Disability.* New York: New York University Press, 2006.
Meisel, Martin. *Chaos Imagined: Literature, Art, Science.* New York: Columbia University Press, 2016.
Micale, Mark S. *Beyond the Unconscious: Essays of Henri F. Ellenberger in the History of Psychiatry.* Princeton: Princeton University Press, 2016.
Miller, Sarah Clark. "From Vulnerability to Precariousness: Examining the Moral Foundations of Care Ethics." *International Journal of Philosophical Studies* 28, no. 5 (2020): 644–61.

Mitchel, David T. and Sharon L. Snyder. "Disability as Multitude: Re-Working Non-Productive Labor Power." *Journal of Literary and Cultural Disability Studies* 4, no. 2 (2010): 1–10, doi: 10.3828/jlcds/2010.14.

Murakami, Haruki. *A Wild Sheep Chase*. Translated by Alfred Birnbaum. New York: Vintage International, 2002.

Mussett, Shannon M. "Irony and the Work of Art: Hegelian Legacies in Robert Smithson." *Evental Aesthetics* 1, no. 1 (2012): 45–73.

———. "Irrationality, Entropy, and Nature: The Aesthetic Collision of Hegel and Smithson." In *Rendezvous with the Sensuous: Readings on Aesthetics*, edited by Linda Ardito and John Murungi. Newcastle upon Tyne: Cambridge Scholars Publishing, 2014.

———. "Death and Sacrifice in Hegel's Philosophy of Nature." *Epoché*, Nancy Tuana 22, no. 1 (2017): 119–34.

———. "Life and Sexual Difference in Hegel and Beauvoir." *Journal of Speculative Philosophy* 31, no. 3 (2017): 396–408.

———. "Robert Smithson, Entropic Art, and the West." In *Philosophy in the American West: A Geography of Thought*, edited by Gerard Kuperus, Brian Treanor, and Josh Hayes. New York: Routledge, 2020.

Nietzsche, Friedrich. *Philosophy in the Tragic Age of the Greeks*. Edited and translated by Marianne Cowan. Washington, DC: Regnery Publishing, 1962.

———. *The Birth of Tragedy and the Case Against Richard Wagner*. Translated by Walter Kaufmann. New York: Vintage Books, 1967.

———. *The Will to Power*. Translated by Walter Kaufmann and R. J. Hollingdale. Edited by Walter Kaufmann. New York: Vintage Books, 1968.

———. *Thus Spoke Zarathustra*. Translated by Walter Kaufmann. New York: Penguin Books, 1978.

———. *Beyond Good and Evil*. Translated by Walter Kaufmann. New York: Vintage Books, 1989.

———. *On the Genealogy of Morals and Ecce Homo*. Edited and translated by Walter Kaufmann. New York: Vintage Books, 1989.

———. *Twilight of the Idols*. Edited and translated by Richard Polt. Indianapolis: Hackett Publishing Company, 1997.

Padui, Raoni. "The Necessity of Contingency and the Powerlessness of Nature: Hegel's Two Senses of Contingency." *Idealistic Studies* 40, no. 3 (2010): 243–55.

———. "Hegel's Ontological Pluralism: Rethinking the Distinction Between Natur and Geist." *The Review of Metaphysics* 67 (2013): 125–48.

Park, Peter K. J. *Africa, Asia, and the History of Philosophy: Racism in the Formation of the Philosophical Canon, 1730–1830*. Albany: Statue University of New York Press, 2014.

Pepper, Stephen. *World Hypotheses: Prolegomena to a Systematic Philosophy and a Complete Survey of Metaphysics*. Berkeley: University of California Press, 1961.

Pigliucci, Massimo. "Neil deGrasse Tyson and the Value of Philosophy." *Huffpost*. May 16, 2014. https://www.huffingtonpost.com/massimo-pigliucci/neil-degrasse-tyson-and-the-value-of-philosophy_b_5330216.html.

Pinkard, Terry. "Speculative Naturphilosophie and the Development of the Empirical Sciences." In *Continental Philosophy of Science*, edited by Gary Gutting. Maldan: Blackwell Publishing, 2008.

Plato. *Five Dialogues*. Translated by G.M.A. Grube. Edited by John M. Cooper. Indianapolis: Hackett Publishing Company, 1981.

———. The *Republic*. Translated by Allan Bloom. Basic Books, 1991.

———. *Plato: Complete Works*. Edited and translated by Donald J. Zeyl and John M. Cooper. Indianapolis: Hackett Publishing Company, 1997.

———. The *Statesman*. Edited by Jeffrey Henderson. Translated by Herald N. Fowler. In the *Statesman, Philebus, Ion*. Cambridge: Loeb Classical Library, 2006.

Prigogine, Ilya. "Time, Structure, and Fluctuations." *Science* 201, no. 4358 (1978): 777–85.

Pritzl, Kurt. "Anaximander's 'Apeiron' and the Arrangement of Time." In *Early Greek Philosophy: The Presocratics and the Emergence of Reason*, edited by Joe McCoy. Washington: The Catholic University of America Press, 2013.

Puar, Jasbir K. "Coda: The Cost of Getting Better: Suicide, Sensation, Switchpoints." *GLQ: A Journal of Lesbian and Gay Studies* 18, no. 1 (2012): 149–58.

———. "Precarity Talk: A Virtual Roundtable with Lauren Berlant, Judith Butler, Bojana Cvejić, Isabell Lorey, Jasbir Puar, and Ana Vujanović." *The Drama Review* 56, no. 4 (2012): 163–77.

Purdy, Jedediah. *After Nature: A Politics for the Anthropocene*. Cambridge: Harvard University Press, 2015.

Pynchon, Thomas. *Slow Learner: Early Stories*. New York: Little, Brown and Company, 1985.

Rand, Sebastian. "The Importance and Relevance of Hegel's Philosophy of Nature." *The Review of Metaphysics* 61 (2007): 379–400.

Reece, Erik. "Bright Power, Dark Peace." *Harper's Magazine*, September 2020, 52–59.

Reuters Staff. *Reuters. Fact check: The causes for Texas' blackout go well beyond wind turbines*. February, 19 2021. https://www.reuters.com/article/uk-factcheck-texas-wind-turbines-explain/fact-check-the-causes-for-texas-blackout-go-well-beyond-wind-turbines-idUSKBN2AJ2EI.

Roberts, Jennifer L. "The Taste of Time: Salt and Spiral Jetty." In *Robert Smithson*, edited by Eugenie Tsai with Cornelia Butler. Berkeley: University of California Press, 2004.

Ross, Daniel. "The End of the Metaphysics of Being and the Beginning of the Metacosmics of Entropy." *Phainomena: Journal of the Phenomenological Society of Ljubljana* 29, no. 112–113 (June 2020): 73–100.

Sale, Peter F. *Our Dying Planet: An Ecologist's View of the Crisis We Face*. Oakland: University of California Press, 2011.

Sallis, John, ed. *Plato's Statesman: Dialectic, Myth, and Politics*. Albany: SUNY Press, 2017.

Sartre, Jean-Paul. *Nausea*. Translated by Lloyd Alexander. New York: New Directions Publishing Corporation, 1964.

Scarre, Geoffrey ed. *The Palgrave Handbook of the Philosophy of Aging*. London: Palgrave Macmillan, 2016.
Schelling, F. W. J. von. *On the History of Modern Philosophy*. Translated by Andrew Bowie. Cambridge: Cambridge University Press, 1994.
———. *Philosophy of German Idealism*. Edited by Ernst Behler. New York: Continuum, 2003.
Schweda, Marc, Michael Coors, and Claudia Bozzaro, eds. *Aging and Human Nature: Perspectives from Philosophical, Theological, and Historical Anthropology*. New York: Springer International Publishing, 2020.
Searcey, Dionne. "No Wind Farms Aren't the Main Cause of the Texas Blackouts." *The New York Times*. February 2, 2017. https://www.nytimes.com/2021/02/17/climate/texas-blackouts-disinformation.html.
Shakespeare, William. *King Lear*. New York: Bantam Books, 1988.
Shapiro, Gary. "Entropy and Dialectic: The Signatures of Robert Smithson." *Arts Magazine*, Summer 1988, 99–104.
———. *Earthwards: Robert Smithson and Art After Babel*. Berkeley: University of California Press, 1997.
Sharp, Hasana and Chloë Taylor, eds. *Feminist Philosophies of Life*. Montreal & Kingston: McGill-Queens University Press, 2016.
Shaw, Michael M. "Unqualified Generation in Aristotle's Natural Philosophy." *Proceedings of the Boston Area Colloquium in Ancient Philosophy* Leiden: Brill (2014): 77–106.
———. "Parataxis in Anaxagoras: Seeds and Worlds in Fragment B4a." *Epoché: A Journal for the History of Philosophy* (March 2017): 273–88.
Shusterman, Ronald. "Anish Kapoor and the Anti-entropy of Art." *Proceedings of the European Society for Aesthetics* 4 (Winter 2012): 472–88.
Slade, Joseph. "Entropy and Other Calamities." In *Pynchon: A Collection of Critical Essays*, edited by Edward Mendelson. Uppler Saddle River: Prentice-Hall, 1978.
Smithson, Robert. *Robert Smithson: The Collected Writings*. Edited by Jack Flam. Berkeley: University of California Press, 1996.
———. *Spiral Jetty*. Directed and performed by Robert Smithson. New York: VAGA at ARS, 1970. 16mm film on video.
Sophocles. *Ajax*. In *The Complete Greek Tragedies*, edited by David Grene and Richmond Lattimore. Translated by John Moore. vol. 2, Sophocles II. Chicago: The University of Chicago Press, 1969.
———. *Oedipus at Colonus*. In *Sophocles I*, edited by David Grene and Richard Lattimore. Translated by David Grene. 2nd ed. Chicago: University of Chicago Press, 1991.
———. *Oedipus the King*. In *Sophocles I*, edited by David Grene and Richard Lattimore. Translated by David Grene. 2nd ed. Chicago: University of Chicago Press, 1991.
Staude, John Raphael. "From Depth Psychology to Depth Sociology: Freud, Jung, and Lévi-Strauss." *Theory and Society* 3, no. 3 (1976): 303–38.
Stauffer, Jill. *Ethical Loneliness: The Injustice of Not Being Heard*. New York: Columbia University Press, 2015.

Stengers, Isabelle, and Ilya Prigogine. *Order Out of Chaos: Man's New Dialogue with Nature.* Boulder: Shambahala, 1984.

Stone, Alison. *Petrified Intelligence: Nature in Hegel's Philosophy.* Albany: SUNY Press, 2005.

Sweet, Kristi. *Kant on Freedom, Nature, and Judgment: The Territory of the Third Critique.* Cambridge: Cambridge University Press, 2022.

Szerszynski, Bronislaw. "Gods of the Anthropocene: Geo-Spiritual Formations in the Earth's New Epoch." *Theory, Culture and Society* 34, no. 2–3 (2017): 253–75.

Terranova, Luciana and Tiziana Parisi. "Emergence and Control in Genetic Engineering and Aritificial Life." *CTheory* (May 2000): https://journals.uvic.ca/index.php/ctheory/article/view/14604/5455.

Tisdale, Sallie. "Out of Time: The Un-becoming of Self." *Harper's Magazine*, March 2018, 63–69.

Tran The, Jessica, Jean-Phillippe Ansermet, Pierre Magistretti, and Francois Ansermet. "From the Principle of Inertia to the Death Drive: The Influence of the Second Law of Thermodynamics on the Freudian Theory of the Psychical Apparatus." *Frontiers in Psychology* 11 (February 2020): 1–8.

Tribus, M. "Information Theory and Thermodynamics." In *Heat Transfer, Thermodynamics and Education: Boelter Anniversary Volume*, edited by H. A. Johnson. New York: McGraw Hill, 1964.

Trott, Adriel. *Aristotle on the Matter of Form: A Feminist Metaphysics of Generation.* Edinburgh: University of Edinburgh Press, 2019.

Tufayl, Ibn. *Hayy ibn yaqzan.* Translated by Lenn Evan Goodman. Chicago: University of Chicago Press, 2009.

Turner, Terrence. "On Structure and Entropy: Theoretical Pastiche and the Contradictions of 'Structuralism.'" *Current Anthropology* 31, no. 5 (1990): 563–68.

Vij, Ritu. "The Global Subject of Precarity." *Globalizations.* Routledge 16, no. 4 (2019): 506–24.

Warman, Matt and Mattwarman. "Stephen Hawking Tells Google 'Philosophy Is Dead.'" *The Telegraph.* May 17, 2011. http://www.telegraph.co.uk/technology/google/8520033/Stephen-Hawking-tells-Google-philosophy-is-dead.html.

Wolchover, Natalie. "New Quantum Theory Could Explain the Flow of Time." *Wired.* April 25, 2014. https://www.wired.com/2014/04/quantum-theory-flow-time/.

Yanagisawa, Hideaki. "Chaos Theoretical Explanation to Operating Time and Space in Literature: A Writer Shows a Chaos State Intentionally in a Novel and Gives Illusory Joy of Entropy Decreasing to Many Readers." SSRN. July 17th, 2019. https://papers.ssrn.com/sol3/papers.cfm?abstract_id=3408257.

Zencey, Eric. "Some Brief Speculations on the Popularity of Entropy as Metaphor." *The North American Review* 271, no. 3 (1986): 7–10.

———."Entropy as Root Metaphor." In *Beyond Two Cultures: Essays on Science, Technology, and Literature*, edited by Joseph W. Slade and Judith Yaross Lee. Ames: Iowa State University Press, 1990.

———. *Virgin Forest.* Athens: University of Georgia Press, 1998.

Index

age, 9, 27; the aged, 11, 108–10, 125n7; ageism, 110, 115–18, 178; ageless, 39, 41, 45, 50–51, 58n47, 109; age studies, 126; aging body, 4, 12, 107, 109, 116, 120, 122–25, 129n57; *The Coming of Age* (*La vieillesse*), 107, 110, 115, 118, 125n1, 126n1; old age, 11–12, 39, 47–48, 58n47, 77, 107–12, 115–25, 128n53, 132; retirement age, 116–22; the working aged, 12, 28, 100, 109–12, 116–25, 129n57

Anaxagoras, 10, 37, 41, 55; cosmology, 27, 43, 57n26, 59n80; matter, 10, 27, 42–43; metaphysics, 42, 58n47; mind, 10, 27, 37, 41–44, 51, 55, 57n26

Anaximander, 10, 37, 41, 43, 46–48, 77; *apeiron*, 41–43, 46, 47, 56n21, 57n23, 77

anxiety, xi, xiv, 109, 113–15; about death, 3–4, 76, 94, 113–15, 148, 156, 164; clinical anxiety, 114, 128n52

apeiron. See Anaximander

Aristotle, 10, 37, 51–52, 74, 77, 89, 92, 102n26, 179; *Metaphysics*, 52–55; philosophy of nature, 27; *Physics*, 52–54, 71, 102n26; prime mover, 37, 54–55; privation, 11, 27, 37, 51–55,

59nn66–67, 59nn71–72, 59n75, 69, 76, 91

arrow of time, 5, 9–10, 18, 32n33, 42, 86, 110, 124, 164

art, xiii, 5, 9, 78; disruptive art, 142, 147, 149; earth art, 167, 169, 170, 174n34; entropic art, 12, 28, 30n5, 142–49, 153n46, 153n55, 163–72, 179, 180; in Freud, 85–86; in Nietzsche, 163–64, 179; of Robert Smithson, 12, 28, 142–49, 164–72, 174n34

artificial intelligence, xi, 3

artist, 3, 5, 169–70, 174; divine artisan, 46–48; entropic artist, 12–13, 29, 125, 141–49, 152nn34–35, 164, 172; in Nietzsche, 163–64

Asimov, Isaac, 35–36, 39, 43, 165

Ball, Karyn, 12, 28, 92, 110–15, 118, 123, 125, 126n17, 126nn19–20, 126n22; poetics of entropics, 111–12, 115, 123, 125

Ballard, J. G., 131

Beauvoir, Simone de, 12, 14n9, 28, 107, 109–10, 115–20, 122, 124, 127n39, 128n52, 180

becoming, 29, 37, 43–44, 46–48, 51, 73, 114, 183n11; in Nietzsche, 13, 157, 162

Benjamin, Walter, 104n44
Bennett, Jane, 28, 137–41; thing-power materialism, 151n19; vital materialism, 12, 137–42, 149, 151n18, 152n32
Berlant, Lauren: slow death, 116–17, 127n32
Big Freeze, 4, 20. *See also* heat death
body, 17, 44, 46, 48–49, 53, 55, 62–63, 74–76, 82, 103n29; aging body, 4, 12, 107, 109, 116, 120, 122–25, 129n57; de-subjectified body, 113, 134, 141; human body as a machine, 12, 88, 110–12; laboring body, 88, 114–15, 126n20; as a system, 19–20, 122; of the world, 15, 47, 69
Boltzmann, Ludwig, 21, 23, 31n31, 57n26, 62
Borges, Luis, 25–26, 29
breakdown, xiv, 2–3, 10–12, 20, 24–25, 28–29, 45, 68, 72, 76, 83–84, 94–95, 97, 133, 139, 141, 144, 153n50, 155, 164, 166–77; entropic breakdown, 12, 54, 76, 110, 124–25, 178–80
Brücke, Ernst Wilhelm von, 88, 102n18
Butler, Judith, 127n32, 181, 183nn11–13, 183n15

capitalism, 12, 85, 94, 96, 111–12, 116–17, 122, 136, 143, 150n14, 170, 177–79; late-stage capitalism, xiv, 108–10, 114–16, 124–25. *See also* industrial revolution
care, 3, 28, 109, 111, 122, 161, 178–79; for the aged, 107–8, 111, 116, 120, 124; call for, xiv, 123, 133, 149; care ethics, 100, 181–83, 183n12; *entrepic* care, 7–10, 12, 14n16, 14n18, 14n20, 109, 123–24, 132, 141, 157, 171, 180, 182n9; in the face of death, 7–9, 55, 181–82; for finitude, 8, 10, 157, 169; human need to, 6, 157, 178; turn toward, 14, 100, 132, 159; for vulnerability, 6, 8, 124, 157, 169, 181

chaos, xiv, 3, 6, 11–12, 24–26, 122–23, 166; in Anaxagoras, 10, 37, 42–43; in Anaximander, 37, 41; in Aristotle, 11, 37, 51, 53; in Beauvoir, 180; as chasm, 38–39, 47; as disorderly, 4–5, 10–11, 27, 36–38, 40–41, 180; entropic, 18, 27, 62; in Freud, 87, 92; generative power of, 5, 12, 28–29, 29n2, 37–38, 133, 166, 173n26, 179, 182n8; in Goethe, 155; in Hegel, 11, 70–73, 76, 78, 80n35; in Hesiod, 6, 10, 12, 28, 38–39, 47–48, 55; as homogeneity, 4, 10, 26–27, 42; in Kant, 11, 63–68, 78; in Lévi-Strauss, 98–99; material, 42, 46–47, 65–69, 73, 76, 78, 180; as natural force, 63, 68, 70; in Plato, 10, 37, 46–50, 72; political, 40; in Pynchon, 62; in Schelling, 63–64, 68–69, 78, 80n26
chora, 47–49, 58n49
Clausius, Rudolf, 6, 19–21, 28, 62, 126n18
control, xiv, 2, 9, 144, 178–80; in Aristotle, 11, 53; of disorder, xiv, 4, 9, 37–41, 45, 49, 51–52, 55, 58n48, 63, 71, 73, 180; in Freud, 91; in Hegel, 76; in Hesiod, 39; in Plato, 49
cosmos, 36, 182; in Anaxagoras, 42–43; in Aristotle, 51, 54; in Heraclitus, 12, 15n23; in Hesiod, 10, 19, 37–39, 46; in Kant, 66; in Nietzsche, 156, 163; in Plato, 10, 46, 48–51, 58n60, 59n61. *See also* universe
creation, 2–3, 84, 155; in Anaxagoras, 37, 43; in Anaximander, 37, 41; in Aristotle, 54–55; in Asimov, 36; and destruction, 9, 156, 158–59, 161, 163–64, 167, 172, 173n20, 179; in Dick, 84; and entropy, 4, 9–10, 12–13, 22, 26, 28–29, 136, 141, 147, 156–57, 159, 165, 179; in Freud, 87; in Goethe, 156; in Hegel, 63, 71–72; in Heraclitus, 166; in Kant, 63, 66–67; in Lévi-Strauss, 97–98; in Lorde, 177; in Nietzsche, 13, 28, 158–64,

171–72, 173n20, 173n26, 179–80; in
  Plato, 47–48, 51, 57n41, 58n47, 72;
  in Schelling, 63, 68–69; in Smithson,
  12–13, 28, 141–49, 164–72, 179–80
Cronus, 39–40, 48–50, 58n54

Darwin, Charles, 88–89
death, xi, xii, xiv, 3, 17–18, 27, 29, 63,
  82n60, 100–101, 104n43, 120–21,
  125, 128n41, 133, 136, 164, 179,
  181–82; in Anaxagoras, 42; in
  Anaximander, 41; in Aristotle, 54–
  55; in Beauvoir, 12, 118; death drive,
  80n27, 85–94, 99, 101n11, 101n16,
  102n16, 102n25, 103n27, 103n39,
  104n53, 110, 112–13, 122, 159–61,
  170, 180; in Dick, 84; in Fanon,
  104n43; in Fechner, 89; heat death,
  2, 4, 9, 13, 20, 22, 24, 28, 36, 42–44,
  55, 62, 93, 97, 99, 102n18, 112, 124,
  132–33, 136, 141, 143, 150n14, 161–
  63, 165, 174n26, 179; in Hegel, 64,
  70–71, 74–78, 82n51, 82n58, 82n60,
  92; in Hesiod, 6, 39–40; in Homer,
  6–9, 55, 156; in Kant, 67–68, 78; in
  Lévi-Strauss, 94–95; in Lorde, 178;
  in Murakami, 17–18; in Nietzsche,
  157, 160–61, 163, 174n26; in
  Plato, 14n18, 44, 46, 48, 50, 63, 76,
  122, 132; in Pynchon, 61–63; in
  Schelling, 71, 78; in Shakespeare,
  107–8; slow death, 116–17, 127n32;
  in Smithson, 107, 149, 166, 168,
  171, 174n38; in Sophocles, 6–9, 55,
  123–24, 156, 157
decay, xii, 2, 12, 27–28, 44, 63, 78,
  83–84, 124–25, 138, 141–42, 149,
  153n46, 164–71, 173n13, 178–79,
  182n8; in Anaxagoras, 43; in
  Anaximander, 43; in Aristotle, 53–
  54; in Dick, 83–84; in Freud, 85, 92;
  in Hegel, 71, 74; in Homer, 7, 124;
  in Ibn Tufayl, 155; in Nietzsche,
  159, 173n13; in Plato, 37, 44–48,
  50, 58n48; in Pynchon, 79n6; in

Schelling, 69; in Smithson, 142, 144,
  149, 164–71; in Sophocles, 149
decline, 7, 9, 11, 22, 39, 45–46, 62–64,
  77, 94–100, 133, 138–39, 148, 156–
  61, 169, 171, 173n12; and old age,
  107–25, 126n19, 127n31, 129n57
de Grasse Tyson, Neil, xii–xiii
Deleuze, Gilles, 127, 137, 150n14,
  150n16, 151n18, 152n32
demiurge, 10, 47, 53, 69, 72
denial (of entropy), 3–4, 12, 99–100,
  109–11, 121–24, 136, 161, 166,
  178–79, 182; in Beauvoir, 115–18;
  in Dick, 83; in Lévi-Strauss, 94,
  97; in Nietzsche, 159; in Schelling,
  70; in Smithson, 169, 174n40; in
  Sophocles, 123–24
despair, xiv, 3, 7, 12, 61, 79n20, 84,
  115, 131; alternative to, 143, 171;
  cause of, 5, 29, 65, 134, 164, 169;
  challenging of, 15n21, 156, 165
destruction, 12, 42, 63, 123, 155, 161,
  164; acceleration of, 86, 96–97, 99,
  109, 123, 178; enabling creation,
  22, 28, 87, 156, 158, 163–67, 169,
  172, 179; entropic, 6, 22, 41, 51,
  109, 123, 171; essential to existence,
  9, 41, 63, 145, 159, 163; forces of,
  2, 7, 12, 66–67, 87, 171; in Freud,
  87, 93, 159, 161, 180; in Hegel,
  75, 77, 81n42, 82n58; humanity
  and, 98, 131, 143, 170, 179; joy of,
  13, 144, 158–59, 165, 172, 181; in
  Lévi-Strauss, 94, 96–99; movement
  towards, 6, 84, 86, 94, 99, 143; in
  Nietzsche, 156, 158–59, 163–64,
  173n20; in Plato, 47–48, 51; in
  Smithson, 143–45, 148, 156, 166–72;
  of the world, xiii, 98, 131
dialectic: in Plato, 45; in Smithson, 166,
  168–70
Dick, Philip K., 83–85, 94, 98
disorder, 26–28, 32n33, 50–51, 62; in
  Anaxagoras, 10, 37; in Anaximander,
  10, 37, 41; in Aristotle, 10, 37,

51–54; as chaos, 10, 27, 38, 47; control of, xiv, 4, 9, 37–39, 40–41, 45, 49, 51–52, 55, 58n48, 63, 71, 73, 180; as entropy, 3–7, 12–13, 22–24, 27, 31n15, 33n35, 36, 127n31, 166; forces of, 37, 40, 48, 58n49, 58n59, 69, 78, 79n6, 80n35; as generative, 4, 6, 36–37; in Hegel, 71–75, 78, 80n35; in Hesiod, 10, 37–41; in Homer, 10; in Kant, 65, 68, 78; movement toward, 4, 6, 7, 50, 75, 79n6, 133, 145; in Plato, 10, 37, 45–51, 58nn48–49, 58n59, 76; in Schelling, 69, 78
dissolution, 3–4, 12, 29, 33n39, 54–55, 126n9, 138, 182; in Darwin, 102n19; in Freud, 93; in Homer, 9, 55; in Kant, 64; in Smithson, 167–68, 170, 172; in Sophocles, 9, 55, 124
diversity, xiv, 2, 29, 43, 50, 78, 95–97, 100, 135, 161, 178, 180, 182
domination, xiv, 2, 14n20, 32n33, 180; in Fanon, 104n40; in Hegel, 63, 73; in Heidegger, 134; in Hesiod, 39; in hooks, 14n20; in Lévi-Strauss, 96; in Nietzsche, 158; in Schelling, 68. *See also* control

earth, 14n21, 15n21, 132, 177–78, 180; in Anaxagoras, 42; in Dick, 83–84; earth art, 146, 153n47, 164, 166–70, 174n34, 175n47; in Freud, 86, 92; in Heraclitus, 166; in Hesiod, 38–39, 55; in Kant, 66–67; in Lévi-Strauss, 97; in Lorde, 178; in Nietzsche, 159, 165, 171–72; in Plato, 49–50; in Smithson, 153n52, 164–65, 167–71, 174n39; in Sophocles, 123
Ehrenreich, Barbara, 83, 95, 122, 128n55, 134, 140–41, 149
energy, 3–5, 10, 12, 27–29, 30n5, 30n11, 43, 84–85, 100, 108, 124–25, 132–36, 141, 156, 179, 182; in aging bodies, 109–11, 116–22; in Asimov, 35–36; in Beauvoir, 116; in Bennett, 137–39; conservation of, 13n6, 21, 50, 92, 112, 162; in Darwin, 102n19; and entropy, 18–24, 31n14, 31nn19–20, 32n33, 150n14; in Fechner, 89; in Freud, 88–93, 113; in Hegel, 74–76; in Le Guin, 2; in Lévi-Strauss, 93, 96–97; in Marx, 112–13, 126n20; in Nietzsche, 159–63, 165; in Plato, 47, 50; in Pynchon, 62–63; in Smithson, 142, 144–45, 164–65, 171, 174n39
entrepic(s), 6–9, 28, 55, 156, 169; and care, 8, 12, 14n18, 14n20, 100, 109, 123–24, 132–33, 141, 157, 171, 179–82; in Homer, 6–7, 9, 55, 86, 133, 156, 179; in Plato, 6, 14n18; reorientation toward, 100, 109, 132, 136, 148–49, 156–57, 169, 179; and reverence, 6–9, 12, 28, 55, 144, 156–58, 169, 179–80; in Sophocles, 7–9, 55, 86, 133, 156, 179
entropia ('Εντροπία), 6–9, 14n18
entropic(s), 3–6, 10–13, 24–29, 31n13, 56n6, 64, 74, 84, 109, 112, 133–42, 148; anti-entropic, 2, 18, 22, 27, 30n5, 39, 41, 47, 50–51, 62, 79n6, 111, 115, 125, 132–33, 161, 179, 183n12; artists, 12–13, 29, 125, 132, 141–47, 152nn34–35, 156, 164, 172; breakdown, 12, 15n21, 54, 76, 103n32, 103n35, 109–10, 125, 179; chaos, 18, 27–29, 29n2, 36–38, 55, 62, 65, 72, 77–78, 133, 166, 173n26, 179, 182n8; decay, xiii, 27, 43, 46, 50, 53–54, 58, 63, 70–73, 78, 84, 92, 124, 149, 153n46, 159, 164, 179; decline, 7, 11, 21–22, 39–40, 44–46, 64, 99, 107–25, 123n31, 126n19, 127n31, 129n57, 133, 138–39, 157, 159–61, 171, 173n12; denial, 3–4, 70, 83, 94, 97, 100, 109–11, 115–18, 121–24, 136, 159, 161, 169, 174n40, 178–79, 182; in Freud, 85–93, 161; in Lévi-Strauss, 94–99; in Nietzsche, 13, 28, 156–64, 171–72,

173n12, 173n20, 174n31, 179–80; philosophy, xi, xiii, xiv, 2–6, 9, 15n24, 28, 37, 42, 63, 68–69, 71, 81n39, 123, 133–34, 160, 179–82; in Smithson, 12–13, 28, 134, 141–49, 152nn33–34, 152n38, 153n46, 153n50, 153n52, 156–57, 164–72, 174n31, 174nn39–40, 175n52, 175n54, 179–80

entropy: in Aristotle, 52–55; and art, 12, 18, 28, 30n5, 32n33, 35–36, 40, 66, 134, 142–49, 153n46, 153n55, 159–60, 163–72, 174n34, 179, 180; and creation, 4, 9–10, 12–13, 22, 26, 28–29, 44–51, 136, 141, 147, 156–57, 159, 165, 174n32, 179, 182n8; and death, 41, 86, 100, 109, 125, 136, 156; as disorder, 7, 13, 27, 33n35, 127n31, 166; entropology, 85, 94–100, 110, 145, 161; in Freud, 92–93, 99–100, 112–13; in Georgescu-Roegen, 19, 30n7, 31n14, 33n35, 103n32, 103n35, 135–36, 182n8; as homogenization, 21, 26, 133, 143; in Lévi-Strauss, 94–100; in Marx, 111–13, 126n20; as metaphor, xiv, 4–5, 9–12, 13n5, 24–29, 32nn28–29, 32n33, 37, 55, 81n48, 84, 93n39, 93n48, 109–12, 114–18, 122–24, 133, 152n38, 156, 179; in Plato, 14n18, 44–51; poetics of, 111–15, 123, 125; in Pynchon, 61–63, 79n4; science of, xiii, 1–6, 15n21, 17–24, 30nn5–7, 30n12, 31nn13–15, 31nn18–20, 32n24, 99, 103n32, 103n35, 105n54, 132, 150n14; in Smithson, 142–49, 153n52, 165–72; and waste, 47, 97–98, 126n9, 134–49, 169. *See also* the second law of thermodynamics

fatalism, 6, 9, 11, 13, 15n21, 62, 99, 123, 178, 180. *See also* nihilism

fear: of aging, 27, 111, 113, 116, 122, 129n64; and entropy, 36, 122, 172; of the other, 117

Fechner, Gustav, 88–90, 93, 101nn15–16, 102nn23–25, 162

finitude, 15n24, 24, 55, 122, 164; in Beauvoir, 122; in Butler, 181; and care, xiv, 6, 9, 10, 28, 86, 124, 181–82; in Hegel, 73–74, 77–78; in Heidegger, 134; in Homer, 6, 9, 86, 157; in Schelling, 69; in Smithson, 164, 171, 174n35; in Sophocles, 6, 8–9, 124, 157

flux, 2, 18, 37, 134, 146, 149, 158, 166

Foucault, Michel, 32n26, 37, 56n7, 158

Freud, Sigmund, 11, 14n9, 61, 102n18, 131, 179; and the death drive, 80n27, 85–94, 98–99, 101n11, 101n16, 102n16, 102n25, 103n27, 103n33, 104n53, 110, 122, 160–61, 170, 180; and life, 27, 78, 85–89, 91–93, 99–100, 102n25, 103n29, 103n33, 160–61; and psychoanalysis, 27, 78, 88, 99–100, 101n6, 112–13

Georgescu-Roegen, Nicholas, 19, 30n7, 31n14, 33n35, 103n32, 103n35, 110, 135–36, 182n8

Goethe, Johann Wolfgang von, 17, 29n2, 103n38, 155–57, 171, 172n7

Guattari, Félix, 127, 137, 150n14, 150n16, 151n18, 152n32

Hawking, Stephen, xii
heat death. *See* death
Hegel, G. W. F., 27, 48, 92, 166, 179; and aesthetics, 174n35; and death, 63–64, 70–71, 74–78, 80n33, 82n51, 82n58, 82n60, 91–92, 104n53, 122, 179; and externality, 70–78, 80n35–36, 81n41, 81n44; and matter, 71–78, 81n44, 81n48, 140; and nature, 11, 27, 63–64, 68, 70–78, 80n23, 80n30, 80n33, 80nn35–37, 81nn39–40, 81n42, 82n50, 91, 140; and Spirit, 11, 27, 70–75, 77–78, 80n35, 81n42, 91, 140

Helmholtz, Hermann von, 30n10, 87–88, 102n18, 126n17

Heraclitus, 12, 15n23, 153n54, 166
Hesiod, 6, 10, 39, 47–48, 59n80, 69, 87, 109, 177; and chaos, 6, 12, 28, 37–40, 55, 173n26; and order, 10, 41, 46
Homer, 10, 40, 61, 157; *entrepic* in, 6–7, 9, 14n16, 55, 86, 100, 133, 156, 179
homogenization, 2, 4, 6, 10, 132, 179; in Anaxagoras, 57n26; in Aristotle, 54; and entropy, 21, 23, 26, 133, 143, 145, 152n34, 163, 165; in Freud, 85, 92; in Lévi-Strauss, 85, 99; in Lorde, 178
hooks, bell, 14n20, 182n9
imagination, 24, 162; collective, 4, 26, 29

immortality, 44, 48, 50–51, 58n54, 103n33, 178. *See also* ageless
industrial revolution, 12, 112
inertia, 28, 112; in Beauvoir, 116; in Dick, 84; in Fechner, 88; in Freud, 85, 87–88, 91, 93, 102n16; in Hegel, 70, 72–73, 77; in Lévi-Strauss, 85, 96–98, 103n39; principle of, 87, 102; in Pynchon, 63; in Schelling, 69, 73; tendency towards, 63, 69, 73, 97, 112, 116
interconnectedness, 3, 125, 138, 158
interdependence, 125, 181–82

Jeffers, Robinson, 131–33, 137, 142, 150n3, 167, 177

Kafka, Franz, 25–26, 29
Kant, Immanuel, 11, 27, 179; and nature, 63–68, 70–71, 74, 78, 81n44

labor, 12, 28, 88, 96, 108–15, 117–22, 124, 126n20, 127n35, 128n49, 129n57, 133, 136, 143, 164; elderly, 12, 100, 107, 109–22, 124; laborers, 107, 111–13, 120–27, 127n39
Le Guin, Ursula, 1–2

Lévi-Strauss, Claude, 11, 14n9, 27, 78, 83–85, 93, 94–100, 101n6, 103n39, 104n53, 135, 145, 179; and entropology, 85, 94–100, 110, 145, 161
life, 24, 29, 37, 63, 100, 103n32, 105n54, 125, 134, 136, 140, 149, 156–57, 179–81; affective, 114–15; in Aristotle, 53–55, 102n26; in Freud, 11, 27, 78, 85–93, 99–100, 102n25, 103nn32–33, 160–61; in Hegel, 11, 63, 70–78, 80n35, 91–92; in Hesiod, 40; in Kant, 64–68; in Lévi-Strauss, 11, 27, 78, 85, 97; in Nietzsche, 12, 157–63; in Plato, 44, 48, 58n54; in Schelling, 69, 81n45, 155
Lorde, Audre, xi, 177–79
love, 62, 123, 131, 180–81; in hooks, 14n20, 182n9; in Schelling, 68–70, 78. *See also* care

madness, 8, 108, 118, 125, 149, 168
Marx, Karl: and Friedrich Engels, 111–12; laborer in, 111–13
materialism, 150n17; vital materialism, 12, 134, 137–38, 140–41, 149, 151nn18–19, 152n32
matter, 9, 12, 20–21, 29, 42–43, 55, 91, 103n32, 114, 131, 133–42, 151n26, 170, 180–81, 183n15; in Anaxagoras, 10, 27, 42–43, 180; in Aristotle, 52–55, 59n72, 59n77, 102n26, 180; in Bennett, 137, 139–40, 151n19, 152n32; conservation of, 13n6, 21, 42, 92, 162; in Freud, 91; in Georgescu-Roegen, 103n32, 135–36; in Hegel, 11, 64, 71–78, 80n35, 81n44, 81n48, 140; in Kant, 67–68, 81n44; in Lévi-Strauss, 97; in Plato, 48, 50–51, 68, 180; in Schelling, 68, 73; in Smithson, 142–49, 153n55, 166–67, 170, 172
Maxwell's Demon, 22–23, 31n19, 47, 50, 136, 145

McRuer, Robert, 117, 122, 127nn36–37
Medicare, 119
metaphor: of body as machine, 88, 109–12; of entropology, 99, 104n47; of entropy, xiv, 4–5, 9–12, 13n5, 24–29, 30n5, 32n28, 32n33, 37, 55, 81n39, 81n48, 84, 93, 109, 111–12, 114, 118, 124, 133, 152n38, 156, 179; root metaphor, 10, 25–26, 32nn28–29, 156
metaphysics, 37, 42, 70; in Aristotle, 52, 54–55, 59n77
mind: in Anaxagoras (*nous*), 10, 27, 37, 41–43, 51, 55, 57n26; in Hegel, 70–72, 80n35; in Schelling, 68
mortality, xiv, 8, 27, 158, 167, 182
Murakami, Haruki, 17–18, 21, 107
myth, 95, 110; of aging, 115, 121–22; of entropy, 32n33, 133; in Freud, 91; in Hesiod, 38–41, 45, 48, 69; in Plato, 44, 48–51, 57n41, 69; in Schelling, 69

nature, xii–xiii, 4, 63, 102n19, 108, 140, 158; in Aristotle, 27, 53–54; in Freud, 86, 92–93, 99; in Georgescu-Roegen, 30n7, 135; in Hegel, 11, 27, 63–64, 68, 70–78, 80n23, 80n30, 80n33, 80nn35–36, 81nn39–40, 81n42, 91, 140; in Heidegger, 134–35; in Kant, 11, 27, 63–68, 74, 78, 180; law of, 30n7, 32n33, 136; in Plato, 37, 45–50, 58n48; in Schelling, 11, 27, 63–64, 69–70, 78, 80n23, 80n30; in Shakespeare, 108; in Smithson, 167–71
neoliberalism, 109, 113
Nietzsche, Friedrich, xii, 13, 15n24, 28, 42–43, 56n7, 156, 158, 171–72, 173n15, 173n26, 179–80; on the artist, 163–64, 174n31; on asceticism, 159–61, 173n13; on the eternal return, 156, 161–63, 165, 173nn20–22
nihilism, 3–4, 158–59, 162, 171, 181

noise, xiii, 3, 10, 21, 23
Nye, Bill, xiii

Oedipus, 7–9, 14n16, 123–24, 157
overcoming, 6, 18, 70, 73, 147, 155, 157, 163, 179

Parmenides, 52–53
Pepper, Stephen, 25–26, 32n28–29
pessimism, 4, 10–13, 14n21, 28, 85, 99–100, 111, 125, 132, 146, 156, 162, 166–67, 171, 178, 180
physics, xii, 19, 26, 30n7, 84, 87–88, 93, 102n18, 162, 174n32; in Aristotle, 52–54, 59n71, 71
planet, 1, 5, 15n21, 22, 83, 127n35, 160, 167, 182; in Anaxagoras, 42; in Beauvoir, 180; in Fechner, 89; in Nietzsche, 159
Plato, 6, 10, 14n16, 14n18, 37, 43–51, 55, 57nn40–41, 58n52, 58n54, 58nn59–60, 63, 68, 72, 76, 77, 89, 132, 162, 168, 179; and demiurge, 10, 48, 51, 53, 58n48, 69, 72; and forms, 45–46, 51; and matter, 48, 50–51, 68, 180
pollution, 1, 15n21, 96, 126n9, 142, 144, 167, 169–70
power: inorganic power, 76, 82n60; thing-power, 137–39, 151n19; will to power, 158, 160–63, 173nn21–22
precariousness, xiv, 3, 136, 144, 181–82, 183nn13–14
precarity, 116, 181, 183nn12–13
presocratic philosophy, 10, 37, 41; of Anaxagoras, 10, 27, 37, 41–44, 55, 57n26, 58n47, 59n80; of Anaximander, 10, 37, 41, 43, 46–48, 56n21, 57nn23–24, 77; of Heraclitus, 12, 15n23, 153n54, 166, 174n38; of Parmenides, 52–53
principle: of inertia, 69, 87–88; of stability, 4, 88–90, 101n16, 102nn23–25, 178–79

progress, 2, 64, 89, 104n44, 133, 137, 143, 148; in Darwin, 89, 102n19; in Freud, 92, 103n33; in Lévi-Strauss, 94, 96–98, 100, 103n39; in Nietzsche, 161; in Smithson, 146–47, 164–66, 170–71
psychoanalysis, 5, 11, 33n39, 84, 88, 101n6; Freudian, 27, 78, 88, 99, 101n6
purpose, xii, 27, 33n35, 63, 135, 137, 148; in Freud, 87, 180; in Hegel, 27, 71–72, 78, 180; in Kant, 27, 64–68, 70, 74, 78, 79n20, 180; in Nietzsche, 158, 162; in Schelling, 27, 68, 70, 78, 180; in Shakespeare, 108
Pynchon, Thomas, 61–63, 70, 79n4, 79n6

QAnon, xiii

racism, 1–2, 56n6, 178
reason, 5, 27, 49–50; in Hegel, 71, 74; in Kant, 63–68, 180; unreason, xiii, 72, 80n35
responsibility, 139, 149; individual, 17, 109, 113, 122, 133, 141; shared, 6, 14n20, 183n9

Sadi-Carnot, Nicolas, 6, 19–20, 28
Sartre, Jean-Paul, 35
Schelling, F. W. J., xi, 63, 80n23, 80n30; and melancholy, 11, 69, 81n45, 99, 155; philosophy of nature, 11, 64, 68–73, 78
science, xi–xiii, 10–11, 14n9, 15n21, 29, 33n39, 78, 122; of entropy, 1–7, 17–24, 30nn5–7, 30n10, 30n12, 31nn13–15, 31nn18–20, 32n24, 99; in Freud, 14n9, 86–88, 93, 99, 102n18; in Hegel, 70; in Kant, 64; in Lévi-Strauss, 14n9, 94, 101n6; in Marx and Engels, 112; in Schelling, xi
Shannon, Claude, 1, 23–24

slackening, 2–4, 9–10, 25, 37, 63, 74, 78, 109, 112, 114, 116, 124, 138, 160, 164
Smithson, Robert, 12–13, 28, 107, 134, 141–49, 152nn33–34, 152n36, 152n38, 152n42, 153nn46–47, 153n50, 153n52, 153n55, 156–57, 164–72, 174n31, 174nn34–35, 174nn38–40, 175nn47–49, 175nn51–52, 175n54, 179; and earth art, 167, 169, 170, 174n34; and Non-Sites, 146–47, 153n47, 153n50, 174n34; and the *Spiral Jetty*, 12, 148, 165–69, 174n42, 175nn47–49, 175n52, 175n54. *See also* artist
Sophocles, 6–9, 14n16, 55, 86, 100, 123, 156–57
Spiral Jetty, 12, 148, 165–69, 174n42, 175nn47–49, 175n52, 175n54. *See also* art
Spirit (Hegel), 11, 70–75, 77–78, 80n35, 81n42, 180

Tartarus, 38–39
technology, 98, 112, 131, 135; in Heidegger, 134–35; in Smithson, 143, 145–47, 165, 168–70
thermodynamics: conservation of energy, 13n6, 21, 50, 92, 112, 126n20, 144, 162; conservation of matter, 21, 42, 50, 92, 144; first law of, 20–22, 42, 50, 162; the laws of, 13n6, 20, 62–63, 88, 92; the second law of, xiii, 4–6, 11, 13, 17, 19–22, 26–29, 30n5, 30n12, 37, 47, 50, 57n41, 87, 89, 93, 112, 121, 142, 148, 162, 165. *See also* entropy
Thomson, William (Lord Kelvin), 132
truth, xiii, 25, 27, 55, 70, 119, 158–59, 165, 171, 173n20; *entrepic*, 138, 164; entropic, 74, 93, 124, 133, 135, 138, 144, 148, 164; in Hegel, 70–74, 77

uniformity, 4, 11, 26; uniforming, 2. *See also* homogenization
universe, 3, 9, 18, 20, 26, 36–37, 63, 132, 140–41, 171, 174n32; in Anaxagoras, 10, 26–27, 41–43; in Anaximander, 41; in Aristotle, 41, 51–55; in Bennett, 140–41; in Fechner, 89, 102n24; in Freud, 87, 93; heat death of, 4, 13, 19–22, 24, 28–29, 30n10, 36, 43, 62, 102n18, 124, 150n14, 164; in Helmholtz, 30n10, 102n18; in Hesiod, 39, 55; in Nietzsche, 162–65, 172; in Parmenides, 52–53; in Plato, 10, 45–51, 55, 58n48, 132; in Smithson, 142. *See also* cosmos
unreason, xiii, 72, 80

vitality, 4, 28, 36, 70, 76, 82n60, 92, 121, 125, 137, 141, 146, 151n19, 159

vulnerability, xiv, 6, 28, 100, 112–14, 116–17, 119, 133, 136, 157, 169, 171, 181–82, 183n14; in Sophocles, 6, 8, 123–24

war, 1–2, 5; against entropy, 110, 116, 146; in Freud, 86, 90; in Hesiod, 38; in Plato, 47
waste, xiv, 12, 15n21, 19–21, 28, 36, 47, 83, 110, 118, 121, 131–36, 139, 146, 162, 167, 178, 180; and entropy, 9, 47, 97–98, 126n9, 149; in Lévi-Strauss, 96–98, 100; in Plato, 132; in Smithson, 142, 144–49, 164, 166–70
wasteland, 67, 84; in Smithson, 142, 144–45, 147, 168

Zencey, Eric, 10, 25–29, 31n20, 32n29, 32n33, 36, 156
Zeus, 7–9, 38–39, 48–49

www.ingramcontent.com/pod-product-compliance
Lightning Source LLC
Chambersburg PA
CBHW021849300426
44115CB00005B/74